Marguerite de Navarre: *Les Prisons*

American University Studies

Series II
Romance Languages and Literature
Vol. 99

PETER LANG
New York • Bern • Frankfurt am Main • Paris

Claire Lynch Wade

Marguerite de Navarre
Les Prisons

A French and English Edition

PETER LANG
New York • Bern • Frankfurt am Main • Paris

Library of Congress Cataloging-in-Publication Data

Marguerite, Queen, consort of Henry II, King of Navarre,
   1492-1549.
   [Prisons. English & French]
   Les Prisons / Marguerite de Navarre ; [edited with a
critical introduction by] Claire Lynch Wade.
      p. cm.—(American university studies. Series II,
Romance languages and literature ; vol. 99)
    Text in English and French.
    Bibliography: p.
    Includes index.
    1. Mysticism — Poetry. I. Wade, Claire Lynch.
II. Title. III. Series.
PQ1631.P713   1989   841ʹ.3 — dc19   88-12976
ISBN 0-8204-0802-6   CIP
ISSN 0740-9257

CIP–Titelaufnahme der Deutschen Bibliothek

Marguerite <Navarre, Reine>:
Les prisons : a French and English edition /
Marguerite de Navarre. Claire Lynch Wade. –
New York; Bern; Frankfurt am Main; Paris:
Lang, 1989.
   (American University Studies: Ser. 2, Romance
   Languages and Literature; Vol. 99)
   ISBN 0-8204-0802-6

NE: Wade, Claire Lynch [Hrsg.] ; American
University Studies / 02

© Peter Lang Publishing, Inc., New York 1989

Printed by Weihert-Druck GmbH, Darmstadt, West Germany

A mon vray amy

ACKNOWLEDGEMENTS

Although naming only a few persons among those to whom I owe gratitude, I hereby express sincere appreciation to all those who supplied their help in this edition. I wish to name my husband, Alex Corson Wade for his unflagging help and encouragement; for evaluative reading, Dr. Edgar Duncan, Dr. Ivan Lou Duncan, Prof. C. Maxwell Lancaster, Dr. Paul Manchester,* Prof. Janet Wilson, and Dr. Sara Whitten; for painstaking assistance with a table of rhymes, Miss Sheryl Harris; for typing, Miss Deborah Whitely, and for proof-reading, Mr. Stanley Matthews. I am grateful to the Bibliotheque Nationale for microfilms and prints of the two basic manuscripts, and to the Joint Universities Library of Vanderbilt University for the loan of many volumes. I acknowledge my foremost indebtedness to the writers of the essential materials credited in the notes and bibliography. I thank Dr. Herbert Gabhart for the privilege of residence on the Belmont College campus.

*Lancaster and Manchester are winners of the Bernard O'Higgins award for translation.

TABLE OF CONTENTS

INTRODUCTION

THE AUTHOR

Marguerite d'Angoulême (1492-1549), sometimes called the "pearl" of the Valois (a pun upon her first name), Duchess of Alençon and of Berry, and Queen of Navarre, is known to history for her activity in four areas: political, feminist, religious, and literary.[1] To place her among familiar names, we may say that she was born in the signal year of Columbus' discovery, a year prior to the birth of Henry VIII. Marguerite herself narrowly missed becoming another of Henry's wives. Elizabeth I was the daughter of one of Marguerite's ladies-in-waiting. As a young princess, Elizabeth was set to translating a poem composed by Marguerite, the *Miroir de l'Âme Pécheresse*,[2] which had created much excitement among seekers of direct relationships with God, provoked the wrath of heretic hunters, and had been banned in France by the Faculty of Theology in 1533.

Though Marguerite's political role was not one of her own choosing, she made good use of it. In 1515, accession to the throne of France by her only sibling, Francis I, two years her junior, made her and her widowed mother, Louise de Savoie, widow of Charles d'Orleans, Count of Angoulême, powerful women in Europe at an auspicious moment. France had gained her territorial unity, and the Holy Roman Empire (Spain, Netherlands, and the German States) had not yet become an encircling dragon under Charles-Quint. Marguerite, who appeared constantly at the side of her brother, her idol, often served France as a surrogate queen. It was a triumph of her tact that she and the true queen remained friends. Claude de France, daughter of Anne de Bretagne and Louis XII, the preceding king, was not prepared, as was Marguerite, to act in an advisory capacity to a monarch; moreover, Claude was occupied with the seven children that she bore in the nine years before she would die at the age of twenty-four. In 1509, Marguerite had been married off to the Duke of Alençon in the interest of preserving the county of Armagnac for France. She was made also the Duchess of Berry and thereby gained patronage rights over the University of Bourges. In this capacity she fostered academic freedom. It was fortunate for Marguerite's promotion of the Renaissance that until 1534 the threat to the monarchy posed by freedom of thought was not perceived. In that year Britain severed diplomatic relations with the Vatican, and placards condemning Catholic practices appeared in France, even outside the door of King Francis's bedchamber. She found herself thereafter increasingly involved in situations where political skill was required.

Brantôme, a memorialist of the French court, who knew her well through his mother and grandmother, who were ladies-in-waiting, reports that Marguerite was always talented in diplomacy. She must have learned much tact from her attendance at *grandes fêtes*, of which she was automatically a part, just as her husband was, by virtue of his position (not his fitness) a participant in all military action of importance. She could hardly have been more eminently placed when, in 1520, she attended the international diplomatic meeting called "The Field of Cloth of Gold," where she served as first lady of France, the king's "Egerie."[3]

Full demand upon her diplomatic expertise came in 1525, when Francis was captured at Pavia in the course of an unsuccessful attempt to recover northern Italy for France and was imprisoned by Charles-Quint in Spain. She set out from Lyons to free him or to share his fate. When, along the arduous journey by litter, she learned that Francis was gravely ill, she abandoned even the meager comforts and rode horseback the rest of the way at forced speed. She found her brother unconscious, confined in deplorable conditions and ill-treated by the Emperor. She succeeded by entreaty in getting better conditions for him, set up an altar in his cell, and undertook intensive nursing. It was no encouragement that the family had recently sustained the loss of several members. Queen Claude had died in July, shortly after Francis's departure for Italy with the army. Their daughter, Charlotte, had succumbed to measles in September while in Marguerite's care. When, after several setbacks, the health of Francis improved, Marguerite tried to arrange an escape for him in which he would replace a Moorish servant. The plot was betrayed by a French attendant.

Francis next planned to escape by abdicating in favor of the Dauphin. He was phrasing the document he would send to France by Marguerite when he recalled that his abdication would not necessarily free him. He concluded instead a pact according to which his two sons were to be imprisoned in exchange for his liberation. What Marguerite carried back with her was appointment to the regency for herself if, before her brother could return to France, their mother, then regent, should lose her health. The proposed exchange of prisoners was made mid-river on a barge at Bidassoa. Francis had returned to rule and never forgot his sister's skill and loyal efforts toward that end. Later Marguerite, along with her mother and Margaret of Austria, was active in the liberation of the children from their harsh captivity.

While Marguerite had been negotiating directly with Charles-Quint she had steadfastly refused concessions of French Burgundian territory. She thus established the basis of the eventual treaty which would be signed at Cambrai in August of 1529. Though she was not a party to the treaty proper, she was conspicuous in the festivities at the conclusion of the conference.

While in Spain she found time to arrange several matters successfully. She had played cupid with skill between Francis and the tender-hearted sister of his captor, Elenore, widowed queen of Portugal. They would be married in 1530. This coup was a rare case in which a female diplomat moved adult males, both monarchs, as marriage pawns.

Blame for the king's capture fell upon Marguerite's husband, Charles d'Alençon. It was thought that had Charles advanced his forces at a critical point in the fray, instead of retreating, he might have saved the day for France. He died April 11, 1526, surviving his disgrace by only a few weeks. Marguerite's account of his death, in Les Prisons, discloses a previously unsuspected affection in the marriage. By returning home, out of the dragon's grasp, Marguerite escaped being married off to Charles-Quint, or to his ally, the defector, Charles, Connêtable de Bourbon.[4] Before the accession of Francis, she had been refused as bride for the son of the King of Naples, for Christian of Denmark, and for Henry VIII. No matter. Subsequently England came seeking twice and twice went away with a refusal. The widowed Marguerite now married the dashing Henri d'Albret, who had shared Francis's capture and had escaped by descending a rope with attractive bravado. She thus became Queen of Navarre, including Béarn. She actively seconded her new husband's long but futile effort to regain from Spain the territory from which his title derived.

There were two children of this marriage, a daughter born in 1529 and a son, who lived but five months, who was born in 1530. The daughter, Jeanne d'Albret, born in 1529, later to be renowned for her support of the Calvinist Condé party, became an important political pawn for Francis as well as for her father. Because d'Albret wished to arrange a marriage for Jeanne with Philippe, son of the Emperor, he was pleased to have Marguerite participate in the two peace conferences with Charles-Quint held in 1538, one at Nice and the other at Aigues-Mortes. When, in 1539, the Emperor crossed northern France on his way to Ghent to put down a revolt, Marguerite, instead of receiving the intruder with hostility, exerted herself to show him hospitality by means of which she hastened his passage and exit. Her daughter caused Marguerite much anguished diplomacy when, in 1541, at her royal uncle's whim, she became the rebellious fiancée (twelve years old) of William, brother of Henry VIII's third wife, Anne de Clèves. Jeanne's mother saw to it that the duke went back to his German province without Jeanne. The union was postponed through Marguerite's efforts until ultimately the whole transaction was dropped because the Emperor, Francis's constant antagonist, had forced Clèves to abandon his former loyalty to France. Eventually she was married to Antoine de Bourbon-Vendôme, a marriage that displeased Marguerite but would make her posthumously the grandmother of Henri IV (Henry of Navarre), the sovereign who was to reunite France after the schismatic wars of religion, and who, in the unitive spirit of Marguerite, became known to history for the religious toleration act, the Edict of Nantes.[5] The political destiny of France was undeniably affected by Marguerite, who even in her failures sowed some eventual successes.

Although Marguerite was often closest political adviser to Francis I, and it was said that no sensible diplomat could have laid his strategy without calculating her reactions, it suited her better to be dubbed unofficially, "the prime minister of the poor." She took much interest in public assistance, reformed hospitals, regulated vagabondage, straightened out ill-administered charity. As a result, the communities of Nérac, Alençon, Argentan, Mortagne, and Ecouche were much benefited. In Paris she founded the Hospital des Enfants Rouges — the color referred only to the uniforms — which was the first charity institution established exclusively to serve children.

She presented a model of modern women in social services while caring for the daughters of Francis, an official appointment, and shirked none of the customary distaff roles of the time.[6] So eminent was she that she was inevitably used by writers as an example of womanhood both good and bad in the literary quarrel of the times over the value of woman in general. Rabelais dedicated to her the *Tiers Livre*, in its introduction inviting her exalted spirit to descend from its habitual heights to this world to read it. Nicholas Bourbon, preceptor to Jeanne, wrote that Marguerite was the superior of all men physically, intellectually, and morally. Court poet Clément Marot addressed to her an epigram saying that she had a feminine body, the heart of a man, and the head of an angel.[7] She had adopted for herself the motto from Virgil, *"Non inferiora secutus,"*[8] and did indeed pursue superior things. It is clear that she enhanced the status of woman at court.

Marguerite was both participant in and analyst of Renaissance woman's roles. Rich in documentation are her prose tales now well known as the *Heptaméron*.[9] These previously, but posthumously, appeared under two other titles, an unauthorized version called *Les Amants fortunés*, and *Le Décaméron* (manuscript edition of Adrien de Thou, 1553); the latter title and Marguerite's prologue point to Boccaccio (1313-1375) as her model. In 1530 she had commissioned André Le Maçon to translate Boccaccio's *Décaméron* into French. Marguerite's *Heptaméron*, unlike its models, in addition to reflecting the lives of women in an entertaining manner rich in psychological observation, makes at least two recommendations important in feminist history: first, a practice of coupling deep affection with marriage (an association frowned upon at the time); and second, a practice of marriage in which there would be reciprocal fidelity. Her biographer, Jourda, has dubbed this work, "a good deed."[8,10]

In support of Marguerite's work as a feminist, E. V. Telle notes that in 1555 Louise Labé of Lyons, in introducing her *Débate de folie et d'amour*, proclaims that the severe laws of men are no longer keeping women from applying themselves to science and the intellectual disciplines, "a liberty . . . so long desired." Telle asserts that for this "liberty," Marguerite, through her example and influence, was largely responsible.[11] Cornelius Agrippa von Nettlesheim, the humanist responsible for convincing Louise's father to have her educated, dedicated to Marguerite his work, *Briefve Declamation du sainct sacrement de mariage*, translated into French at Lyons, in 1524.

Marguerite connects feminist and Reformist trends. Often as she was inspiring women to be informed and outspoken, her topic was religious philosophy, her guests were accused heretics. Her rescue of free thinkers from the stake, her support of Bible translation, and her circulation of German evangelical treatises give her a place in the history of religion. Historians of religion have for better than four centuries either condemned her for weakening Roman Catholic unity or praised her for spreading the Reformation.

Her mother and brother, as well as Marguerite, had at first coveted the cultural enrichment found in humanism for the court of France. Before the affair of the placards, which threatened the king's position and person, the Sorbonne might condemn writings and writers; Marguerite, with Francis' approval, would intervene to save them. In the face of threatened torture and death for herself, an eventuality that the Sorbonne Faculty of Theology, persuaded by the syndic Nöel Béda,[12] requested of the Parlement in 1533, Marguerite protected humanists as diverse as Rabelais and Calvin,[13] — the former roisterous satirist, physician, and pro-Lutheran monk; the latter a stern governor, author of eloquent religious tracts in French, and founder of a predestinationist sect. She received in exchange much erudition. Her failure to shun the "spiritual libertines," Pocques and Quintin, later cost her Calvin's friendship.[14] Some of her protégés, such as Étienne Dolet (translator of Plato's *Hipparchus* and *Axiochus*) and Bonaventure des Périers (author of the *Cymbalum Mundi*) were attackers of all religion, but she principally protected writers and preachers of Lutheran and Fabrist persuasion.[15] Among these were Gérard Roussel and Michel d'Arande;[16] also Guillaume Farel, who took treatises by Frenchmen to be published in Germany; Pierre Caroli, gifted preacher who escaped to Switzerland; and Antoine Papillon, who was commissioned by Marguerite to translate from Latin to French Luther's treatise condemning monasticism, the *De votis Monasticis*.[17] Especially important was Marguerite's protection of the translators of the Bible: Lefèvre d'Etaples; Guillaume Briçonnet, who headed a group of Christian Platonists at his bishopric at Meaux; and Clément Marot, fine poet and translator of the Psalms. Even after 1534 Francis did not interfere when she sheltered religious refugees in her husband's capitals at Nérac and Pau, although it lay well within his power to do so. This alarmed the Catholic powers, who increased their demands for repressive measures. As a result Marguerite's husband ceased to be supportive and actually struck her while she was at prayer with Gerard Roussel.[18]

Jeanne, who reported this incident, was compliant while her father lived, but after his death became a Calvinist. She asked God's forgiveness for her mother's having wavered between two religions. Some critics find Marguerite pro-Lutheran in her writings and defense of Lutheran heretics and their writings,[19] but she stayed within the Roman church, routinely orthodox. She endowed and supervised monastic institutions. She and her mother-in-law, "Marguerite the Blessed," founded the Dominican convent of Sainte-Claire at Argentan. Both made deathbed confessions to Franciscan priests. *Les Prisons* shows Queen Marguerite to have been a Christian and a mystic.

She was eclectic in her choice of doctrines, and much at home with Platonism, but not sectarian. In the 1520's, "Lutheranism," as most free examination of faith was called, had probably appeared to her to be restorative of original Christianity and unitive. It is most probable that she empathized with erudite researchers and bold writers, and acted to give them safety and encouragement because she herself was a researcher and writer, especially concerning the path of spiritual development.

Her aid to the men of letters and arts was as important to the spread of the Renaissance in France as her aid to the reformists was important to the Reformation. Her example as a militant champion of enlightenment and human rights may have helped to turn west European ideals in that direction. She was one of the seven major writers in sixteenth century France before the Pléiade, and her life touched the other six. She preserved the life of Rabelais, Marot, Calvin, and Bonaventure des Périers (who may later have killed himself); we read above how she "liberated" Louise Labé, and was several times honored by Scève, the French Petrarch.

In *Les Prisons*, she presents the phases of her mystical search. For the moment though, the masterpiece and other works grouped in the *Dernières Poésies* were withheld; she joined the history of literature on the strength of other credits. It was her short lyrics that chiefly found audience. Speaking of her *Reveille-toy, Seigneur Dieu* and of her *Penser en la passion de Jesus Christ*, Jourda affirms that these two odes constitute the finest expression of French lyricism between Villon and Ronsard. With Lefranc, he upholds the literary merit of the *Triomphe de l'Agneau*, the *Dialogue en forme de vision nocturne* which commemorates the death of Madame Charlotte, daughter of Claude and Francis, and the spiritual songs, which were published in the *Marguerites;* some critics single out the *Oraison de l'ame fidele*, the *Dialogue*, and the *Miroir* as the most touching expressions of her religious ideas.[20] Outside of poems for special occasions her lyrical work is collected in two volumes: the 1533 edition of the *Miroir* and the *Marguerites de la Marguerite des princesses*, edited in 1547 by André Le Maçon. *Les Dernieres Poésies*, or *Final Poems*, in which *Les Prisons* was found, is sometimes referred to as the second *Marguerites*. Jourda suggests that in her elevated, intimate lyricism she is not unlike Racine, and that she prepared the audience to appreciate the aims of the Pléiade group of poets in presenting examples of serious aspirations for French verse; he further suggests that she helped to prepare the way for the divine afflatus of the Christian epicists, (naming Milton and Goethe) and therefore for the eventual meeting of these elements in the French classical drama.[21] With her witty protegé, Clément Marot, she shares the merit of giving French verse facility. In *Les Prisons* we find the additional achievement of sustaining a message of philosophic worth with its sincere, intense emotional color intact throughout almost 5000 lines, the longest such piece in French before Du Bartas' epic, *Les Tragiques*. Finally, one should not fail to mention the excellence of another of her literary works, one only slightly less sustained, the *Navire*, nor to enroll Marguerite among the writers of excellent morality plays and of a plethora of letters.[22]

Letter-writing was taught her most probably by her preceptress and friend, Madame de Châtillon, and Marguerite corresponded with every major figure of the time, including Vittoria Colonna, her exact age-mate and the inamorata of Michelangelo. It has even been suggested that *Les Prisons* is a reply to Erasmus' *De Libero Arbitrio* (1524), since she seems to have answered all other pieces of correspondence except two letters from the great Dutch humanist.[23]

What had led Marguerite to the search animating her literary work? It came obviously from both writings and people, and there was a rich supply of both. Her intelligence digested with much thoroughness the Bible, Dante, and the Neo-Platonism in the letters of Briçonnet, the mentor during her widowhood.

Lucien Febvre asserts that it was because she had come to eminence from the position of a déclassé in poverty that she was spurred to energetic cultural exertion, but one can note that, like Eleanor of Acquitaine, Marguerite was following in the footsteps of her family. There had been passed on to her not only the Italian culture of her mother's side, the Visconti, but the troubadour lore of her paternal great-uncle, the poet prince Charles d'Orléans.[24] To that we should add the independent mind of her paternal grandfather Jean d'Angoulême, whose library at Blois offered perusal of Boethius, Augustine, Dante, the story of Tristan, the Lancelot in prose, and likely Alain Chartier, Boccaccio, and Chaucer, works superior to the usual rhetoriqueur, hagiographic and patristic elaborations.

She had received careful instruction in many things from her ambitious, intelligent mother. Louise de Savoie, who, married at age eleven and widowed at nineteen, found in her children her principal absorption. Marguerite became, at her mother's insistence, an early participant in co-education, when she shared the formal schooling given her brother and selected male associates at Amboise, where the Marshal Gié vied with Louise to be their chief supervisor. Under the good tutors, François Demoulin, Robert Hurault, and François de Rochefort, she learned Latin, Greek, Hebrew, some theology, and the basics of Franciscan and Platonic philosophy. Her knowledge of European languages was not only a product of contacts with native speakers but, as she grew older, of her acquaintance with philologists such as those of the Vatable and Estienne names. Between the accession and 1534, the "Trinity" (Louise and her two children) was hospitable to scholars, doctors, illuminators, and artists of both achievement and promise. As if Panurge had ordered it, physics, astronomy, and zoology were discussed at meals. Marguerite's life included a variety of talented and enlightened people, the shipfitter Jean Ango, the portraitists Clouet, the architect Serlio, the sculptors Da Vinci and Benvenuto Cellini, to name just a few. Notable among the intellects who became familiars were Guillaume Petit, the King's confessor; the Cardinal de Tournon and Etienne Poncher, diplomatists; Guillaume Cap, physician to the King; and Guillaume Budé, the noted hellenist.

About 1517 Lefèvre d'Etaples joined the court. With the aid of his disciples, he had brought to publication the works of the Pseudo-Denys in 1505, also works attributed to Hermes Trismegistus in 1514 and those of Nicholas Cusa in 1516. He was then to translate the Bible under the patronage of Briçonnet, Bishop of Meaux, with whom Marguerite undertook correspondence in 1521, a correspondence that would last for four years. The well-spring of her writing was grief in the loss of loved ones through death or indifference, but her cultural contacts were paramount for her conceptual development. When Lefèvre was forced to flee the persecution of the ecclesiastical authorities, her interest in Neo-Platonist mysticism became involvement. Another of Briçonnet's disciples, Michel d'Arande came to the royal palace of the Louvre to preach Reform, as did Gérard Roussel in 1533. The former became her almoner; guided by him, she and her companion, Madame de Châtillon, took the "dangerous" step of reading the Bible in new translations. Fabricius, also known as Capiton, who was sometimes host at Strasbourg to Lefèvre, Roussel, and Calvin, dedicated to Marguerite in 1527 his translation of the book of *Hosea*. She and her brother collected the books that would form the nucleus of the Bibliothèque Nationale. Marguerite had the honor of commissioning Amyot's translation of Plutarch, on which North later relied. She and Francis also founded the group of lectureships which would become the Collège de France. The lectures were dedicated to respect for logical, rather than purely authoritarian, reflection, and to advancing the study of medicine, mathematics, architecture, languages, and literature. There Rabelais, Calvin, *and Loyola* (founder of the Society of Jesus) came to learn Greek.

When Marguerite traveled France, Italy and Spain, it was mostly on errands of politics or illness, but she never failed to undertake cultural exchange. Lyons, which served as headquarters where Francis lingered to plan his strategies against Charles-Quint, was a prosperous publishing capital and the flourishing center of humanism, Petrarchism and Neo-Platonism. Marguerite's presence there with her brother encouraged much poetic production; it mingled the two dominant French circles of Petrarchism, her own and that of Louise Labé. Marguerite's group, the "Marotiques," included Antoine Héroët, Bonaventure des Périers, Charles Fontaine, Eustorg de Beautieu, La Borderie, her secretary Victor Brodeau, Mellin de Saint-Gelais, Charles de Sainte-Marthe, and Clément Marot, who was the model of this group. The music and poetry salon of Louise Labé embraced Maurice Scève, Pernette de Guillet, Olivier de Magny, Pontus de Tyard and Jacques Peletier du Mans. Scève was the tutor. The Petrarchists adapted the quasi-religious anguish of the Italian love sonneteer to their French love poetry and were beginning to plunder the Hellenic baggage, Alexandrian and Florentine. They mark the transition between the school of Moret and Ronsard.[25]Scève devoted dixains from his immortal *Délie* to Francis and Marguerite. He commemorated the death of the poisoned Dauphin François in a surviving poem entitled *Arion.*[25] He wrote for Marguerite two sonnets which were published at the head of her *Marguerites de la Marguerite des princesses.* At the moment when Marguerite was particularly interested in Italy, poems were published in Florence under her name. Most interesting among her international cultural exchanges were those touching Germany. She acquainted France with German evangelical literature in several ways. In 1518 Luther released an explanation of the Pater Noster in dialogue form; Marguerite rendered it in French decasyllable verse. In 1524, Antoine Papillon sent her Luther's *De Votis Monaticis*, and for his pains she made him Maître des Requêtes for the Dauphin.[26] Around 1527 Sigismond de Hohenlohe made regular deliveries to Marguerite of Luther's treatises.[27] In 1531 and again in 1533, Simon Dubois, who published almost all the books of Luther that exist from that period, as well as the clandestine translations of Calvin and Marot, also published the *Miroir* of Marguerite. The Queen, newly married to Henri d'Albret, was supervising the translation and printing of quite a series of evangelical writings. In 1537 she was associating with certain Lutheran writers of Strasbourg, Bâle, and Berne.

As Queen of Navarre, Marguerite made her husband's court at Nérac a foyer for men of letters as well as a refuge for heretics. Among her guests there whom we should not fail to mention because of the streams of influence which they represent were: Luigi Alemanni, the Italian poet who passionately promoted the works of Dante; the Cardinal Du Bellay who employed Rabelais; the Petrarchan poets, Mellin and Octavien de Saint-Gelais; Marguerite's secretary, Victor Brodeau;[28] the soldier memorialist, Montluc; and Antoine Héroët, author of the *Parfaite Amie*, which was one of two prime documents in the Querelle des Femmes. Along with Simon Dubois we seen Calveau, the Bishop of Senlis whom Marguerite had caused to translate the Missal into French and revise it for use in all the churches and chapels of her husband's domain. Lefèvre took refuge in Nérac in 1531, having made the year before a complete translation of the Bible according to Jerome. He was given a royal pension and table privileges. Translators Marot and Farel were transient guests as was Gérard Roussel, who had charge of the Abbey of Clairac in Agenois.[29] It seems justifiable that some have associated the Queen of Navarre with the origin of the French literary salon that was to flourish in the next century.

The work of Marguerite owes as much to contact with various people as it does to her reading, for humanity was as important to her as was humanism. As she saw it, it was divine love that motivated human love. The divine manifestation was illumination, a direct relationship between a person and God, unalterable on the part of God, and discoverable on the part of the individual only with the aid of a mystical light which appeared after long study, especially of the New Testament, a light that brought not only joyous Christian liberation from troublesome cupidities but the spirit of solidarity with others. Her quest for this illumination furnished the dynamics of her life and of her long work.

Her political, feminist, religious, and literary significance was expressed in the wave of superlatives that broke after a temporary hush at her death. She died of pleurisy and stroke at the castle of Audaux (Odos) in the Basses-Pyrénées, on December 1, 1549, and was buried at Morlas, near her husband's summer capital at Pau. At the time, she was residing in a new house near the Abbey of Tusson, where she at times participated in the chanting and other exercises of the nuns, hoping to lift her spirits. The onset of the final illness had struck her eight days before her death, as she was watching a comet light the sky. She associated the phenomenon with the imminently expected death of Pope Paul III. Brantôme says, "But possibly it appeared for her."[30]

The illustrious Jane Seymour, along with her sisters Anne and Marguerite, composed a tribute of one hundred verses in Latin. It was first published in 1550 and subsequently appeared in translations into French and Italian made by their tutor, Nicholas Denisot. A tombeau of tributes was assembled; Ronsard, Du Bellay, and Dorat of the Pléiade published laments and odes, as did several lesser poets. Charles de Sainte-Marthe of Lyons, whom Marguerite had greatly influenced, wrote a condensed history of her life in Latin and a version of the same in French, his masterpiece. Later the historians de Thou and Colletet rendered homage to her learning, wisdom and virtue. Etienne Dolet, the translator of Plato who was martyred in 1546 after Marguerite had thrice saved him from the stake, had left an ode in Latin which celebrated her good deeds in the service of letters. Among the men who praised her humanity were Marot, Nicholas Bourbon, Jean de la Haye (publisher and translator of Ficino), Jean Frotté (Marguerite's secretary of financial matters) and Jacques Peletier du Mans (Lyonnais, member of the Pléiade).

Calvinists Théodore de Bèze and Melancthon gave her complimentary mention, but it was Valentine Denisot who, in the epitaph composed by him, achieved the pinnacle of praise in calling her, "the tenth muse and the fourth grace."[31]

Her nephew Henri II, who succeeded his father to the throne in 1547, said, "If it were not for my aunt Marguerite, I should doubt the existence of such a thing as genuine goodness upon this earth, but I have never been disappointed in her." "She is never tiresome or stupid," her brother and idol said of her once.[32]

It is *Les Prisons* that offers documentary evidence of Marguerite's compelling personality and deep reflection. One can evaluate her fully only after studying her long philosophical work, her masterpiece, for it is at once authentically personal and conclusive. It did not appear in French print until two hundred fifty years past its completion, in 1549. Only with this present edition does it make its first appearance in English. *Les Prisons* is a rightful part of the early Renaissance and Reformation heritage, for Marguerite was the hub of that dual development in France.

THE WORK

HISTORY OF PUBLICATION

The publication of *Les Prisons* was delayed for over 250 years. This is irregular especially because the collection in which it was found appears to constitute a *tombeau* designed to honor Francis I at his death, which occurred in 1547 . It is likely that Marguerite finished the compilation only shortly before her death in 1549 and for reasons of declining health and political disadvantage could not personally attend to the publication of her work. She had long been a target of leaders of the orthodox Roman Catholic faction. There had been cries of "Sew her in a sack and throw her in the Seine!" Students at the College of Navarre had produced dramas which ridiculed her. The Bishop of Condom had attempted to poison her with noxious incense. During the reigns of Francis's son and grandsons, heretical utterance became ever more dangerous. Marguerite's husband, Henri d'Albret, had turned against the reformists. The political position of their surviving child, wife of Antoine de Bourbon, was very delicate. As the government came under the influence of the Guises, it exacted the direst penalties for unorthodoxy. Marguerite's posthumously published *Heptaméron* appeared with evidences of expurgation.

Les Prisons, which equated all inspirations and asserted that Francis, after his death, ruled with God in Heaven (v. 4576), was far from orthodox. The arrival on the literary scene of Ronsard's Pleiade buried the queen's poetry beneath a figurative blanket of roses.

We are indebted to Abel Lefranc, former secretary of the Collège de France, and to the Société d'histoire de la France, his sponsors, that the queen's final work at last came to the attention of French scholars. Lefranc brought to publication approximately 12,000 previously unprinted lines of verse by Marguerite in his volume entitled *Les Dernières Poésies* (Paris: Champion, 1896). He had discovered the works in MS. 24.298 of the *fonds français*, the Bouhier collection, explicitly titled in red capitals: *Les Derniers* [sic] *Œuvres / de la Reyne de Navarre / Lesquelles n'ont este imprimées*. *Les Prisons* is the longest poem of the group, in which there are ten other items. The watermark and script date this manuscript before 1575.

Homonymic errors such as *temps* for *tant* and *regret et* for *regretté* suggest dictated material or a bad model. Transposed, mingled, and even omitted lines signify an inattentive copyist, a bad model, or both. At least we are sure that we have a non-original.

The weaknesses are fewer in the slightly later B. N. MS. 1522, where *Les Prisons* appears in a more legible script. This MS, in a cursive Gothic script of the late 16th or 17th century, is entitled *L'Hepatméron ou Histoire des Amants fortunés, les Nouvelles de la Royne de Navarre—un poéme en trois livres, intitulé les Prisons, par la même Royne*. On the verso of the title page one reads, "Pour ma sœur, Marie Philander." This gift inscription, when considered with the circumstance of a male protagonist and Marguerite's mention of herself in the third person, served to confuse certain 19th century critics as to its authorship; among them were the brothers Haag of *La France Protestante*, as well as Leroux de Lincy and his continuator, Anatole de Montaiglon, who published sections of Livre (Canto) III, ascribing it to Philander, an architect from Rodes in the service of the Alençon family, that of Marguerite's first husband.

Lefranc, having discovered both manuscripts, worked mainly from MS. 1522 to publish the first complete printed copy but adjusted his text occasionally to accord with MS. 24.298 and spellings used customarily by Marguerite elsewhere.

The present work is the first bi-lingual edition of *Les Prisons* by Marguerite de Navarre, also the first best-text edition of the French.

SUBJECT MATTER AND SOME SOURCES

This is a dramatization of Luther's favorite passage, from Paul, 2 Cor. 3:17. As does Luther, Marguerite takes "Where the Spirit is there is liberty" to mean that there is liberation from Adamic taint through divine Spirit. The liberation comes only through grace, this being granted because of Jesus' sacrifical love for mankind. The three writers stress the concept that human effort can not earn it, that what is required is that the seeker identify with Christ. This, according to Luther, should be the chief aim of a Christian.[34]

Marguerite next draws upon Neo-Platonism. It is apparent that the quest of the mystical was a part of the queen's inner dialogue and helped to sustained her through a stress-filled life. The Hermetists and Dionysians around her, chiefly Briçonnet and Lefèvre, fanned this enthusiasm. It is a common mistake to read into the *Poimandres* attributed to Hermes Trismegistus of ancient times a prophecy of Christ's coming. This interpretation was seemingly reinforced by similarities between the Hermetica and writings of the pseudo-Dionysius, assumed to be the convert of St. Paul; it seemed to authorize a fusion of the pagan and Christian traditions into one theology. Such was the premise of Ficino, head of the fifteenth-century Medici Florentine academy, whose work was to spread it. It is small wonder that we find it in *Les Prisons*. Pervading the third canto is the theory of the negative way, which has a history too long to relate here except to point out that it was espoused by Nicholas Cusa in his *De Docta Ignorantia*, a work translated by Lefèvre. The idea is that man's wisdom lies in recognizing his ignorance so that he may apprehend God by intuition when, in a state of exaltation, he finds comprehension total and all limitations gone. The Nothing is then seen to be comprehended in the All, free and invincible. Marguerite holds the Bible as touchstone for judging all books yet specifically praises the *Pimander* [sic] attributed to Hermes, which was published by Briçonnet, in 1514.[35] She approves Dante, taking no notice of his separate treatment of the pagans. Although a lover of letters, she pays tribute to an untutored mystic, most likely Saint Catherine of Sienna, author of *Libro della divina dottrina*, who exemplifies for her the importance of divine inspiration in the case of all worthy writers.

The *Legende Dorée* (Lives of the Saints) figures as another of Marguerite's sources when she gives a brief chronological martyrology. To update it she adds a Christian Turk of then recent renown, the purpose being to show the continuing spiritual stamina of the Christian succored by Christ; the account is eloquently silent upon the proto-protestant and Catholic martyrs of Marguerite's personal acquaintance. Still on the subject of the Christian manner of meeting death, she relates, in most confidential style, the death scenes of four cherished members of her family: her mother-in-law, husband, mother, and brother; respectively, Marguerite d'Alençon, Charles d'Alençon, Louise de Savoie, and François d'Angoulême. She posits a joyous mystical marriage of the soul at death with Christ for folk of Christian faith. Since she supposes it to leave visible traces on the faces of the dead, she peers at them with inquisitorial, as well as clinical curiosity.

The work ends on a plaintive query addressed to the Nothing-become-All. It can not answer, having become ineffable. There is a sense of abandoned stress in struggle but increased freedom to explore the totality.

One may observe that the protagonist has tried unsuccessfully on his own to achieve the three attributes traditionally ascribed to God by Bonaventure, Abelard, and others: goodness, power, and wisdom. These are attained through a recognized unity with the All, a unity that has brought liberation and wholeness.

In *Les Prisons* Marguerite has set forth familiar elements of St. Paul, the *Légende Dorée*, Luther, Dante, and Neo-Platonism both Alexandrian and Florentine, but so blended that they form an original syncrisis.

STYLE, METER, AND RHYME

It has been alleged that Marguerite was unconcerned for ornamental style. She writes with simplicity that is disarming and usually sounds spontaneous. She salutes rhetoric in Canto III: 1914-42, but expresses more reverence for fluency that comes from divine inspiration (verse 2682). She withholds praise from one who is full of wisdom without benefit of scholarship, passing the credit on to the love which informed and inspired the writer. This makes a statement regarding her attitude on style. The rhetorical figures that she uses are found in her extensive reading, but her primary concern is subject matter, her search for something worthy of her worship impulse. Her style is by turns effusive amplification and caustic brevity, now and then irony, and finally prayer.

It is useless to ask why she chose verse once we recall the esteem in which it was held in her time. There survives in English a *cliché*, "neither rhyme nor reason," reminiscent of the superstition once attached to rhyme as a confirmation of truth. That a felicitous rhyme should come to mind at a required moment seemed to the miracle-oriented period to be miraculous, conferring the stamp of truth. The surprise is only that she wrote in French and not in Latin. It was due in the prevalent patriotic attitude toward French which would culminate in the *Deffense* of DuBellay.

Decasyllabic line in Marguerite's verse is most often given a cesura following the fourth syllable, and this is the likewise true in *Les Prisons*. Rarely does a different distribution occur, such as 6-4:

Qui plus espaisse estoit, plus m'estoit belle (v. 112)   or
Le bruit d'estre ung homme sage et scavant (v. 1012)

or 7-3:

A regarder tenebres? Mon desir (v. 586).

She shows a strong preference for the lyric cesura over the epic type. In the latter, a mute *e* meets a consonant in the initial word of the second hemistich, there being already four syllables in the first hemistich besides the weak *e*:

A mon oreille, la ou il se tenoit (v. 82)
L'une après l'autre, gardant leurs ordonnances (v. 116)

In *Les Prisons* there are nine examples of epic cesure:

Je vous confesse, Amye tant aymee (v. 1)

Similar *e*'s appear in verses 1248, 1527, 1725, 3380, 4328, and 4669. Verse 146 might be divided either 4-6 or 5-5.

Of the lyric types, 288 of the 4928 verses offer elision where the weak *e* meets a vowel opening the second hemistich. There are ten verses where two vowels meet and both must be pronounced to conserve the ten syllables of the line (hiatus type). One must note that the final weak *e* of the line is never counted in the complement of ten. Another type of lyric cesura shows two consonants meeting at the coupe (leonine); and still another type, the most frequent, shows a vowel and consonant meeting, either preceding. If the vowel precedes, it is the fourth syllable. To illustrate the above lyric patterns, we note:

Elision caused by two vowels meeting: Jusqu'a la moindre; et voila mes esbatz. (v. 118)
Hiatus: Car il n'y a au monde chose seure (v. 1609).
Leonine: Et apres mort reçoit une couronne (v. 2041).
The most frequent type: Et de l'Amour a l'amant demandée   or
Tant y en a que le seul remembrer (v.1818)

Like Marot, Marguerite preferred a reject of four syllables; for example:

Celluy quy Est sans doubte il connoissoit
Et a luy seul sa complaincte adressoit
Illuminé de ceste charitable
Clarté de Dieu; c'est l'esprit veritable (vv. 2409-2412).

Thus we see that although she used *rime plate*, the couplets are not necessarily closed; some are left open to hasten the arrival of a new line and break up the military monotony. She allows the parade to halt with the thought.

A table of rhymes is found in the Appendix. The most frequent vowel of the rhymes is *e*. The *er* of the first conjugation infinitive is the rhyme syllable in 290 instances; the *é* of the past participle accounts for 286 rhymes, the *ée* or *ées* comprising another 64. Couplets rhyming in *ent* or *ient* number 80 (160 instances of which 68 are adverbs ending in *ment*). There are 52 instances of final -*ere*, 50 of -*essse*, and 48 of -*ez* (chiefly verb forms).

In the 1250 forms in *i*, which is the vowel of second highest frequency, 760 are verb forms, the largest groups being the 86 infinitives in -*ir*, the 112 forms of the imperfect tense in -*oit*, and the 52 forms in -*oir*. *Faire* and its compounds in forms other than the imperfect tense represent 47 lines.

The third most frequent vowel is *u*. Past participles in *u* and in *eu* account for 70 verses; there are 46 rhyme words in -*ulx* (grouping -*eulx*, -*aulx*, and -*oulx*), 90 in -*eur*, 22 in -*our*, 74 in -*ure* (including -*eure*).

Fourth in frequency are the rhymes in -*able* (chiefly adjectives), 56 nouns in -*ance*, and 126 words in -*ant* (101 present participles, the feminine and plural accounting for another 29).

Fifth in frequency is *o*, with the final -*on* (74 nouns ending in -*tion*) comprising 134 lines.

Of the *y* group, totalling 127 words, 55 are verb forms in which -*i* or -*is* would occur in modern times with absolute regularity.

We conclude that in *Les Prisons*, Marguerite follows a verb-dominated rhyme practice.

[1]For general historical data we are relying upon the works listed in the bibliography under "Biography," mainly on Pierre Jourda, *Marguerite d'Angoulême* . . . *Étude biographique et littéraire*, (Paris: Champion, 1930. Bottega d'Erasmo Reprint, 1966), and on Lucien Febvre, *Autour de l'Heptaméron , Amour sacré, amour profane* (Paris: Gallimard, 1944).

[2]*A Godly Medytacion of the Christain Soule* . . . 1513. Marbourg: Hans Luft, 1580, and London, 1570. Included is a transposition of the familiar Salve Regina (addressed to Mary) to a Salve Rex (addressed to God). The lack of emphasis on the intercessory figures, as well as the psalm translation by Clément Marot in this volume were of a nature displeasing to the Catholic authorities. The king protested the condemnation and declared that his sister believed whatever he did.

[3]Lucien Febvre, *Autour de l'Heptaméron: Amour sacré, amour profane*. (Paris: Gallimard, 1944), p. 32. *Égerie*, female inspiration.

[4]*Queen of Navarre: Jeanne d'Albret*. A motive sometimes mentioned for Bourbon's defection to the side of Charles-Quint is that he was annoyed by Louise's wish to marry him.

[5]Emile Jourda, *Étude* I, 160.

[6]Michel François, *Marguerite de Navarre: L'Heptamérom*, Her pupils included Catherine de Medici whom Marguerite instructed in mathematics, classical language and poetry. (Paris: Garnier, 1967), pp. viii-xvii.

[7]"Corps feminin de Madame la Duchesse d'Alençon," in Floyd Gray, *Anthologie de la poésie française du XVIº siècle* (New York: Appleton-Century-Croft, 1967), p. 67.

[8]Leroux de Lincy and Anatole de Montaiglon, *L'Heptaméron des Nouvelles* (Geneve: Slatkine Reprint, 1969) I, 132 indicates *Aeneid*, VI, 170.

[9]A. J. Krailsheimer, "The *Heptaméron* Reconsidered," in Alan Martin Boase festschrift: *The French Renaissance and its Heritage* (London: Methuen, 1968), 55-90, indicates that there was a live re-enactment of the Decameron adventure by Marguerite and the pseudonimous ladies presented in the *Heptaméron*, and that the compilation of the *Heptaméron* tales was undertaken in autumn of 1546, on Marguerite's return from Cauterets, where the group had discussed love both sacred and profane.

[10]Jourda, *Etude, I* cited by Emile V. Telle, *Œuvre de Marguerite d'Angoulême, Reine de Navarre et la Querelle des Femmes* (Geneva: Slatkine, 1969), p. 370.

[11]Telle, *Œuvre de Marguerite d'Angoulême*, p. 378.

[12]Noël Béda, Syndic of the Sorbonne, was required to apologize for the insult to Marguerite in proscribing her book, *Le Miroir de l'âme pécheresse*, before being exiled at Mont-Saint-Michel.

[13]François Rabelais, verbal virtuoso, roisterous satirist, physician, and monk, shows a Lutheran penchant in his tales of Gargantua and Pantagruel. Jean Calvin, born at Noyen, in Picardy, was leader of the Huguenots, organizer of a theocracy at Geneva, and author of *L'Institution Chrétienne*, the first document giving respectable status to French as a language of serious discourse.

[14]The *"Libertins spirituels"* believed two conditions essential to salvation: love of God and sublimation of self. They scorned learning and revered "Spirit," which they held to lead them to the state of Nothing whence they would be absorbed in God.

[15]Etienne Dolet, philologist and printer, translator of Luther and Erasmus, as well as Plato, was both hanged and burned for agressive opinions.

Bonaventure des Periers, was author of the *Cymbalum Mundi* and as well of *Nouvelles Recréations et joyeux dévis*.

[16]It was Gérard Roussel, author of *Exposition familière*, who, by his Reformist preaching at the Louvre, brought down the wrath of Noël Béda upon Marguerite, who had invited him. Cf. Nancy Lyman Roelker, *Queen of Navarre Jeanne d'Albret* (Harvard University Press, 1968), p. 14.

[17]Guillaume Farel is reputed to have composed the placards which Marcourt of Neuchatel is known to have posted on the king's bedroom door at Amboise.

[18]Roelker, *Queen of Navarre: Jeanne d'Albret*, p. 15.

[19]Pierre de Sébiville, a monk of Dauphiné, wrote to a Zwinglist, Anemond de Coct, that there was no one of that moment in France more evangelical than the Dame of Alençon, for had she not just commissioned "a noted evangelist, Antoine de Papillon to make for her a translation from Latin into French the *De Votis Monasticis*, the explosive treatise of Luther against vows?" Febvre, *Autour de l'Hepatméron*, p. 118.

[20]Jourda, *Etude*, I, 377, 391, 426, 627. Cf. Abel Lefranc. *Dernières Poésies* de Marguerite de Navarre (Paris: Champion, 1896), introduction.

[21]Jourda, *Etude*, I, 482.

[22]Cf. Robert Marichal, *La Navire* (Paris: Champion: 1956). Marichal, *La Coche* (Geneva: Droz, 1970). V. L. Saulnier, *Marguerite de Navarre: Théâtres profanes* (Paris: Textes Littéraires français, 1946. Saulnier, "Etudes critiques sur les comédies profanes de Marguerite de Navarre," in *Bibliothèque d'Humanisme et Renaissance*, t. IX, 1947, p. 36.

[23]Samuel Putnam, *Marguerite of Navarre* (New York: Grosset and Dunlap, 1936), pp. 352-353.

[24]Maurice Allem, ed. *Anthologie poétique française: XVI° siecle* (Paris: Garnier. Flammarion, 1965), I, 10-15.

[25]Bertrand Guégan, ed. *Œuvres poétiques complètes de Maurice Scève* (Geneva: Slatkine, 1967) intro., pp. xiii, xv, xlii.

[26]Febvre, *Autour de l'Heptaméron*, pp. 118, 119.

[27]W.G. Moore, *La Réforme allemande et la littérature française* (Strasbourg, 1930), pp. 109-184.

[28]Victor Brodeau was author of *Les Louanges de Jésus*.

[29]Roelker, *Autour de l'Heptaméron*, p. 127.

[30]Leroux de Lincy et Anatole de Montaiglon, eds., *Marguerite de Navarre: L'Heptaméron des Nouvelles, I*, 140 cites the Lalanne edition, VIII, PP. 214-226.

[31]"Musarum decima et charitum quarta: inclyta regum et soror et conjunx, Maguarites illa jacet," cited in Martha Walker Freer, *Life of Marguerite d'Angoulême* (Cleveland: Burrows, 1895), II, 353.

[32]Putnam, *Marguerite de Navarre*, pp. 352-53.

[33]Denis de Rougemont, "L'Amour courtois:Troubadours et Cathares," in Marc Blanchard et Serge Gavronsky, eds., *Le Moyen Âge* (New York: Macmillan, 1972, p. 89), summarizes the laws of the "cortezai: le secret, la patience, et la mesure . . . Et surtout, l'homme sera la servant de la femme." See C.S. Lewis, *The Allegory of Love* (Oxford University Press) for discussion of courtly love in English.

[34]W. G. Moore, *La Réforme allemande et la littérature française* (Strasbourg, 1930), pp. 200-220. For the grace versus merit debate of the 16th century, see Bishop Bradwardine's *De Causa Dei*.

  Frances Yates, in *Giordano Bruno and the Hermetic Tradition* (London: Rutledge and Keagan Paul, 1963), p. 50, indicates that works toward salvation included more, in the 16th century, than acts of charity and religious observance: the term was apt to signify also acts of talismanic magic related to astrology.

[35]Symphorien Champier published hermetica at Lyons in 1507.

[36]Marguerite makes a direct statement on her style in a poem entitled, "Pensées de la Reine de Navarre étant dans sa litière durant la maladie du roi":

"Mes larmes, mes soupirs, mes cris
Dont tant bien je sais la pratique,
Sont mon parler et mes écrits,
Car je n'ai autre rhétorique."

  Maurice Allem, ed. *Anthologie poétique française*, XVI° Siècle, i, Paris: Garnier-Flammarion, 1965).

FRENCH AND ENGLISH EDITIONS

PRINCIPLES OF THIS EDITION AND PARAPHRASE

The intention here is to offer a "best text" edition of the French, based on MS. 1522 (Bibliothéque Nationale) with B. N. MS. 24.298 and the Lefranc edition serving as controls along with the critics credited in the textual notes. Brackets in the French text below signal the existence of variants, which are explained in the textual notes.

Clarity and fidelity to the original are the general aims of the English paraphrase: fidelity first to sense and feeling, and second to the pattern of the form. It has been a special hope to preserve Queen Marguerite's mysticism, lyrical intimacy, and facility. Fortunately her mysticism does not depend on obscure words or special poetic vocabulary, and her lyricism does not depend on poetic phrasing; there are a negligible number of rhetoriqueur figures.

In considering fidelity to sense, one readily admits that word for word rendition of idioms and idiomatic syntax is undesirable; tense, voice, and number changes are therefore admitted to accommodate English usage. It has been possible, however, to make the end of line English word equivalent in sense to the French end word in over 50 per cent of the lines.

It is not likely that Marguerite's present readers will react with the emotions that she expected from her contemporaries. We are not awed when she looks upon the face of a dead person and purports to read there proof that the soul has been recently espoused by Christ. When she paints Platonic love metaphorically in terms of a prison, we tend less to sympathize with the resentment of the protagonist than to wonder about his identity. We have tried, however, not to deprecate the appreciative regard in which the queen held these matters. Our purpose was to convey her feelings and preserve her tone of confessional intimacy.

In preserving fidelity to form we have waived the question of difficulty and honored the queen's choice of verse over prose, thereby embarking upon our act of faith. The early placement of the grammatical object and the trailing of the adjective in French are more nearly acceptable in English verse than in English prose, especially in that of the 16th century, and are occasionally admitted here. French verse is not metered in the lurching manner of English verse, but the number of syllables is easily held equivalent in corresponding lines without damage to sense by not confining expression of all the ideas in the French line to the line of corresponding number in English. Iambic pentameter was chosen as the English meter closest to Marguerite's facile decasyllabic line. Her preferred pause after the fourth syllable has been preserved in sample. She has relieved the monotony of masculine couplets with a scattering of feminine ones; these do not occur with any regularity but are the reason for our having in random fashion ended a few lines in trochees.

We have adjusted the number of syllables as did Marguerite, through addition or omission of connectives such as *and, for, then, thus,* and the relative pronoun *which.* We have sometimes repeated an established idea in adjectives and phrases. We have manipulated adverbs such as *there, ever, while, so, all,* and *indeed.* In keeping with the aim of clarification, we have added syllables, expanding from absolute, infinitive, or participial construction to the phrase or clause; conversely, we have on rare occasions reduced a long construction to a basic adjective. We usually counted the word *every* in two syllables.

MS. 1522 does not use the apostrophe and usually relies on liaison to maintain the meter in places where elision has since become standard; however, one finds "quil" in verse 4513 and "sestimoit" in verse 4635. "Jusques a" is treated as a liaison in both MSS. "Si elle" is usual in MS. 1522; "selle" is more common in MS. 24.298. In the latter, in verse 3640 "selle" is found bridged with an arc. The Lefranc édition shows standard 19th century apostrophes, and this modern elision is followed in the present text. Punctuation, hyphens, italics, distinguishing accents, and some capital letters have been added in the interest of clarity. Spacings of *en fin* and *par tout* are closed or open in the modern manner according to meaning.

The folio numbers have been preserved, but we have taken the liberty of numbering the lines.

Although rhyme is apt to exercise a tyranny detrimental to the sense and feeling of the original, in *Les Prisons* there are encouraging circumstances. There is no *terza rima* as in the queen's *Dialogue* and *Coche*, merely *rime plate*. Marguerite is a virtuoso of facility, and rhyme is almost the only ornament she has used to effect this distinction. The return of the same phoneme at a fixed moment conveys a quality of assurance on the part of the poet and carries a complementary capability of assuring the reader. The ear exercise of anticipation and fulfillment is also consonant with the quest subject of the work and would be missed without the rhyme. It was frequently found possible to make the English rhyme word cognate with the French one.

LES PRISONS
de la Reine de Navarre

<table>
<tr><td>Livre I</td><td>Canto I</td></tr>
<tr><td>B. N. MS. 1522. Fol. 265.</td><td></td></tr>
</table>

Je vous confesse, Amye tant aymée,	Friend so beloved, to you I here confess
Que j'ay longtemps quasi desestimée	That I long rather spurned for something less
La grand doulceur d'heureuse liberté	The sweetness vast in blesséd liberty,
Pour la prison où par vous j'ay esté,	For prison, where, through you, I came to be, 4
Car j'en trouvoys les tourmentz et lyens	Because I found its torments and bond-chains
Doulx passetemps et desirables biens.	To be sweet pastimes and beguiling gains.
Tenebre lors me sembloit lumineuse	The darkness then appeared to be the bright,
Et le soleil lumiere tenebreuse;	And sunshine seemed to me the shaded light, 8
Larmes et pleurs j'estimoys riz et chants,	The tears and wails were mirth and melody;
Et si trouvoys plus plaisans que les champs	I found more pleasing than to be alea
D'estre enfermé entre ferrées portes,	To be confined between the iron-clad gates,
Grilles, barreaux, chaines et pierres fortes;	Stern stones and pickets, chains, and barring grates. 12
La volerie et la chasse et le jeu	Not falconry, nor hunt, nor games of chance
Ne me plaisoient si fort que le gros neu	Would please me like this knot of circumstance
Qui piedz et mains me tenoit attaché,	That bound me hand and foot, in whose restraint
Dont ung seul jour ne me trouvay fasché.	No single day I found the least complaint. 16
Pener, jeusner, veiller soirs et matins,	To labor, fast, keep watch both day and night
Me plaisoient plus que triumphans festins.	Were, more than victors' revels, my delight.
O! que souvent voyant les passetemps	Oh! Often seeing how the gentry spent
Que prennent ceulx qui se trouvent contans	Their leisure, those who think themselves content, 20
Tout seul disoys: «Helas! gens sans raison,	I said, aside, "Alas, you witless race!
«Si vous sçaviez le bien de ma prison,	If you but knew what boons my bonds embrace,
«Vous laisseriez armes, chiens et oyseaulx,	You'd quit arms, dogs, and birds, and you would spurn
«Prez, boys, jardins, et trouveriez plus beaulx Fol. 265 v°	The meadows, woods, and parks, and you would learn 24
«Mes fortz lyens et ma ferme closture	That finer are my bonds and cloister found
«Que tous les biens qu'a sçeu creer Nature.»	Than all the boons that Nature can compound."
Ainsy longtemps, tout seul m'entretenant,	A long while being entertained apart,
Heureux tout seul en ung lieu me tenant,	Remaining in one place with joyous heart, 28
Sachant que vous aussy seul me teniez	And knowing that in turn you held but me,
Et que moy seul sans plus entreteniez,	My comp'ny to be your sufficiency,
Demouré suys en si plaisant sejour	I tarried, having such a pleasant stay,
Que j'y trouvoys l'an plus court que le jour.	The year I measured shorter than the day. 32
Quelz doux lyens de regret tant honneste	What gentle bonds of longing without guise
Des yeulx plantez en si très saige teste,	In your most prudent head, from deepest eyes,
Qui se tournant vers moy non sans propoz,	That, turning to me, not without kudos,
En m'esveillant, m'apprestoient ung repoz	Arousing me, pledged me such sweet repose 36
Voire si doulx que jamais nul veiller	That never stint, regardless of its length,
Par sa longueur ne me peult travailler.	Could ever then have overtaxed my strength.
Et tout ainsy que l'oeil qui ne prend garde	And quite as any eye that takes no care
Le clair soleil en plain midy regarde,	May look at full noon into bright sunglare 40
Longtemps après en demoure esblouy,	And long time after have the sight erased,
Bien qu'il ayt peu de sa beaulté jouy,	Although the radiance was briefly faced,
Tant que partout pense veoir ung soleil	Will think to see a sun in every place

Ou que tout est ou doré ou vermeil:
Pareillement, croyez qu'après vous veoir,
En regardant ailleurs n'avoys povoir
D'appercevoir rien, fors vostre visaige,
Dont en mes yeulx empraincte estoit l'ymaige.
Donques pensez si ma prison cruelle,
En vous voyant partout, me sembloit belle,
Si vostre oeil fut mon lyen et ma corde,
Vostre parler, que souvent je recorde,
Fut mes durs fers et ma pesante chaisne,
Qui me faisoit, ainsy qu'en forte
   gehenne,   Fol. 266
Dire souvent, en eslevant ma voix,
Ce que plustost taire et celer devoys,
Et si taisoys ce que je vouloys dire,
En desirant alonger mon martyre.
Martyre, quoy! mais mon très grand plaisir!
En est il nul tel que d'estre à loysir
Pour escouter si plaisante lesson?
N'av'ous point veu qu'ung trop extreme son
Rend pour ung temps sourde une bonne oreille,
Cuydant ung bruyt ouyr qui l'esmerveille;
Car elle n'oyt rien de ce qu'on luy dit,
[S'on] la benist ou si on la maudit:
Tout luy est ung, car ung bruyt seulement
Tient occupé sens et entendement.
Las! moy aussy, oyant ung tel parler,
Je ne vouldroys jamais loing m'en aller.
Je me moqouys de celluy qui s'aplique
Et prend plaisir à la doulce musique;
Vostre parler m'estoit toute armonie
Qui ma prison rendoit si bien garnie
D'un son, en quoy gist ma felicité,
Que je n'avoys point de necessité,
D'orgues, de lutz, de fifres, de violes:
Je trouvoys tout en voz doulces parolles.
Si ung bon mot ouyr de vous povoys,
Croyez pour vray [que parolle] ne voix
N'estoit, sinon ce mot qui revenoit
A mon oreille, là où il se tenoit;
Tout le parler qu'onques depuis ouy
Ne m'exemptoit sinon ce doulx ouy.
                         Fol. 266 v°
Parquoy mon œil, mon oreille et mon cueur,
Ceste prison ne toute sa rigueur
N'estimeront tant que je fiz jadis,
Fors ung plaisant terrestre paradis.
Ouyr et veoir fut mon salut, ma vie,
Ma passion en qui estoit ravie
Ma liberté, jusques à ne sentir
Le mal duquel j'estoys tousjours martir
Et ce mal là, dedans le cueur planté,

Till red or gold, each new thing bears the trace;   44
Likewise, believe that after seeing you,
On looking elsewhere I could have no view
Of anything except your face, whose guise
Was lingering, imprinted in my eyes.   48
Consider whether, then, my bitter lair,
Where it was always you I saw, seemed fair,
Your eye were bond and cord attaching me,
Your speech, which I remember frequently   52
Were cruel irons to me and heavy chain,
Which made me, as if in Gehenna's pain,

Speak frequently and in loud tone reveal
What I had better silenced to conceal;   56
And, too, I silenced what I meant to voice,
Prolonging then my martyrdom by choice.
What? Martyrdom! But pleasure most sublime!
Is any like one's having leisure time   60
To listen on to such a pleasant theme?
Have you not known one note played to extreme
To ruin a good ear for a little while
So that it thinks to hear sweet sound beguile?   64
Of what one says it hears not anything,
If it be blessed or called accursèd thing;
All's one to it. One sound and naught beside
Keeps sense and understanding occupied.   68
Alas! I too, on hearing such a speech,
Would never wish to wander from its reach.
I scoffed at one whose dedication showed
He relished music in the new sweet mode;   72
Your speech to me was all of harmony,
And it enriched my cell so well for me
With sound in which lay my felicity
That I had simply no necessity   76
The organ, viols, fifes, or lutes to hire:
In your sweet words I found the choir entire.
If I might hear a blessèd word from you,
No other speech nor voice—trust this as true—   80
Existed, only this word which returned
To that one place, my ear, where it sojourned.
All parlance that I subsequently heard
Would fail to grip me except this sweet word.   84

Therefore my eye, my ear, my heart no more
Will judge this prison as they did before
Nor take its utter rigor otherwise
Than for a pleasant earthly paradise.   88
To hear and see was life and my mainstay;
My passion, state in which was snatched away
My liberty, till I became inured
To martyrdom that always I endured,   92
And that pain planted in my heart then would

2

M'estoit pour lors souveraine santé.
Brief, qui eust veu le grand contantement
Que je prenoys en ce cruel tourment
Et d'estre ainsy rudement enchayné,
Il eut jugé mon sens aliené.
Car sans cesser sçavez que je faisoys
Estant tout seul: mes chaines je baisoys,
Puys j'embrassoys, d'amour par trop espris,
Les pesantz ceptz où courbé j'estoys pris,
Puys me tournoys à la porte ferrée
Qui de verroulx redoublez fut serrée
Tout doulcement sa force regardoys,
Ou y touchois et puys baisoys mes doigtz;
Après, alloys contempler ma fenestre,
Où, en saultant, n'eusse sçeu de[la]dextre
Ne d'un baston de deux toises toucher;
A deux genoulz, en lieu d'en aprocher,
Je l'adoroys et sa grille rebelle,
Qui plus espaisse estoit, plus m'estoit belle;
Et les pierres de ceste grosse tour,
Que je voyoys en grand nombre à
l'entour   Fol. 267
Je saluoys aveques reverences,
L'une après l'autre, gardant leurs ordonnances,
En commençant aux plus grosses du bas
Jusqu'à la moindre; et voila mes esbatz.
Lors, ayant fait ces tours par ma prison,
Je commançoys faire telle oraison:
«O belle tour, O paradis plaisant,
«O clair palais du soleil reluysant,
«Où tout plaisir se voit en ung regard!
«Las! qu'il me plaist d'estre icy[seul] à part
«Pour contempler vostre perfection,
«Vostre beauté, vostre condition;
«Par quel amour ne par quel artifice
«Peult estre fait si parfaict édifice?
«Fi des chasteaux, des villes, des palais!
«Au pris de vous ilz me semblent tous laidz.
«Boys et jardins, blez, vignes et
    prairies
«Dignes n'estoient sinon de moqueries,
«Ayant esgard au plaisir de ce lieu
«Qui passe tout fors celluy de veoir Dieu;
«Mais tout plaisir que çà bas a donné
«Pour ma prison doit estre habandonné.
«O digne tour d'avoir toute louange,
«Pour autre bien jamais je ne vous change;
«Je vous requiers aussy ne me changer
«Pour recevoir prisonnier estranger,
«Et que jamais vostre porte ne s'ouvre
«Qui le dedans de mon repoz descouvre.
«Pour cest effect voys les verroulz mouiller,

Appear to me to be health's sovereign good.
In brief, had someone seen the great content
I took in torment cruel, violent,   96
To be thus pitilessly chained and bound,
He must have judged my mind to be unsound;
For, mark you what I did without remiss
When left alone: my chains I used to kiss;   100
I then embraced, by love extremely wrought,
The weighty stocks where, huddled, I was caught
And turned round to the door with iron secured,
Which, locked with double bolts, was twice insured. 104
I meekly looked and stretched my fingertips
To feel its strength, then pressed them to my lips,
Proceeded next to view my windowlight,
Where, leaping, I could never reach with right   108
Hand nor would touch with double-fathom pole;
I knelt; since I could not approach my goal,
I worshipped it and its resistant grill,
Which, where it thickened, seemed but finer still; 112
And all the stones of this great tower stout
Which met my eye in foison thereabout
I greeted with deep bows of reverence,
This one, then that, to keep their ordonnance   116
Beginning with the stoutest, the support,
And ranging to the least; behold my sport.
Then, having made the rounds of my abode,
I undertook petition in this mode: 120
"O, tower fair — O, heaven of delight,
O, glowing residence of sunray bright,
Where every pleasure in one glance is shown,
Oh, here I'm pleased to be apart, alone,   124
To ponder your perfection and to sense
Your beauty coupled with all excellence!
Through love of what kind, nay, what artistry,
Can such a perfect structure come to be?   128
Fie! Castles, towns, and villas I disdain.
Compared with you, they all to me seem plain,
Their woods, grain fields, their vineyards, parks, and
    leas
Are things deserving of mere obloquies   132
When one compares the pleasure of this place —
Which passes all except to see God's face.
Yes, every pleasure earth did once afford,
For this, my prison, is to be ignored.   136
O, tower worthy to have praise's range,
For other good I could not ever change
You, and implore that you do not exchange
Me, taking prisoner some person strange;   140
And opened never let that portal be,
Disclosing its inside, repose for me.
To this end I will make the hinges damp —

3

«Pleurant dessus pour plus les enrouiller. Fol. 267 verso	By weeping thereon, tighter rust their clamp. 144

«Pleurant dessus pour plus les
  enrouiller.   Fol. 267 verso
«Il vous plaira renforcer voz barreaux,
«Redoubler grilles, multiplier carreaux
«Et reunir mes lyens si très près
«Que departir du lieu ne puysse après.
«N'ayez pas peur, lyens, de me blesser,
«Tant seulement ne me vueillez laisser;
«Soyez certains [que plus fort] me tenez
«En fers pesans, plus doulx vous devenez.
«Ne vous ouvrez, fenestre, pour le jour,
«Car j'ay icy la lumiere d'amour,
«Par qui je voy le bien qui me fait vivre,
«Dont je vouldroys jamais n'estre delivre.
«Empeschez donq le soleil de loger
«Icy dedans, car je ne veulx changer
«A sa clarté mes lyens et ma chayne.
«Pour me monstrer ma prison et ma peyne,
«Las! il a[beau] au midy m'esclairer,
«Il ne me peult malheureux declarer,
«Prisonnier bien: c'est ce que je veulx estre.
«Or fermez vous contre lui, ma fenestre,
«Car je ne veulx aÿde ne moyen
«Pour saillir hors de ce plaisant lyen.»
Voilà commant, [Amye,] je parloys
A ma prison où enferré j'aloys
Puys çà, puys là, plus aymant sa beautlé
Que nul empire ou nulle royaulté.
Je possedoys le seul bien que desire
Pour vivre heureux, tout royaulme et empire:
C'est seureté d'amour vraye et loyalle,
Qui vault trop myeulx que la gloire
  royalle;   Fol. 268
Car estre grand et puyssant terrien
Sans estre aymé et aymer, ce n'est rien.
J'estoys donq roy, car j'aymoys si très fort
Qu'il n'y avoit fin en moy que la mort;
Et vous tenoys par amour aprouvée
Semblable à moy, vous ayant esprouvée.
Il est bien vray qu'en ces plaisans discours
Craincte souvent disoit: «Ilz seront cours,
«Ces grans plaisirs, et ne pourront durer;
«Pensez au mal qu'il vous fault endurer
«Quand la prison sera par le vieulx temps
«Mise à neant, et tous ses passetemps.»
Lors, tout mon cueur se troubloit dedans moy,
Mais tout soudain me mettoit hors d'esmoy
La seureté que donnoit sans cesser
Vostre parler de point ne me laisser,
En m'affermant que ma prison antique
Demourroit ferme sans en rompre une brique,
Sinon que moy mesme en fisse rompture,

By weeping thereon, tighter rust their
  clamp.   144
You will be pleased to reinforce your stocks,
To double grills, to multiply stone blocks,
And join my bondage links so very tight
That I may never from this spot take flight.   148
Do not fear, bonds, that you may give me wound
So long as you won't let me come unbound.
Know, As your grip approaches maximum
In heavy irons, the sweeter you become.   152
Pray, Window, do not open to daylight;
For I have here the lamp of love quite right
To show the boon that meets my vital need,
From which I wish not ever to be freed.   156
Impede sunlight, then, lest it should arrange
To lodge herein, for I will not exchange
Against its clarity my bonds and chain.
To show to me my prison and my pain,   160
In vain it turns on me at noon its light;
It can not show that mine's a wretch's plight.
True prisoner: that's what I want to be.
Be closed against it, Window made for me,   164
Because I wish no aid, nor, to abscond,
Convenient means from this most pleasing bond."
You see there, Dear, the way my tongue would race
While, trapped within my prison, I would pace,   168
Its beauty loving with more loyalty
Than any empire or than royalty.
I had the only good I would desire
To live with joy, full kingdom, and empire.   172
Certainty of love both true and loyal
Has more value far than glory royal;

For, to be lord of might and strong domain
And not be loved or loving is in vain.   176
I then was king. I loved with every breath.
There was no end of it in me but death;
And I took you to be, like me, approved
For love, since testing had such doubts removed.   180
True it is, in times of pleasant meeting,
Fear would say, "These pastimes will be fleeting,
And pleasures great as these can not remain.
Consider agonies you must sustain   184
When time brings this, your hermitage, to dust,
And pleasures pass away, as pleasures must."
Then was my whole heart troubled within me.
But instantly to cure this misery   188
Came surety you never ceased to give,
Your promise not to leave me, positive.
In stating that my ancient bailiwick
Would firmly stand without one loss of brick,   192
Unless, myself, I might its confines break

Qui plus tost eusse enforcy ma closture.
Las! je vous creuz par si très ferme foy
Que dame Craincte et sa perverse loy
Je mys dehors de mon entendement,
En vous croyant seule parfaictement.
O quel repoz, quel bien je possedoys,
Estant au lieu que parfaict je cuydoys
Et perdurable, où tout plaisir et biens
Pensoys avoir sans nul soucy de riens!
Mais Cestuy là, qui seul est incongneu
Fors de luy seul, voyant le temps venu
Fol. 268v°
[De liberté qu'il avoit limité
Pour me tirer hors de calamité,]
Fist vostre cueur[pour]mon bien si muable,
Qu'il proposa, non par voie amyable,
Me delivrer, non pour ma liberté,
Mais par sa trop grande legereté,
De ma prison,[par]ouverture plaine,
Non en ung jour ny en une sepmayne,
Mais peu à peu, par le temps qui la fist:
La voulut donc deffaire à son prouffit.
Diray je icy ou l'oseray je dire?
Mais ce plaisir de faire ung lecteur rire
De ce qui est ma folie et ma honte,
Mais le desir, qui ma gloire surmonte,
De declairer la fin de ma fortune,
Me contrainct dire à chacun et chacune
Le comble et fin de ma fole folie,
Mon ignorance et ma melancolie.
Ung jour, ainsy ma prison regardant
Comme le bien dont plus j'estoys ardant,
Le soleil viz entrer par la rompture
Que j'apperceuz dedans la couverture.
O que ce ray, qui me donna dans l'œil,
Me fist grant mal et me causa grand dueil!
Car il me fist, par sa grande beaulté,
Appercevoir ung peu de cruaulté
De ma prison; mais, pour ne plus la veoir,
Fermay mes yeulx et feiz si bon devoir
De rabiller le lieu où il passoit,
Que le soucy plus ne m'apparoissoit.
Le lendemain, j'en viz encore autant,
Et tous les jours alloit en augmentant; Fol. 269
Moy qui cuydoys que le Temps, qui descouvre
Toutes maisons, me fist ce beau chef d'oeuvre,
Compte n'en fiz, pensant bien le gaigner.
Lors jour et nuict me prins à besongner
Et conservay, nonobstant sa puyssance,
Ma couverture, où il ne fist nuysance.
Incontinant, sentiz pierres abattre:
C'estoit le Temps qui me souloit combattre,

Who'd sooner reinforcement undertake.
Oh! I believed you with so firm a trust
Dame Fear and her contrary law I thrust   196
Out of my mind as if they were unknown,
To trust you absolutely, you alone.
What wealth I did possess! Oh, what repose
To be where it was perfect and suppose   200
It durable! All boons and pleasure there
I thought to have, and not the slightest care!
But that One solitary who's unknown
But to Himself, on seeing, as is shown,   204
The moment come that He had set for me
To be diverted from calamity,
Turned your heart fickle, so that it designed
To free me — not by way of being kind,   208
Nor in the interest of my liberty,
But through its monstrous immorality —
From prison; through an op'ning base to peak,
Not in a day, nor in a single week;   212
He willed such time as built it, bit by bit,
Tow'rd your heart's ends then to demolish it.
Shall I relate, dare I? But both the glee
To have the reader laugh at comedy   216
In that which is my folly and my shame
And wish that supercedes my pride of name
To make clean breast of my good fortune's end
Compel my telling all whom fate may send   220
The final climax of my madcap folly,
Ignorance, and depths of melancholy.
One day, as I considered my bastille
The blessing worthy of my utmost zeal,   224
I saw the sun make entry through the rent
That I perceived across the tegument.
Oh, how this ray that gave me in the eye
Such pain did cause me sorrowful outcry!   228
Because, through its great beauty, it caused me
Within my prison to see cruelty
To some degree; and so that I might view
The ray no more, I closed my eyes to do   232
Such good repair as should refill the crack
So my concern should not again come back.
But then, next day, I saw as much again,
And every day it went on growing then.   236
For I, I thought that Time, that doth denude
All houses, gave this work infinitude.
I paid no heed, thought victory ahead.
I took to working day and night instead;   240
And notwithstanding weight to cause alarm,
I patched my roof to where it did no harm.
Then, all at once, I felt some stones descend.
This was mere Time, accustomed to contend   244

5

Ce me sembloit; parquoy de toutes partz
Je m'efforçoys de faire des rempars
Par le dedans, à l'endroit de la bresche,
Tant qu'il n'y peult passer ne dard ne flesche.
Pour renforcer ceste muraille ferme,
J'appetissoys mon limite et mon terme,
Prenant plaisir de faire plus cruelle
Ceste prison, pour la rendre eternelle.
Mais quoy! je vis et grilles et verroulz
Rompre et lascher; j'en euz trop de courroux,
Car je pensoys tout le povoir d'enfer
Ne povoir rompre ou lascher tant de fer.
Ce que je peuz toucher je[reparay],
Sinon ung lieu, où mon sens esgaré
Se trouva trop, car la grille tant haulte
Me garda lors de reparer la faulte.
O quel ennuy, quand tout mon passetemps
Fut converty à combattre le Temps,
A reparer non de telle matiere
Que faicte estoit la muraille premiere,
Laissant mon doulx penser pour travailler
Et mon repoz pour ung songneux
veiller! Fol. 269 verso
O ma prison, qu'estes-vous devenue?
Je luy disoys: «Moy qui vous ay tenue
«Mon paradis, ô beauté enlaidie,
«O ma santé tournée en maladie!
«J'ouvre mes yeulx comme faire cuydoys,
«Mais je n'y voy que l'œuvre de mes doigtz:
«Ce n'est plus vous qui me tenez icy,
«C'est mon labeur, ma peyne et mon soucy.
«Si veulx je icy faire ma demeurance,
«Tant que de vous je verray apparence.
«Je relieray voz pierres de mortier
«Et voz grilles de ce qu'ilz ont mestier,
«Ne pour le temps ce que j'ay entrepris
«Ne laisseray, et si ne seray pris,
«Ny jà de moy flesche n'approchera,
«Ne dard doré mon cueur ne touchera.
«Jà ne rendray la place que je tiens,
«Si je ne meurs, cela je le mainctiens.
«Ny le soleil passant par la fenestre,
«Pour me monstrer le mal où je puys estre,
«Ne me fera jamais par là saillir;
«J'ayme trop myeulx à ma vie faillir.»
Velà commant mon propoz obstiné
Se conformoit, myeulx n'aymant estre né
Que n'estre point prisonnier langoureux,
Ne vray captif du Dieu des amoureux;
Croyant avoir pour ceste fermeté
Vous, vostre cuer, amour et seureté.
Ce propoz ferme effaçoit ma douleur

With me, it seemed, and so on every hand
I tried to build some ramparts that would stand
Inside, at point of breach, and of such mass
That neither spear nor arrow might there pass.   248
To reinforce this strong defensive wall
I made my bounds and cloister still more small,
And, taking pleasure, made more adamant
This cell, with hopes to make it permanent.   252
But lo! I saw both bars and bolts, my cage
Crack and give way; I felt excessive rage;
For I had always thought that hell's full force
Could never such iron slacken or divorce.   256
What I could touch I then repaired except
One place, where my brain found itself inept,
Too much awhirl; the grill so high to reach
Prevented my attempt to bridge the breach.   260
Oh, what chagrin when all my past delight
Was yielded to my fight with Time, the fight
To make repair with matter not at all
Like that of which was made the former wall: 264
Forsaking my sweet dreams to take up work,
And for a haunted watch my rest to shirk!
"My prison, what has now become of you?"
I said to it, "I held you in my view   268
My paradise; O beauty turned to dross,
My health turned into malady, what loss!
My eyes I open, or so think to do;
My handiwork is all that I can view;   272
It is no longer you who keep me here;
It is my pain, my labor, and my fear.
Yes, I still want to make my dwelling here
As long as I shall still see you appear.   276
With mortar I shall bind the stones entire
And mend your gates with that which they require.
I'll not release to Time what I've assumed,
Nor shall I be by any force subsumed,   280
Nor yet shall shaft reach me in any part
Nor fatal golden arrow touch my heart,
Nor e'er shall I give up the place I hold
Unless I die; it's this I will uphold.   284
No sunshaft passing through the windowlight
To show me evil that may be my plight
Will ever force me through its frame to spring;
I'd sooner forfeit life than do this thing."   288
See, that was how my vow so obstinate
Was phrased, I loving less the living state
Than not to be a prisoner forlorn,
True captive of the God of those lovelorn;   292
I thought to have as pay for this endurance
You, your heart, your love, and full assurance.
Steadfast resolve still cancelled all my pain,

Et me faisoit ignorer mon malheur Fol. 270
Tenant pour vray que le Temps batailloit
Seul contre moy, et qu'il ne me failloit
Fors tenir bon et bien opiniatrer,
Rediffier, rabiller, replastrer
Ce qu'il gastoit, et qu'enfin par victoire
Triompheroys de sa honte, à ma gloire.
Qui m'eust dit lors: «Vous n'avez ennemye
«Ny ennemy que vostre seule amye,
«Ce n'est le Temps, c'est sa main variable
«Qui peu à peu son chef d'œuvre louable
«Veult mettre à rien et tout aneantir.»
Jamais mon cueur n'eust voulu consentir
A donner foy à chose si estrange;
Et n'y avoit homme, ny saint, ny ange,
S'il fust venu d'un tel cas m'advertir,
Que j'eusse crainct soudain le desmentir.
Si fut ce vous, ce ne fut autre main,
Qui, soubz mainctien gracieux et humain,
Soubz ung parler digne de m'asseurer,
Soubz ung regard pour me faire endurer
Dix mille mortz, m'avez en trahyson
Par les petis demoly ma maison.
Mais, en pensant de moy tout le contraire,
Je ne cessoys moy mesmes la reffaire,
Dont prisonnier de moy mesmes j'estoys,
Non plus de vous, et si ne m'en doubtoys
Jusques au temps que le soleil, plus chault
Qu'il ne souloit, enflamba ung lieu hault,
Où de bruller chacun ne se feignoit,
Fust il de glace, au moins on s'en
     pleignoit. Fol. 270v°
En ce temps là, je veillay une nuict,
Disant tout seul: Qui est ce qui me nuict?

A qui desplaist le repoz où je suys?
Qui veult avoir le bien que je poursuys?
Qui sent le lieu où je suys[de] la place?
Qui entreprend m'en chasser par audace?
Qui que ce soit, il perdra et sa force
Et son labeur, car mon cueur plus s'efforce
De demeurer en ce lieu fermement,
Plus reçoit d'ennuy et de tourment.
Ainsy, passant la nuict à ce beau jeu,
Je me [trouvay] environné du feu,
Non de celluy qui estoit avec moy,
Mais, d'autre estrange. O l'incroyable esmoy
[Qu'il] me faisoit, en voyant ma ruyne
Inevitable invention et fine!
Ce feu brulla et pierre et brique et boys,
Et moy j'estoys ung sanglier aux [a]boys:
Car, d'une part, la mort me menassoit;

Helped me ignore my hurt, cease to complain, 296
And trust, since it was only Time that fought
Me singlehandedly, I merely ought
To hold steadfast and stubbornly maintain,
Renew, replaster, or should build again 300
His waste — by victory at last proclaim
My triumph to his shame, and build my name.
Whoever then had said: "You have no foe
Female or male; your sole friend is one, though. 304
This is not Time, but your friend's restless hand
That bit by bit would set at nothing and
Would desecrate the most praiseworthy hall,"
My heart would never have agreed at all 308
To granting credence in a thing so strange.
No man, nor saint, nor wraith of heaven's range
Had he come cautioning of such conflict,
Would I have feared at once to contradict. 312
So it was you, it was no other hands
That 'neath a gracious mien and humane stance,
Beneath a speaking suited to assure,
Beneath a glance for which I must endure 316
Ten thousand deaths; you with dishonesty
By bits were wrecking what was home to me.
But holding of my myself the other view,
I did not cease, myself, to build anew. 320
Thus I was my own prisoner-elect,
No longer yours, and so did not suspect
Until the sun, inordinately hot,
Inflamed a certain elevated spot 324
Where each to set a brand without fear pledged,
Were it of ice; at least so one alleged.

Now, at that time, I stayed awake one night
And asked myself: Who plagues me? Why this
     plight? 328
Who is annoyed I should in this place be?
Who wants the boon that I would seek for me?
Who prowls here where I have priority?
Who hopes to oust me by audacity? 332
Whoever it may be wastes both his force
And his hard work; my heart tries more, of course,
With stubbornness to hold my tenement,
The more it gets of harm and punishment. 336
For having spent the night at this fine game
I found myself enveloped in a flame,
Not by the one that was with me always,
But strange! Oh, the incredible amaze 340
It caused me, seeing fated ruin mine,
A subtle, inescapable design!
This fire burned wood and stone and brick away;
And, as for me, I was a boar at bay; 344
For death upon one hand with closeness pressed;

7

De l'autre, Amour, qui sans craincte passoit,
Me commandant plustost ferme mourir
Qu'à nul moyen pour eschapper courir.
Desjà estoit brullé mon vestement,
Quand je vous viz jecter joyeusement,
Par la fenestre où vous estiez, brandons
Dessus ma teste. O quelz piteux guerdons!
En vous voyant fusse devenu cendre,
Car contre vous ne me vouloys deffendre;
Mais aussy tost que vous euz apperceue,
Cuydant parler, je vous perdis de veue.

Fol. 271

Lors, congnoissant vostre extreme finesse,
Vostre cueur faulx qui dissimulant blesse,
Par tous les lieux de ma prison rompue
Gravay au lieu où je vous avoys veue,
Par là saultay en hazardant mon corps:
Le feu estrange et vous m'en myrent hors.
De ce malheur j'euz ung bien non pareil,
Car, en laissant tenebres, le soleil,
Que tant et tant, tant j'avoys refuzé,
Me vint monstrer que j'estoys abusé.
Premierement, me fist veoir clairement
Vous seulle, Amye, aymant trop doublement,
Qui en passant par une galerie
Aviez façon d'une femme marrie.
Moy, tout soudain, je ne le puys nyer,
Tenant encor ung peu du prisonnier,
Couruz à vous pour sçavoir que c'estoit;
Mais le soleil, qui ma lumiere estoit,
Dist: «Non, tais toy, car son ennuy ne vient
«Sinon du bien qu'elle voit qu'il t'avient
«De liberté, où maintenant tu entres;
«Elle vouldroit te tenir dans le ventre
«De sa prison jusques au jugement,
«Pour le plaisir qu'elle a de ton tourment;
«Voire et pour toy ne vouldroit porter peyne
«Sinon autant que son plaisir la meyne;
«Mais en voyant que plus ne te tourmente,
«C'est le seul poinct qui la rend mal contante.
«Si de mon dire as doubte ou deffiance,
«Je t'en donray plus grande experience,

Fol. 271 v°

«Car je m'en voys retyrer ma clarté
«Et ma chaleur;[donc,] comme homme eshonté,
«Regarde et voy ce que sans plus la lune
«Te monstrera.» Lors, contre ma coustume,
J'entray au lieu et grand et spacieux
Où je vous viz, m'Amye, de mes yeulx,
Des vostres faire, à moy non, mais ailleurs,
Les tours que j'ay de vous tenuz meilleurs.

In conflict, fearless love swept me and stressed
That I should rather take my stand and die
Than to some means of exit promptly fly. 348
Already was my clothing set aflame
When I saw you release, in gleeful game,
Firebrands! Seen through the window where you were
Above my head. Oh, what rewards less fair! 352
On seeing you, to ashes I was turned.
My own defense against you I then spurned;
But, just as soon as I caught sight of you
And thought to speak, I found you lost from
view. 356
Then, recognizing your extreme finesse,
Your false heart, hiding, causing me distress,
Through all the crannies of my crumbling tomb
I clambered to reach where I'd seen you loom. 360
To risk of life and limb I was impelled;
By you and that strange flame I was expelled!
This mishap brought me good beyond compare.
When I came out of darkness, sunlight flare 364
That I had so, so many times refused,
Came in to show me I had been abused.
Foremost, it made me see you lucidly:
My sole friend, expert at duplicity, 368
One who in passage through a gallery
Portrayed a lady vexed in modesty!
I forthwith then (deny it I could not,
Still clinging to the captive's ways somewhat) 372
Ran up to you to ask how this might be.
But lo, the sun that was a guide to me
Said, "No, be silent, for her pique derives
But from your gain she sees which now arrives, 376
The liberty on which you may embark.
She would have kept you in the womblike dark
Of her stronghold until the Judgment Day
For her delight in your tormented stay; 380
Indeed, for you she would not take much pains
Except as pleasure of her own constrains.
But seeing she can no more torment you
Is all the point her discontent comes to. 384
If you have doubt of this or arguments,
I offer you still greater evidence:

For I will now retreat, withdraw my flame
And warmth. Then, like a man devoid of
shame, 388
Go look and see what no more than the moon
Will show you." Counter to my custom, soon
I entered at the place of space and awe,
Where it was you with my own eyes I saw 392
Do tricks that I esteemed especially
With yours, but for another, not for me!

J'y demouray ce soir, d'autres assez
Pour regarder tous mes plaisirs passez;
Et tout autant qu'en aviez [desployez]
En mon endroit, les voyoys employez
En autre lieu qui bien les recevoit,
Car vostre cueur comme moy ne sçavoit:
Vous bastissiez, il bastissoit aussy
Une prison fundée sans mercy;
Dieu vueille enfin qu'elle vous soit meilleure
Que la premiere, et que nul œil n'en pleure.
A mon soleil libre je retournay,
Le suppliant que, s'il[m']avoit donné
La congnoissance et claire verité
De ce que n'ay envers vous meritté,
Que ma prison par dedans me monstrast,
Et que luy seul, non plus moy, y entrast.
Je n'euz sitost ma parolle finée
Que ma prison viz toute enluminée
De sa clarté, me monstrant tout partout
Les fundemens, le hault de bout en bout.
Helas! mon Dieu, ame trop aveuglée,
D'un fol plaisir, hors du sens
                    desreglée,   Fol. 272
Dis je à moy mesme, est il possible croyre
Qu'ayez esté si longtemps sans memoire
Du bien perdu, pour si meschante ordure,
Où je ne voy que ruyne et laidure!
Avoys je tant perdu le souvenir
Des maulx passez et du bien advenir,
Que je[me peusse] en ce lieu contanter
De ce qui plus me devoit tourmenter?
Fy, qu'elle est layde et sale la prison
Que j'aymoys tant par sa doulce poyson!
Les fondementz de ferme seureté
Ont trop duré par leur grand dureté,
Mais, à la fin, sur le sablon assis,
N'ont peu durer bien qu'ilz fussent massifz,
Car le sablon mouvant les desmolit
Et l'eau muable enfin les amolit.
Je ne devoys donc pas edifier
Sur ce où nul ne se doit confier.
Puys regardant ceste grosse muraille
Que j'estimoys de grans pierres de taille,
Je n'y viz rien sinon boue et crachat,
Et que trompé je fuz en tel achapt,
Quand je donnay pour telle servitude
Ma liberté! O quelle multitude
De gros monsseaux de terre viz à bas
Qu'à reparer j'avoys pris mes esbatz!
Ma servitude estoit si voluntaire
Qu'incessamment je ne me povoys taire,
Par mes[sermens] dont faisoys ceste boue,

I stayed that night, also sufficient more,
To watch from my past joys the total score!   396
And just as many as you had employed
In my direction I beheld deployed
Another, saw that they found welcome there.
Like me, of your heart he was unaware: 400
As you once built, he now built in my place
A prison founded without pity's grace.
God grant, then, it may be a better keep
Than was the first, lest any eye should weep!   404
Freed, to my sun I turned again, for aid,
To beg that, if to me it had conveyed
Impression that was accurate and true
Of what I'd not deserved to have from you,   408
My prison inside out it might make clear,
It might go in where I could not appear.
No sooner was my pleading terminated
Than I saw my lair illuminated   412
By His own light, revealing me the whole
From top to bottom, end to end, my role.
Alas, my God, my soul had been purblind!
For one fool pleasure I had lost my mind.   416
And to myself I said, "Can one believe
You'd be without recall so long you'd leave
Behind the good for trash so ill-begot
Where I see only ugliness and rot!"   420
Had I so wholly lost the memory
Of by-gone ills and good things yet to be
That I could in this place find my content
With what should rather fill me with torment?   424
Phew, but it is vile and foul, the prison
Thanks to whose sweet bane my love had risen!
Footholds resembling firm security
Endured too long through their rigidity;   428
But, in the end, these being set in sand,
However firm, could not forever stand;
For the shifting sand at last dispersed them,
And the restless waves at length immersed them.   432
For me to build here was a poor design;
To such a place no person should consign
Himself. Then, scanning this substantial wall
That I once saw as ashlar thick and tall   436
I now saw nothing if not clay and spit.
I saw that I was duped in buying it
When I exchanged for such a servitude
My liberty! Oh, what a multitude   440
Of dunes of fallen dust now met my sight,
That to repair had once been my delight!
Mine was such a voluntary fiat;
I could not consistently keep quiet   444
All my vows, of which I made a mortar

9

De m'enfermer; et fault que je me loue, Fol. 272v°	Binding me. Blame must lie in my quarter;
Car plus m'ostiez pierres d'occasion,	When you moved random stones from my surround,
Ouvrant ma tour par plus forte lesion,	My tower opening with greater wound, 448
Par où povoys[vistement] m'en aller.	Where it were quickly done if I withdrew
Soit de m'oster la veue ou le parler;	By cutting off my speech, or dropped from view,
Je rabilloys ceste bresche disant:	I patched this breach each time with words of grace:
«Elle est trop myeulx, en mon cas advisant,	"She is more apt at planning in my case 452
«Que je ne suys, c'est pour meilleure fin	Than I, It's better in the end, I find,
«Qu'elle le fait»; et de ce mortier fin	That she does it." And with such grout refined
Amour et moy reparions ce passaige,	True-love and I repaired the passageway,
En me louant de mon ferme couraige.	Pride praising me for courage that would stay. 456
Or estes vous murailles abattues	But now, O Walls, you have been overthrown
Après avoir esté fort combattues.	In wake of fierce engagements you have known.
Jamais sus bout ne puyssiez revenir	And may you ne'er return to stand upright
Pour prisonnier autre foys me tenir!	To hold me prisoner another night! 460
O gros lyens, doulx regardz traversans,	O stout bonds, sweet glances radiating
Qui dans mon cueur fustes si[transpersans]	That were in my heart so penetrating,
Que doulcement, lyé myeulx que de corde,	You held more firm than rope, yet gently reined.
Soubz vostre trop faincte misericorde	Beneath your mask of mercy wholly feigned, 464
Le conduysiez là où il vous [plaisoyt],	You led it where it pleased you it should be
Car voluntiers en tout vous complaisoyt!	Because it humored you quite willingly.
Je vous ay veuz, ce me semble, dorez,	It seems I saw you gilded when, before,
Je vous ay tant aymez et adorez	I loved you so, and so much did adore 468
Qu'en ce temps là ne povoys avoir myeulx	You, then I could have had no better prize
Que de myrer en vous mesme mes yeulx.	Than to admire my own inside your eyes.
Or n'estes vous plus que chanvre et ferrasse;	Now you are no more than hemp and irons.
Maudit soyez et toute vostre race,	Curses be on you and all your scions! 472
Car trop longtemps m'avez humilié!	Too long you have humiliated me.
Plus ne seray par vous pris et lyé	Now no more fettered by you will I be
En voz durs fers et chaynes et parolles,	By your stern irons and chains and binding word
Que je trouvoys gracieuses et molles, Fol. 273	Which I thought gracious—yielding, I inferred, 476
Tant me plaisoit d'estre par vous tenu,	So pleased was I so long to be detained
Soir et matin longtemps entretenu.	By you, and night and morning entertained.
Que de chesnons, de comptes et de songes,	My, what webs of fibs and vain delusions,
D'inventions, d'histoires, de mensonges,	Falsehoods, tales, deliberate confusions, 480
De louanges, de courroux et de plainctes,	Tirades and protests, and sundry blandishments,
D'appoinctemens et de promesses feinctes,	False promises and such emoluments,
De jurementz, de tant d'autres propoz!	Wordy vows and other disquisition,
Et les chesnons que[forgeoys] sans [repoz,]	Links of chains I forged without remission! 484
La nuict au jour, souvent, comme il me semble,	Unwearied by them, oft I used to see
Voyoys par eulx sans ennuy joinctz ensemble.	The night joined to the day, it seems to me,
Las! Ceste chayne, en grant plaisir forgée,	Oh! this chain of pleasure fabricated
Fut tous les jours par nous deux alongée,	By us both was daily elongated 488
Par vous rompue et par la menterie	But by you was snapped, due to weak matter
Qu'avez mellée en ceste batterie,	That made, when you mixed it in the batter,
Qui le metal rendoit tant imparfaict	A metal so imperfectly alloyed,
Qu'enfin failloit qu'il fust par vous deffaict.	Inevitably, it would be destroyed. 492
O pesant faix, chaynes laides et rudes,	O heavy load, crude concatenation,
Ne pensez plus par voz faulces estudes	Don't expect by cunning calculation
De m'arrester, car vous ne valez pas	To detain me; For you are no more worth
Que plus pour vous je retarde ung seul pas	My halting for you any step on earth 496

D'avoir le bien de mon contantement,
Que j'ay par vous perdu trop longuement
A les lyer. Satan ou Lucifer,
Je ne veulx plus [l']enfer de vostre fer:
Et vous, où tant j'ay trouvé de doulceur,
Ceptz d'union, dont je me tenoys seur
Que pour nul temps je n'en departiroys,
Mais garderiez que nulle part yroys:
Teste, mains, piedz me bouschiez rudement,
Mais si très doulx m'estoit l'attouchement
                        Fol. 273v°
Que je n'euz onq de ce plaisant toucher
Mal ny ennuy, bien que marque en ma chair
Souvent parut, et en mes mains estrainctes
Et piedz foulez j'en aye bien veu mainctes.
Mon œil bessé et mes genoulz pleyez,
Que nuict et jour teniez humiliez,
N'eurent jamais telz biens qu'ilz possedoient
Ou posseder en ce temps là cuydoient.
Qu'est ce de vous maintenant, fascheux ceptz?
Pas je ne viens pleurer vostre decés,
Comme autres foys j'ay fait la folle craincte
De vous laisser; or est ce par contraincte
Que pour mon bien vous estes tout laschez,
Plustost de moy que moy de vous faschez.
O foible boys pour faire telle force,
Tout vermoulu et le cueur et l'escorce,
Est ce par vous que j'ay esté tenu
Pis que captif? Or le temps est
         venu
Que maulgré moy et vous j'ay alegeance;
J'en laisse au feu à faire la vengeance.
Mais est ce là ma couverture antique
Qui nous fut chere autant qu'une relique,
Où je n'osoys toucher non plus qu'au feu,
Craignant l'oster ou destourner ung peu?
Helas! qu'Amour en moy à l'heure ouvroit
Quand je voyoys qu'elle se descouvroit,
Que je n'osoys par là saillir aux champs,
Car j'estimoys les tours saiges, meschans,
Et me sembloit que de la conserver
C'estoit la loy d'amytié observer.   Fol. 274
O couverture, o seure fiction,
O trop double dissimulation!
Souvent par vous j'ay cuydé eschapper,
Comme par vous l'on m'a sceu attrapper!
En mille partz maintenant je vous voy;
Plus n'estre riens, chascun vous monstre au
       doigt:
Je n'ay regret sinon que d'un tel rien
J'ay eu la peur qui monstra mon grant bien.
N'estes vous pas où il vous appartient,

That I might have the good of my content,
Which I've too long delayed for you, time spent
In forgery. You, Satan, Lucifer,
No more of your steel hell will I incur!   500
And you—in whom such sweetness I have found—
The jointed stocks I used to keep me bound
So, at no time, from that place I should stray,
You would take care I did not go away: 504
Head, hands, and feet, quite roughly you would act
And yet, so sweet to me was your contact,
That I'd never from this pleasant pressure
Hurt nor fret, although upon my flesh your   508
Mark ofttimes appeared; on the hands you strained
For me I saw a number, and feet sprained.
My downcast eye, knees bent in supplication—
Day and night kept in humiliation—   512
Had never had such boons as they possessed,
Or thought to have in that time, while distressed.
What's now become of you, vexacious trap?
I have not come to mourn your own mishap,   516
As once I pitched a foolish, fearful fit
On losing you. More requisite is it
For my own good that you should be relieved
Of me, than that by you I should be grieved.   520
O feeble kindling, counterfeiting strength!
Worm-eaten both in core and bark, full length!
By such a one as you I was deprived
And worse than slave? The time, though, has
         arrived   524
That, mauger you and me, I have relief;
For all I let the fire repay the grief.
But can this be my former sanctuary
Dear to us as any reliquary   528
Where I would no more touch than reach for flame,
Lest I destroy or leave it not the same?
Alas that love, in me, in that late hour
As I watched the uncovering, should flower!   532
I did not dare plunge there for fields I saw:
I felt smart moves to be obscene and raw;
And then it seemed to me that to conserve
It were the law of true-love to observe.   536
Oh sanctuary! What protective figment!
Doubly false the sacrosanct depictment!
Oft I thought to find through you release
When people knew me trapped by your caprice. 540
A thousand places now I see you, views
Where you cut no more figure. All
         accuse:
I've no regret but that for thing so slight
I had the fear that measured my delight.   544
But are you not where it befits you stay?

11

Moy où je veulx? Jouons à qui tient tient.
Mais vous, Amye, or pleurez sa deffaicte;
J'en ay desjà lamentation faicte:
Refaictes la,[s'elle] vous peult servir
Pour myeulx à vous autre esclave asservir.
En regardant la fenestre, tout coy
Je m'arrestay et ne diray pourquoy,
Car vous sçavez que par là l'impossible
Possible fut, l'invisible visible;
Louer la veulx, en lieu de la blasmer
Car je sortiz par là hors de la mer
De tous ennuys et folie evidente:
Contantez vous d'elle et je m'en contante.
De quel fer fut ne de quelle matiere
Le petit huys? Nul verroul ne barriere
N'a delaissé, je le voy tout entier
Et tourjours cloz, las! il en est mestier,
Car bien celer, quelque cas qu'il advienne,
Ou quelque mal qu'ung vray amant
    soustienne,
C'est le seul poinct qui faict entretenir
Parfaicte amour. O! que le souvenir.

Fol. 274 v°

Du mal passé, combien qu'il a fasché,
Est gracieux quand il est bien caché
Et que nul tiers n'en peult jamais parler!
Je m'esjouys de veoir l'huys bien celler.
De mon costé entier non descouvert,
Du vostre aussy sans estre en rien ouvert,
Et par nous deux jamais il ne sera;
Mais toutesfoys à travers passera
Ma foible plume, estant si bien couverte
Que l'huys n'aura par elle mal ne perte;
Vous le pourrez, Amye, très bein veoir
Mais autre nul n'en pourra rien sçavoir.
Las! est ce icy ceste prison plaisante
Où j'ay passé ma vie languissante
En tel plaisir, que tout le bien du monde
N'estimoys tant que ma prison profunde?
Moy miserable ay je tant estimé
Ce creul lyen? Las! comme l'ay je aymé!
Comant a pris mon œil tant de plaisir
A regarder tenebres? Mon desir,
Comant a il esté si fort lyé
Et à mes fers et lyens alié,
Qu'il ne pensoit aux choses trop plus dignes
Dont je feroys et miracles et signes?
Comme longtemps mes mains furent oysives!
Comme mes piedz de leurs façons nayves
Furent tournez, myeulx aymant sejourner
En lieu fascheux que de se proumener!
En suys je hors, en suys je du tout suer?

I, where I wish? Let's finders-keepers play;
To mourn its downfall falls this time to you;
Of lamentation I have done my due: 548
If it can serve you well, rebuild the lair
That you may better some new slave ensnare.
While looking at the window on the sly
I stopped myself: I shall not say just why. 552
For the impossible, you know, was near
To being, the invisible was clear.
I wish to praise instead of laying blame
Because thereby I left what one might name 556
A sea of troubles, fool's play evident.
Be happy with it and I am content.
The small door, of what matter was it, nay
What steel? No bolt nor barrier gave way. 560
I see it closed, it is perpetually
Entire. Alas! There is necessity;
For, to hide well, whatever may occur
Or what the hurt a true-love
    may incur, 564
That is the sole point that effectively
Keeps perfect love. But, oh the
    memory
Of past pain, although once it ill-befell,
Is gratifying when it's hidden well, 568
And by third-parties never can be told!
I'm glad to see the door with staunchness hold.
On my part it is wholly unrevealed;
On yours also not in the least unsealed; 572
By neither of us will it ever be.
Yet, since my pen's so clothed in secrecy
It can trespass and still be delicate:
The door will not have hurt nor loss through it. 576
You can, my dear, see all this very well
While no one else learns anything to tell.
Alas! Is this my pleasant prison cell
Where once I spent my life in languid spell, 580
In such delight that all the good on earth
I set at less than my deep prison's worth?
Wretch that I am, held I in such high view
Mean bondage? Ah, what love for it I knew! 584
How was it that my eye took such delight
Pursuing shadows —I desired this plight?
How came desire to be so firmly tied
And with my irons and bonds so fast allied 588
That it would not consider things more fine
Of which I should make miracle or sign?
How long my hands were idled in this phase!
Just as my feet from their more natural ways 592
Were turned aside, preferring then to stay
In duress rather than be on their way!
Am I outside? Quite certain it's all true?

12

Ay je parent, ou pere, ou mere, ou
    seur,   Fol. 275
Qui ayt pour moy ung tel bien procuré?
Non, car je suys de vous si asseuré
Que jurer puys qu'amy, pere, ne frere
N'ont jamais sceu ung mot de ce mistere,
Ny ne sçauront; parquoy, sans nulz moyens,
Ma liberté et tous mes lyens tiens
De mon soucy, de qui l'amour gentille
N'a eu repoz que, par façon subtille,
Ne m'ayt mys hors du labirinthe estrange
Là où j'estoys; à luy soit la louange,
Car ce ne fut jamais à ma requeste:
Je n'avoys pas ce vouloir si honneste.
Or, adieu donc ma prison et ma tour,
Où je ne veulx jamais faire retour.
Adieu l'abisme où j'estois englouty,
Adieu le feu où souvent fuz rosty,
Adieu la glace où maincte nuict tremblay,
Adieu le lac de larmes assemblé,
Adieu le mont pour moy inaccessible,
D'y retourner il ne m'est plus possible:
Par vous de vous plus compte je ne faiz.
Adieu vou dy pour la seconde foys.

FIN DU PREMIER LIVRE DES PRISONS.

Have I kin, father, mother, sister who   596
Has such a benefit for me procured?
Oh, no, for of you I rest so assured
That I can swear: no father, brother, friend
Has ever learned the secret herein penned   600
Nor word shall learn, how I, without the means,
Retain my liberty and all the liens
Of my concern, and whose gentle passion
Did not rest until in subtle fashion   604
He'd extricated me from this strange maze
Where I had been; to Him must go the praise.
For my escape was not by my design,
As I had not intention quite so fine.   608
Adieu then, tower, cell of my concern,
Where I have no wish ever to return.
Adieu, abyss wherein I disappeared;
Adieu, O fire, where I was often seared;   612
Farewell, ice where many nights I trembled;
Farewell, lake of many tears assembled;
And mount to me e'er inaccessible;
Return there is no longer possible.   616
The fault is yours I care no more for you
And for a second time bid you adieu.

END OF THE FIRST CANTO

	Fol. 276	
Amour, qui n'est subject à la fortune,	Love that to fortune's changes is immune,	
Qui ne congnoist ne mouvement de lune,	That neither knows the movement of the moon	620
Ne de soleil, ne changement de temps,	Nor of the sun, nor of the time's fickleness,	
[Ne]veult, pour l'heur que posseder pretendz,	Does not wish, for the bliss I would possess,	
Me retarder de mes vers adresser,	To stop me from addressing rhymes I make	
Amye, à vous que je ne veulx laisser.	To you, my friend whom I would not forsake.	624
J'entendz laisser portant de vous le soing	I have a charge in you I would acquit;	
Qui au salut de l'amy fait besoing;	Your true friend's own salvation calls for it;	
Mais j'ay desir, après ma passion	I desire, in view of recollection,	
Et les lyens de mon affection,	Passion, and the bonds of my affection,	628
De vous monstrer le bien de ma franchise,	To show to you the good in my franchise,	
Pour essayer partout, en toute guyse	To try in every area and wise	
Que je pourroys vous faire desirer	I can to win you to it or to cause	
Ung tel plaisir ou vous y attirer.	You to desire such pleasure till it draws	632
Or donc, Amye, à ce commancement,	You there. Now, Dear, to my beginning here:	
Le beau soleil me monstra clairement	The fair sun shone about me, making clear	
L'ouvrage grand de ceste pomme ronde,	To me the great work of this apple round,	
Le ciel, la terre et la grandeur	The earth and sky, the grandeur,	
profunde,	so profound,	636
Dont l'œuvre en est tant excellente et grande	So excellent in workmanship, so grand	
Qu'il fault penser que Celluy qui commande,	That one must think that He who has command,	
Qui la regit, la gouverne et la meult,	Who rules, governs, and with motion fills	
Peult ce qu'il veult et qu'il veult ce qu'il peult.	It does what He can and can as He wills.	640
Car qui pourroit tel chef d'œuvre parfaire,	For who could such a masterpiece have wrought	
Fors que Celluy qui de rien peult tout faire?	Except that One who can make all from naught?	
Je regardoys hault, bas, de tous costez,	I looked above, below, and all about,	
Fort esbahy, Amye, n'en	In great amazement, True-friend, —have no	
doubtez,	doubt—	644
Comme celluy qui eut les yeux bendez	Like one who'd had his eyes wrapped with a band	
De cest amour que bien vous entendez,	Too long by that love you well understand,	
Trop longuement, ne pensant que	Nowise thinking Nature'd meant to	
Nature Fol. 276v°	feature	
Eust fait ça bas nulle autre creature	Under heaven any other creature,	648
Sinon vous seulle, où ma veue estendue	For on you my gaze had been expended	
Fut sans cesser, non ailleurs espandue,	Constantly and nowhere else extended;	
Mais aveuglée en autre lieu estoit,	It was blind in every other locus,	
Car de vous seulle elle se contantoit.	While it was content with you as focus.	652
Je regardoys par grande nouveaulté	So with much novelty I now would view	
Le ciel d'asur plain d'extreme beaulté,	The sky, of rarest beauty, full of blue,	
Puys mon soleil le jour illuminant,	My sun, also, by day producing light,	
La lune aussy de nuict clarté donnant,	The moon, too, giving clarity by night.	656
Estoilles quoy! en tel ordre et tel nombre	Stars in such array and in such number	
Que nul ne peult de ceste mortelle umbre	No one who is of this mortal umber	
Voire et d'avoir permission d'en faire,	Indeed and get permission for wrong acts	
Puysque j'avoys de quoy les satisfaire.	Since I had wherewithal to pay their tax;	660
Car, pour six blancz faisant dire une messe,	For, having mass said for six blancs, I paid	

Les unes plus qu'autres claires et nettes,	Some, more than others, clear, with light endued,
Desquelles est le cours et la nature	Their nature and paths of their procedure
Bien peu congneu à toute creature,	Very little known by any creature: 664
Mais leurs effectz des corps humains se sentent	But their effects are felt by humankind
Qui plus qu'à Dieu à elles se consentent,	And sooner than to God, to them consigned.
Car l'homme heureux sur les astres domine	But lucky man can over stars preside
Quand Sapience et la Foy l'ilumine.	When Wisdom and the Faith light him as guide. 668
En regardant, je voyoys les nuées	On gazing upward, cloud-forms I beheld
Couvrir le ciel, et puys soudain muées	To veil the sky, then all at once propelled
De lieu en lieu par ventz, aspres effors	From place to place by winds, like coins hoar
Que le Puyssant produict de ses tresors,	That the Almighty summons from His store, 672
Qui souvent sont par la pluye deffaictes,	Such are often by the rain diluted,
Puys par vapeurs incontinant reffaictes	Then at once by mists reconstituted;
Aucunes foys, et par neige et par grelle;	Sometimes with snow, sometimes with hail they're fixed
Et quand le chault avec le froid se melle,	And when the heat is with the coldness mixed, 676
Creve et prent fin ceste nuée obscure Fol. 277	This dark cloud meets its end, rent asunder
Par tonnerre et par fouldre laide et dure.	By the jagged lightning and hard thunder.
Car le Seigneur de tout cest exercite	For oft the Lord of all this host contrives
Pour nostre myeulx bien souvent s'excercite	With flare of fire to send what then arrives 680
Mander ça bas ses message(r)s qu'il fait	Below for our good, messages of His
De feu ardant: c'est ung œuvre parfaict.	That He designs; a perfect work this is.
Je ne sçavoys pourquoy Dieu fist la teste	God made the head of man, I know not why,
De l'homme en hault differente à la beste,	Unlike the animals', a head raised high. 684
Mais mainctenant je puis bien advouer	But, confidently now, I can submit:
Que ce ne fut sinon pour le louer.	To have man's praise was His one aim in it.
En regardant ce beau trosne luysant	While I beheld that splendid, gleaming throne
Du Salomon, qui tout est conduysant,	Of Solomon's, directing all things known 688
Je ne povoys mon œil en bas besser,	I could not rightly cast my eye below,
Ny ce regard si très plaisant laisser;	Nor this most pleasing spectacle forego.
Mais ma foiblesse enfin par forte guerre	But my weak nature, through tough war, here won,
Le contraignit de regarder la terre,	At length it forced my eye to look upon 692
[Là où] je viz tout le plaisir que l'œil	The earth; I saw all pleasure eye can see,
Peult regarder, qui souvent fine en dueil.	Which frequently results in misery.
Je viz les champs, les prez herbuz et verdz,	Fields I saw, the meadows green and swarded,
Arbres portans fueilles, fleurs, fruictz divers.	Trees that bore leaves, blooms, and fruits assorted;696
[J'advisay] lors ces profundes foretz,	By stages I beheld the forests deep,
Ces grans estangs, fontaines et marez,	Great pools and springs and swamps where waters seep
Pour abruver cerf[z], sanglier[s], loups et daims,	For stags, does, boars, and wolves, to furnish drink
Chevreulx, connilz et lievres bien soudains.	To conies, roe, and hares swift as a blink. 700
O qu'il fait beau veoir courir et trotter	What thrill to see deer trot, on fleet hoof borne,
Cerfz, et aux boys leurs grands testes frotter,	And on the branches hone their lofty horn!
Pour myeulx povoir des princes se deffendre,	Better to defend themselves they tend them
Qui nul travail ne[prennent]pour les prendre!	Lest, with no work, princes apprehend them! 704
Moy qui avoys desprisé ce plaisir,	I, who had always scorned this pleasant aim
En les voyant en sentiz le desir.	Felt, seeing them, desire to hunt this game.
Mais quoy! partout où mon regard se jette,	So what? Wherever my survey is cast
Beste ne voy qui ne soit très subjecte,	I see no beast not subject at the
Fol. 277 v°	last, 708
Quelque fureur, puyssance ou cruaulté	Despite the wildness, strength, or cruelty
Qui soit en eulx, dessoubz la royaulté	That lurk in it, to human sovereignty;

De l'homme seul et dessoubz son empire;
Et si l'honneur qu'il en reçoit l'empire
En l'ignorant, il sera fait semblable
A la jument et plus abhominable.
Donques je viz mainctes bestes passans
Par boys, par champs, et veneurs les chassans:
Les uns à force, les autres de cordages.
Brief, j'apperceuz les façons, les usaiges,
Dont les veneurs sçavent les bestes prendre:
Ce que n'avoys par devant sceu entendre,
Pour ne penser qu'à la seulle entreprise
De bien garder celle que cuydois prise.
Or, mainctenant commance à pourchasser
Le grant plaisir que l'on prand à chasser.
D'autre costé, je voyoys fauconniers
Portans faucons, esperviers et laniers,
Et tous oyseaulx et de leurre et de poing,
Dont par avant je n'avoys eu nul soing;
Prandre je viz le heron dans la nue,
Millan, perdrix et la pie et la grue,
Dont je trouvay le passetemps nouveau,
Et toutesfoys ne me sembla moins beau.
En tournoyant, je regarday rivieres
Portant bateaulx de diverses manieres,
Par le moyen desquelz pays se hantent,
Et comme amys estrangers se frequentent;
Car par la mer où les rivieres vont
Navigages increables se font.   Fol. 278
Que ceste mer je trouvay admirable!
Que la congnoistre est chose desirable!
Je prins plaisir de veoir ceste balaine
Qui là dedans se joue et se promaine,
Et semble bien que peu l'homme elle prise
Duquel enfin par les faictz elle est prise.
De ceste mer rochers sont combattuz
Dont les aucuns je voyoys abattuz.
Et, dessus tout, je m'esmerveillay fort
Voyant venir les undes sus le bort,
Ronflant, bruyant, et comme une montaigne
Haulte, et puys il semble qu'elle se feigne
A l'aprocher, ceste mer: sa puyssance

A son facteur rendant obeyssance
Sans riens passer son limitte borné
Come s'il eust de verroulx ordonné
Pour la garder de couvrir ceste terre.
O quel pouvoir a ceste main qui serre
Ung si grand corps en ung limitté lieu!
Autre elle n'a sinon celluy de Dieu.
Voyant cecy, je pensay aux voyaiges
Qu'ont fait les preuz rempliz de haulx courages,

All fall exclusively to human rule.
And if this honor makes the man worse fool   712
When he makes nothing of it, it finds fruit
When he's made like the mare and more the brute.
I watched the many forest creatures race
Through fields and woods, and huntsmen giving chase: 716
Some using force and others, netting-gear;
In short I learned their ways, use they revere
By which they've learned to bring their prey to hand:
What earlier I could not understand,   720
Distracted by that single enterprise
Of guarding her whom I had deemed the prize.
Now, at this point, I set about to court
The mighty pleasure found in hunters' sport.   724
Across the way I saw the fowlers set
Bear-falcon, sparrow-hawk, and lanneret,
All birds both of the lure and of the fist,
An interest that formerly I'd missed;   728
I saw the heron taken in the sky,
The kite, the crane, the partridge and magpie,
And so I would absorb a new pastime;
Each new one seemed to me no less sublime.   732
While roving, I observed the rivers float
A great variety in kinds of boat,
By which means the lands are populated,
Foreigners, like friends, associated;   736
Across the high sea where the rivers lead,
Incredible, sea-going trips proceed.
Oh, how I found the sea to be admired!
How much her lore a thing to be desired!   740
I took delight in looking at the whale
That plays therein, appearing to regale
Itself; it seems that whales but little size
Up man and so at length become his prize.   744
By sea itself the greatest rocks are churned
And some of them I saw thus overturned.
And, topping all, I marvelled even more
To see the waves advancing on the shore,   748
Loud, roaring, looming like a mountain chain
In height; and then it seems this sea may feign
Encroachment, her strength to God surrendered.
Her obeissance to her Maker tendered   752
Nowhere passing where by earth she's bordered
As if He some bulwark might have ordered,
Restraining her lest she should flood the earth.
What power has this hand that folds its girth   756
To keep so large a mass in one set place!
The ocean has no curb but God's embrace.
Observing this, I thought upon the trips
Courageous men had made in sailing ships;   760

Et desiray de faire ainsy comme eulx
Pour aquerir le bruyt des vertueux.
Je [lessay] là la mer et ses bateaux
Pour aller veoir et villes et chasteaux,
Palais, jardins, paradis de delices,
Dont les beaultez font ignorer les vices.
Jamais n'avoys congneu l'architecture,
Ne prins plaisir en dorure ou paincture

Fol. 278 v°

Car ma prison, bien qu'elle fust mal faicte,
Trouvée avoys si belle et si parfaicte,
Que je n'avoys œil ny entendement
Jamais tourné sur autre bastiment.
Mais, délivré de ma prison antique,
Ambition, dont le feu brulle et pique,
Me vint saisir par desir de bastir
Mille maisons et de les assortir,
Et d'aquerir possessions et terres,
Dont souvent sort procès, debatz et guerres.
Puys, j'advisay marchans et marchandises
Qui ont du gaing senty les friandises,
Gens de justice, officiers, commissaires,
Qui souvent sont plus griefz que necessaires.
Là viz le gain multiplier plus grant
Par les estatz dont j'avoys eu desdaing,
Estimant plus l'estat de serviteur
Que j'euz de vous, que d'estre conducteur
D'un grant empire, ou d'estre connestable,
Ou chancellier, ou le plus prouffitable
Estat qui soit; mais perdant ma maistresse
Pers mon estat, parquoy toute richesse
Qui me faschoit, maintenant me plaist fort.
Dont je concluz de faire mon effort
De ces grans biens par estatz aquerir
Et les tresors amasser et querir,
Estimant bien d'en faire mon devoir,
Mais mon soucy n'estoit que d'en avoir.
L'ambition je trouvoys raisonnable
Qui me haulsoit à l'estat honorable, Fol. 279
Cuydant vertu ce desir de haultesse
Qui veult monstrer en tous lieux sa noblesse.
D'autre costé me poussoit avarice,
Qui si très bien sçavoit couvrir son vice.
Qu'en souhaittant biens en diversité
De tous pensoys avoir necessité:
Une heure après, ung estat honorable,
Une heure après, ung riche [et] prouffitable,
Couvrant mon cueur, mon desir, mon penser.
Soit pour gaigner ou bien pour m'advanser,
Je m'en allay ung petit plus avant,
Prenant chemin droict au soleil levant:
Eglises viz belles, riches,[anticques,]

And I desired to do as much as they
To gain renown for merit in some way.
There I left the sea and all her vessels
That I might inspect the towns and castles,   764
Villas, gardens, delight-filled paradise
Where beauties make one ignore the vice.
Fine architecture I had never learned,
No joy in gilt nor painting yet discerned.   768

Because my prison, though it was ill-wrought,
I'd deemed so beautiful, amiss in naught,
I'd never turned my eyes nor fixed my mind
Upon another house of any kind.   772
But from my ancient prison I was freed,
Ambition with its stinging spark of greed
Came to ignite me with desire to build
A thousand homes, as varied as I willed,   776
Acquire possessions, also real estate,
Which breed lawsuits, great wars and long debate.
Next I watched merchants with their merchandise
Who knew the thrills of profit on their buys   780
And lawyers, captains, and commissioners,
More troublesome ofttimes than useful sirs.
I saw the swiftly multiplying gain
Among the classes I'd held in disdain   784
Because I deemed it high'r a servitor
To be, as I'd been yours, than pilot for
An empire, constable, or chancellor,
Whichever the most gainful place to score   788
Might be; but, losing mistress, I my post
Too, lost; and all the wealth that vexed me most
Before, now came to please me much thereby.
So I decided henceforth I should try   792
Through positions to acquire a measure
Of those riches, seek and lay up treasure.
Though I thought thereby to do my duty,
My concern was but attaining booty.   796
I deemed it sound, my wish to elevate
Myself to the most honorable estate
And took for virtue my wish for an air
Parading royalty no matter where.   800
Too, I was pushed by avariciousness
So wise in covering its viciousness.
In seeking goods of wide diversity
I thought of all to have necessity: 804
An hour later, honorable estate!
An hour more, a post both rich and great.
Disguising my true heart, desire, and thought.
To push myself or see what gain it brought   808
I forged along a little way ahead
Pursuing paths that straightway eastward led:
I found fine churches rich and truly old,

[Clochers,] portaulx triumphans, autanticques.
Entrant dedans, j'y viz divers ouvraiges,
Tables d'autelz fort couvertes d'ymaiges
D'or et d'argent, monstrant n'estre pas chiches
Ceulx qui les ont donnez si beaulx et riches,
Et qui plus est grandes fondations,
Sans espargner terres, possessions;
Tant qu'il sembloit que de ces fundateurs
Tous les prians fussent les redempteurs,
En rachaptant leurs pechez par prieres,
Dont j'en[oÿs] en diverses manieres:
L'on en disoit les unes en chantant,
Les autres bas seulement, en contant.
Je prins plaisir d'ouyr ces chantz nouveaulx,
De veoir ardans et cierges et flambeaux,
D'ouyr le son des cloches hault sonnantes
Et par leur bruyt aureilles estonnantes

Fol. 279 v°

«C'est paradis icy, me dis je alors,
«Se le dedans est pareil au dehors;
«Je n'oÿs riens que chantz melodieulx,
«Orgues sonnant pour resjouir les dieulx;
«Je n'y entendz sinon parolles sainctes,
«Prestres devotz, predications [mainctes,]
«Pour consoler tous les devotz espritz
«Et ramener à bon port les perilz.»
Les sacremens j'y viz administrer
Et les petis en evesques mistrer.
Bref, je viz tout ce que font les prelatz
Officiant, dont souvent ilz sont las;
En les voyant j'y prins devotion,
Car par avant jamais affection
Ny avois eu. Ma prison m'estoit temple
Pour moy assez riche, beau, large et ample;
Vous seulle estiés mon autel mon ymaige,
Le but et fin de mon perlerinage;
Mais, n'ayant plus devant moy telle ydole,
Il fault qu'ailleurs mon esprit se consolle,
Parquoy bientost dedans ma fantasie
Se vint loger madame Hypocrisie,
Me remonstrant que j'aquerroys honneur
Si à l'église estoys devot donneur;
Et la croyant, pensay d'edifier
Temples et chantz, où me vouloys fier,
Pour delaisser aux pierres ma memoyre
Et aquerir par les pierres la gloyre
De vray salut, estimant par telz chantz
Povoir purger mes pechez trop meschantz,

Fol. 280

Voire et d'avoir permission d'en faire,
Puysque j'avoys de quoy les satisfaire.
Car, pour six blancz faisant dire une messe,

Triumphal archways, spires where bells were tolled. 812
And entering, saw works more than one kind
Where altars filled with images combined
Gold and silver, showing those unstinting
Who gave gifts so fine and richly glinting, 816
What is more, magnificent foundations
Even land and their accumulations
Till it seemed that, for the founding schemers,
All those praying might be the redeemers 820
Ransoming the donors' sins through prayers.
I heard them pray with many different airs:
Certain of them, one would say, while chanting,
Others only counting, softly canting. 824
How pleased I was these new chants to discern,
To see the torches and the tapers burn,
To hear the sound of church bells ringing clear,
And by their clangor deafening the ear. 828

"It's heaven here," I told myself right then,
"If that within is what the shell has been."
I hear no sounds except melodic songs,
The organs boom to please the godly throngs; 832
There nothing but the sacred words I hear,
And many sermons from divines sincere,
Bringing faithful spirits consolation
And to good port those in trepidation. 836
The sacraments I saw administered
And bishops' mitres on the small conferred;
I saw the prelate routines myriad,
Officiants at them often wearied; 840
Watching brought a pious predilection.
Never to that moment such affection
Had I known. My prison had been temple
Rich enough for me, fair, wide, and ample; 844
You were my altar, idol, hermitage,
The end and aim of my soul pilgrimage;
Having you no more for adulation,
I must seek elsewhere the consolation 848
Of my mind. Soon into my fantasy,
There came to lodge Madame Hyprocrisy,
Arguing to me it would deliver
Honor if to church I were a giver. 852
Believing her, I thought to build, to spend
For church and chant on which I would depend,
Bequeath to stones the keeping of my name,
Acquire of stones my glory and the fame 856
Of true salvation; for I thought by songs
To have the pow'r to purge my sinful wrongs,

Indeed and get permission for wrong acts
Since I had wherewithal to pay their tax; 860
For, having mass said for six blancs, I paid

19

Quicte j'estois de rompre ma promesse,
Voire et absoubz de ce qu'en mariage
Povoys faillir, en donnant quelque ouvrage,
Ou de l'argent, ou quelque reliquaire
Que Charlemaigne apporta du grant Quaire.
Ainsy resvant, sailliz hors et[entray]
Dans ung chasteau, auquel je[rencontray]
Allans, venans, riches,[povres, chetifs,]
Saiges, prudentz, audacieux, craintifs;
L'un va le pas, l'autre par ardeur tournoys;
Lors j'entendiz ung qui dis: «C'est la court.»
J'ouvriz mes yeulx pour myeulx veoir qui
   c'estoit:
Mais d'un costé je viz que l'on mettoit
En triumphant estat plusieurs chasteaux,
D'autre costé l'on proumenoit chevaulx;
Et peu après viz commancer tournoys,
Renverser gens et rompre de groz boys,
Et, à la fin, au myeulx faisant donner
Ung riche pris pour bien le guerdonner.
J'ouys cryer heraulx, sonner trompettes
Pour hault louer les faictz des gens honnestes.
Las! par avant je n'avoys point apris
Qu'il se fallust armer pour gaigner pris,
Le pris estiez, pour qui travail et peyne
M'estoit repoz et joye souveraine;
Lance et harnoys ne m'y firent besoing,
Parfaicte amour fut ma force et mon
   soing;   Fol. 280 v°
Puysque tel pris j'avoys par bien aymer,
Nul autre pris ne povoys estimer.
Je ne l'ay plus, parquoy desir d'aquerre
Ung plus parfaict me fait les armes querre,
Aymer chevaulx, priser l'art militaire,
Dont ne se doit cueur vertueux retraire,
Car par vertu la noblesse est venue
Et la vertu par les armes a creue.
Quant du tournoy chacun eut son butin,
J'entray au lieu où ung très grand festin
L'on prepara, si plain de friandises
Qu'il incittoit gourmandz à gourmandises,
Et le bon vin, tant delicat et souef,
Se faisoit boire a tel qui n'avoit soif.
Et puys je viz sortir de l'habundance
Les enyvrez et commancer la danse:
Masques, mommons, farces et comedies
Entrerent lors, dont furent estourdies,
Tant des haulxboys que du bruyt, mes aureilles
D'ouyr ainsi musiques non pareilles;
Mais le plus beau qui fust en ce teatre,
C'estoit de veoir[non]ymaige de plastre
Mais des dames vives la compagnye,

My fees to break the promises I made.
In matrimony I could then fall short
Absolved if I gave artwork of some sort,   864
Wrought in silver, or some reliquary
Brought from Cairo by great Charles' equerry.
Thus musing, I dashed forth to penetrate
A castle town where I might contemplate   868
The traffic, the rich, the poor, the caitiff,
Prudent, well-behaved, the bold, the craintive,
I watched one pace, one run (the eager sort);
I heard one then who said, "That is the court!"   872
To see what this might be, I stared
   wide-eyed
But saw that they were putting, on one side,
Pavilion bowers in triumphal state,
And opposite, put horses through each gait,   876
And shortly after, saw the jousting start,
The knights capsized, the wood-lance split apart;
Last, the best performing one awarded
A rich prize to show him well-regarded.   880
I heard the trumpets blare and heralds raise
Their cries, the deeds of worthy men to praise.
Till then I had not learned that if one rise,
He must take arms for winning of the prize!   884
You were the prize for whom the work and strain
Were my repose and pleasure sovereign.
For, lance and armor did not make me yearn
While perfect love was strength and full
   concern;   888
Since such a prize I had through my true-love,
No other prize might I esteem above.
'Tis mine no more: so yearning to acquire
A better makes me into arms inquire,   892
Love horses, prize the military feat
From which the heart of worth must not retreat.
For, noble ranks come through this virtue; too,
With use of arms the virtue must accrue.   896
Then, when, from jousting, each one had his spoil,
I came upon the place where feasting royal
Had been prepared, so plentiful in sweets
That it incited guests to gourmand feats.   900
The goodly wine, so delicate and smooth,
Was drunk by such as had no thirst to soothe.
Some I watched who turned from the abundance
And began to dance; they'd drunk redundance.   904
The masks and mummers, farce and comedy
Made entrance then; musicians equally
With noise as with their oboes filled my ear,
Which was made numb by uproar without peer.   908
Best in this theatrical cadaster
Wasn't any image cast in plaster,
But the company of ladies witty,

20

De grans beaultez et de vertus garnye.	Armed with talents, also very pretty. 912
Dancer les viz et chanter en doulx son,	I watched them dance and sing sweet notes with art
Dont il me print au cueur une frisson,	At which a sudden shudder stirred my heart
Car des lyens il me vint souvenir,	Because there came to me the memory
Qui en prison longtemps m'ont fait tenir.	Of bonds that long in prison fettered me: 916
Et tout ainsy qu'un grant coup adressé	Quite as does a heavy blow directed
Dessus ung bras, ung peu devant blessé, Fol. 281	To an arm but recently affected
Fait double mal et donne peur et craincte,	Increase the hurt in dread and fearfulness,
Aussy mon cueur, où vous fustes impraincte,	Also my heart, where you had left impress, 920
Se print par peur si fort à tressaillir	With fear began so strongly then to pump,
Que je pensoys qu'il deust de moy saillir,	I thought it from my chest must surely jump;
Craignant tumber par grace et par beauté	I feared to fall through beauty, grace, or charm
En la prison plaine de cruaulté;	Into a cruel prison of fresh harm. 924
Qui me fist tost destourner mon regard,	This made me quick to turn aside my gaze
De ces beaultez, le jectant autre part,	From those new beauties, casting it oddways;
Car jamais plus ne vouloys asservir	For, not another time would I reserve
Mon cueur d'aymer une aultre ou la servir,	My heart to love another or to serve. 928
Pensant que myeulx vault des femmes user	Of women it were better to make use
Qu'idolastrer d'elles ou abuser,	Than idolize them or give them abuse,
User ainsy comme fait une beste,	To utilize as does an animal
Sans passion. De cest amour honneste	Quite passionless. On courtly principle 932
Vous seulle, Amye, aymée avez esté	You only, Dear, were ever loved by me
De moy, par vraye amour d'honnesteté,	With true-love in my heart for probity,
Qui me faisoit voz vertuz honorer	Which made me to your virtues honor do,
Et vox beaultez et graces adorer,	Adore your beauties and your graces woo, 936
Sans y penser villennye ou malice.	Not thinking malice there, nor villainy,
Mais myeulx aymant mourir que veoir ung vice	Preferring death before a vice I'd see
En vostre cueur, ne de veoir tache noyre	Vice in your heart, or discoloration
En vostre blanc, car mon plaisir, ma gloire	Black upon your white. My reputation 940
Et mon honneur fundoys sur l'amour pure	And my joy made pure-love their prime feature;
Dont vous aymois, non comme creature,	I loved you with pure-love, not as creature
Mais comme ung Dieu dont le seul regarder	But as a deity, of whom the sight
De tous ennuys me povoit engarder.	Sufficed to guard me from all troublous plight. 944
Tant que l'amour dura, chaste je fuz,	I was chaste as long as love was lasting,
De tous plaisirs vilains faisant refuz,	From all villain pleasures I was fasting,
Pour ressembler à ung [que] comme ung ange	To be like her, a cherubim or higher,
Nette tenoys de la mortelle fange. Fol. 281 v°	Whom I was keeping clean of mortal mire. 948
Las! ceste amour tant pure estoit durable	Such a pure love boded long duration
Si vostre cueur n'eust esté variable!	Had your heart not run to variation!
Variable est, parquoy je varieray,	But since it does, then I shall wander too.
Mais toutesfoys je ne me marieray	Still, I shall never marry, thanks to you, 952
Ny ne seray jamais lyé de femme,	And never shall I be to woman feal,
Soit pour espouse, ou pour maistresse ou dame,	To mistress, wife, or ladyship ideal,
Mais j'useray de toutes à loysir,	But shall resort to all of them at will
Sans nul travail pour y prendre plaisir.	And heedlessly of pleasure take my fill; 956
Je m'essayray de farder mon visaige	Now, I shall take the pains to paint my face,
Et d'acoustrer et pollir mon langaige,	To be well-dressed, and polish language grace,
De deviser nouveaulx habillemens,	To put some thought on new habiliments
De bien danser, de jouer d'instrumens,	To dance with skill and play on instruments, 960
De manier chevaulx et porter armes,	To manage horses and to carry arms,
De feindre avoir souvent aux yeulx les larmes,	Feign often having tears at small alarms,
De les tourner doulcement contremont,	And sweetly turn my eyes to look uphill

Monstrant le blanc comme amantz transiz font,
Et de couvrir ma pensée vilaine,
Faignant souffrir jusqu'à perdre l'alayne.
Bientost partiz de ce lieu, dangereux
A qui n'a sceu que c'est d'estre amoureux,
Mais qui d'aymer a le tourment apris,
Sçaura bien prendre et n'estre jamais pris.
Je regarday des Empereurs et Roys
Les magestez et triumphans arroys,
Le grant povoir qu'ilz ont de commander
Voire et de prandre au lieu de demander,
Comment ilz sont serviz et obeys
Souvent de ceulx dont ilz sont bien haÿs,
Car, tant que Dieu les mainctient en puyssance,
De leurs subjectz ilz ont obeyssance. Fol. 282
Devant leurs yeulx je viz genoulz fleschir
Et par leurs dons povres viz enrichir,
Et gens de peu en haulx estatz monter,
Et les plus haulx à force desmonter.
Quant leur fureur s'esmeut comme tempeste,
Lors, il n'y a sur corps si belle teste
Qu'ilz ne facent des espaulles voller,
Ny nul si fort qu'ilz ne facent branler
En ung gibet, par ung mot seulement:
Telle puyssance a leur commandement!
Je m'estonnay de veoir oster la vie,
Et la donner ainsy qu'ilz ont envie
A leurs subjectz, et dis: «Ceulx-cy sont dieux,
Car Dieu ne peult, ce me semble, avoir myeulx:
Ilz ont plaisirs tant qu'ilz en veullent prendre,
Ilz ont honneurs[s'ilz]y veulent pretendre,
Ilz ont des biens plus qu'il ne leur en fault.
S'ilz ont santé, rien plus ne leur deffault,
Et si plus fort de bien veulent aquerre,
Gens et argent ilz ont pour faire guerre,
Et s'ilz ayment leur repoz et leur ayse,
En leurs maisons n'ont rien qui ne leur plaise.
Et pour venir au degré de l'empire
Où tout grant cueur ambicieux aspire,
Je viz chacun qui d'estatz en estatz
Montoit, gravoit jusques aux potestatz.
Les uns par force et armes aqueroient
Ces grans estatz, les autres les queroient
Par leurs amys et support et avoir,
Autres mais peu par vertu et sçavoir,
Et bien grand part par finesse et
    cautelle: Fol. 282v°
C'est le chemin de la plus courte eschelle.
Car, qui à Dieu tourne l'espaulle, on dit
Que tout soudain aura biens et credit,
Et que long temps ung vray homme de bien
En grant travail et peyne acquiert du bien.

To show the whites as stricken lovers will,   964
Pretend, while curtaining my villain thought,
To suffer till more breath can not be caught.
I promptly quit this place where danger ruled
For someone in the sense of love unschooled,   968
But he who of love's torment has been taught
Will well know how to catch and ne'er be caught.
On emperors and kings I came to gaze—
Triumphant and majestic, their arrays—   972
And saw their awesome powers to command:
Indeed, to seize instead of asking, and
How they're served, obeyed, accommodated
Often by the ones by whom they're hated.   976
For, while God keeps them in pow'r as regents,
From their subjects they receive obedience.
In royal presence, lo, the bended knee,
And, by their gifts, the poor made rich I see!   980
And folk from low to high estate ascend
As those who are above perforce descend.
When kingly fury, like a storm, is noised,
No head's so fine, on any body poised   984
But kings may make it from its shoulders spin,
Nor man so strong but he will tremble in
The gibbet; all done at a single word.
Such power has the order [(though absurd)!]   988
I was amazed to see these rulers kill,
Take life, or give it, equally at will
Among their subjects. I said, "These are gods!
God can not have better, I give you odds.   992
All pleasure's theirs, however much they claim;
Fame, too, if that direction draws their aim;
Whatever their requirements, goods exceed;
If they have health, no more exists to need.   996
But if still further wealth they would acquire,
They've men and coin, through war to meet desire;
And if they like to take their rest and ease
Inside the house, they let no thing displease." 1000
And then to reach the stage of the empire
To which all great ambitious hearts aspire,
I marked each man as he would change estate,
Ascend, and clamber to be potentate.   1004
While certain ones by force and weapons gained
These offices, some sought till they obtained
By means of friends, possession and upkeep;
Few gained through virtue and a wisdom deep,   1008
A major part through slyness and
    cunning
Up the shortest ladder those were running.
He who turns his back on God (they've said it)
Quickly will have goods and likewise credit,   1012
While a true righteous man acquires his gain
In lengthy spans of labor and with pain.

22

Lors m'advisay et le chemin cherchay	I then took counsel and I sought the way
Duquel pensoys avoir meilleur marché,	By which I thought to have the least to pay; 1016
Et me trouvay à ce commancement	I found myself upon this fresh outset
Bien recueilly de tous humainement,	By every person tolerantly met.
Dont me voyant par faveur commancé,	So, seeing that I started with a chance,
De mon povoir et force m'advancay,	On my own force and power did advance, 1020
Perdant souvent le boire et le manger	Foregoing often food and beverage since
Pour le plus près du prince me renger;	In order to stand nearest to the prince;
Et peu à peu et degré à degré	Bit by bit, in stages never failing
Montay tousjours, tant que j'eus vent à gré.	E'er advanced as I had wind for sailing. 1024
J'aquiz honneur par travail et fuz riche	Honor I acquired through my endeavour,
Soudainement, à force d'estre chiche;	Gained quick wealth by dint of being clever.
Tant me brulloit ceste concupiscence	So fired was I with this concupiscence
Que je n'avoys moyen, force ou puyssance	I came to lack the strength, the means, or sense 1028
De vivre en paix, ne de me reposer,	To live in peace and make my pace less brisk;
Mais sans dormir ne cessoys d'exposer	So, without sleep, I did not cease to risk
Mon temps, mon corps, ma vie et ma santé,	My time, my person, very health and life
Pour avoir biens et honneurs a planté	In getting rich possessions, honors rife. 1032
Plaisir m'estoit d'endurer froit et chault	The cold and heat were pleasure to endure
Pour aquerir chose qui trop myeulx vault;	To get what might have most worth and allure.
De çà, de là, je couroys sans cesser,	This way and that, without surcease, I'd run.
Importuner sçavoys bien et presser	How well I learned to beg or press someone 1036
Tant qu'à la fin j'emportoys quelque plume.	Till, in the end, I carried off the plum!
Changé j'avoys, Amye, de coustume:	For I had changed my ways, my Dear; in sum:
Mon cueur, qui fut contant en vous voyant, Fol. 283	My heart, that seeing you had been content,
Alloit ainsi le monde tournoyant,	To whirl away about the world thus went, 1040
En grant travail, par terre et mer profunde,	Now over earth, now deep, much effort gave
Souffrant la peur de la guerre et de l'unde,	While suffering the fears of war and wave;
Et qui plus est, je me persuadoys	And what's more, I was myself persuaded
Que d'aquerir ce que bien je cuydoys	Getting what I took for good and rated 1044
[Et]vray honneur, c'estoit louable chose,	The True Honor should be celebrated,
Monstrant vertu dedans le cueur enclose.	Showing virtue in the heart instated.
Je cuydoys donc, par ce cuyder puissant,	I thought by such inflated thinking then
Moy inutile en valoir plus de cent,	To equal better than a hundred men 1048
Et meritter tous les biens qu'onques eurent	And merit all the goods they e'er possessed,
Des vertueux les plus qui onques furent,	Though I were useless, they the doughtiest,
Ausquelz mettoys peyne de ressembler.	Those whom I was trying to resemble.
Cela me fist des livres assembler,	Hence the books that I would now assemble, 1052
Pour myeulx sçavoir racompter[les]histoires	So I might grow in telling history's
Dont les escriptz ramenent les memoyres,	Fine tales, whose records furnish memories
Pour myeulx parler des sciences exquises	For talking sciences dubbed "exquisite"
Qui sont si fort des curieux requises,	That to the curious are requisite, 1056
Pour bien sçavoir prononcer toutes langues,	For learning aptly to pronounce each tongue
Affin de faire en tous pays harangues;	To speak in all the lands I go among
Car à tous ceulx qui font de longs voyaiges	Because for all who make long voyages
Est bien requis de sçavoir tous langaiges,	It is required to know all languages; 1060
Et a l'on veu par estre embassadeur	We've seen, by being an ambassador
Et bien parler parvenir à grandeur.	And speaking well, some do to greatness soar;
Des advocatz chanceliers ont esté	From advocates are chosen chancellors
Par leur parler bien propre et affetté,	And cardinals from glib ambassadors 1064
D'embassadeurs cardinaulx on a faictz,	Because their speech is mannered and correct,

De cardinaulx, papes sainctz et parfaictz;
Faictz ont esté empereurs et vaincueurs
Ceulx qui ont sceu gaigner hommes et cueurs
Par bien parler, par vives oraisons, Fol. 283v°
Par art subtil, par très fortes raisons.
Donques je veulx avoir doresnavant
Le bruyt d'estre ung homme sage et sçavant:
Par ce sçavoir du prince on a l'oreille,
Par bien parler au conseil on conseille,
Le bien parlant trouve assez qui l'escoute,
Du bien parlant nul ignorant n'a doubte.
Je parleray myeulx que tous si je puys:
Les livres j'ay qui sont la porte et l'huys
Par où l'on va à l'honneur de science,
Repoz n'auray, ny paix, ny passience,
Qu'à bien parler ne soye parvenu,
Qui à sçavoir toute chose est tenu
Ainsy trotant et par tous lieux allant,
Ainsy passant seul et tout seul parlant,
Cuydant pour vray qu'il n'y eust nul semblable
A mon plaisir et gloire inestimable,
Au plain midy le soleil m'esclaira
Qui mon estat plus plaisant declaira.
Car je trouvay par son rayon luysant
Ce monde bas desirable et plaisant,
Mais d'autre part me monstra ung vieillart
Blanc et chenu, mais dispost et gaillart,
De très joyeuse et agreable face,
D'audacieuse et grave et doulce grace,
D'un marcher lent; ainsy le viz venir
Tout droit à moy, dont ne me peuz tenir
De m'incliner et faire reverence
A l'ancien qui donnoit esperance,
Le regardant seulement à sa myne, Fol. 284
De recevoir de luy quelque doctrine,
Car le sçavant, à dire verité,
A d'un chacun grant honneur meritté.
Ma reverence à la fin me valut,
Car j'euz de luy profitable salut:
«Amy, dist il, d'autant que j'ay pitié
«De mon semblable et luy porte amytié,
«Je viens à vous, voyant vostre couleur
«Qui montre assez que vous sentez douleur,
«Ou que si fort le plaisir vous transporte
«Que prenez joye à souffrir douleur forte,
«Ou que saisy est d'avarice[horde]
«Tout vostre esprit, plus lyé que de corde,
«Ou que soufrez, remply d'ambition,
«Sans la sentir, mortelle passion.
«Quoy que ce soit, vous portez le visaige
«D'homme troublé en corps ou en courage;

Popes, saints, and prophets from them they select.
Some emperors and conquerers are made
Of those who learn that men and hearts are
   swayed 1068
By good speech, by spirited orations,
Wily art, and forceful disputations.
Henceforth I shall aim to have it bruited:
Man both sage and savant, I am suited. 1072
One gets princes' ears by sounding wiser;
Speaking well in court, he's made adviser
And finds sufficient who will hear him out.
Of him, the ignorant can have no doubt. 1076
In speech I'll try to pass what others do.
My books are doors that offer passage through
Which one to honor of true knowledge goes;
I'll have no peace, not patience, nor repose 1080
Until I have arrived at speaking well,
Which art, for knowledge of all things, is held.
Thus at a trot and going everywhere,
Alone and talking to the empty air, 1084
I thought for sure that nothing could compare
With joy like mine, my boundless debonair.
At full midday the sun enlightened me,
Declared my state soon pleasanter to be; 1088
For, while I found by its translucent ray
This nether world desirable and gay,
It showed me now, upon another hand.
A pale and grey, yet pert and hearty man 1092
Of quite agreeable and cheerful face,
With forthright, dignified, yet kindly grace
And stately step. I saw him come present
Himself to me; I could not then prevent 1096
Myself inclining, doing reverence
To this old man who gave encouragements;
If one but looked at him, peered at his face,
To learn some doctrine that there left its trace. 1100
To tell the truth, when any man has learned,
Great honor from all persons he has earned.
My rev'rent bow availed me in the end:
For I'd a worthwhile greeting from him. "Friend, 1104
To me said he, "since I have sympathy
For my own kind and bear him empathy,
I come to you. I note your cheeks have stain
Which shows effectively that you feel pain 1108
Or pleasure transports you so far amain
That you take joy in suffering great strain.
Either, seized with horrid greed, all your mind
Is yet more tightly bound than rope would bind; 1112
Or you suffer bloating from ambition
And know not its fatal disposition.
At any rate, your face betrays the smart
Of someone troubled in his flesh or heart. 1116

«Et sans sçavoir de vos faiz plus avant,
«En vous voyant cercher d'où vient le vent,
«Je congnois bien que prisonnier vous estes
«De troys tyrans, les plus cruelles bestes
«Que l'on sçauroit estimer ne penser.
«Las! s'ilz ont peu sur vous leurs mains lancer,
«Ilz vous ont priins par si grande finesse
«Que leurs tourmentz vous estimez lyesse;
«Leurs cordes sont de si subtile soye
«Qu'en estranglant ilz font mourir de joye,
«Tant que nully leur danger n'apperçoit.
«Car leurs beaultez le sens humain deçoit,
«En regardant le plaisir qu'ilz promettent,
                                    Fol. 284 v°
«Non le malheur où leurs servantz ilz mettent.»
Je respondis: «Monseigneur, j'ay esté,
«Je le confesse, en prison arresté,
«Plus de dix ans, et d'amour enyvré,
«Mais, Dieu mercy, j'en suis bien délivré;
«Je suys dehors de prison et de peyne,
«En liberté partout je me promayne,
«Et qui plus est, je vous jure et prometz
«Que plus contant suys que ne fuz jamais,
«Car de plaisir, d'honneur et de richesse
«M'a departy Fortune à grand largesse.
«J'ay d'un chacun l'amour et la faveur,
«Et mon sçavoir, aprins à grand ferveur,
«Me fait avoir au monde telle estime
«Qu'arrivé suys, ce me semble, à la cyme
«De mon desir, qui me rend très contant,
«Car la beaulté du monde me plaist tant
«Que l'Eternel, que je prie jours et nuitz,
«Me donne plus de plaisirs que d'ennuyz;
«Et si vous dy, voyant tant de profit,
«Honneurs, plaisirs, que pour moy il suffit:
«Ainsy vivant tousjours demeurer veulx.
«Voicy le temple où j'apporte mes veuz,
«Il ne me fault que bonne et longue vie,
«Car d'estre icy sans amour j'ay envie.
«Povre aveugle, ce me respondit il,
«Vous estes hors d'un lyen bien subtil,
«Doulx et plaisant et assez excusable,
«Pour estre pris d'un trop plus dommageable, Fol. 285
«Car la jeunesse à follie est excuse
«Et la vieillesse apporte sens et ruze.
«Vous qui devriez estre fin et rusé
«Plus qu'en jeunesse, estes plus abusé;
«Voz jeunes yeulx ont vostre cueur tiré
«A la beaulté, puys il a desiré
«De ce bien là, dont avoit congnoissance,
«Par ung plaisir en avoir jouyssance,
«A quoy bien fort l'a poulsé la nature

Of your doings nothing further knowing
Than the way you test what wind is blowing,
I know you for a captive at the feasts
Of tyrants who are three: the meanest beasts   1120
That one could think of or appraise as such.
Alas! If they have caught you in their clutch,
They caught you with such artful sublety
Their torments you mistake for jollity.   1124
Such fine silk ropes these felons do employ,
In strangling, the poor victim dies of joy.
By no one are their menaces perceived.
The human sense by pretties is deceived: 1128
It eyes the promised pleasures they'll bestow,

Not seeing that they send their slaves to woe."
— "Your lordship, I have been," I now explained,
"Ten years and more in durance vile detained,   1132
I confess, on love inebriated.
Thanks to God, I am well liberated,
Outside of pain and prison I am found;
In freedom, everywhere, I move around.   1136
And what is more, I'll make you any vow
That never was I happier than now;
For, of pleasure, honor, and of treasure,
Fortune's dealt me in abundant measure.   1140
I've found favor, love from everyone.
My learning, which with fervor I have won
Gives me, among the world, such great esteem
That I have reached the summit, it would seem,   1144
Of my desire; which makes me quite content;
For worldly frills thrill me to such extent
That I petition God both day and night
To send me more such joys than troublous fright. 1148
I tell you, with such profit it entices,
Fetes and honors me, that that suffices:
That's the way of living I espouse.
Behold the temple where I bring my vows.   1152
A good long life is all that's lacking me.
Here, free of love, is how I want to be."
"Why you are blind, poor man!" said he to me.
"The bondage you escaped was subtlety,   1156
Pleasant, sweet, one rather to be pardoned;
But you're caught in one where danger's hardened.
Because, for folly, youth is the excuse,
More age brings plan and ruse along for use.   1160
You who should be astute, with sense transfused,
More than you were in youth are now abused!
The eyes of youth attracted your poor heart
To beauty; Heart then wished you to take part   1164
In that boon known instinctively a bit,
And on a whim to make full use of it;
Nature strongly pushed it there, a feature

25

«Que Dieu a myse en toute creature:
«C'est ung vouloir de se perpetuer.
«Mais en voyant, pour vous evertuer
«[Et] travailler, ne povoir avoir myeulx
«Que le parler et le regard des yeulx,
«Amour de plus avoir ne vous tenta,
«De soy, sans plus, vostre cueur contanta.
«Aussi le vray amour a tel povoir
«Que qui le peult parfaictement avoir
«Et en remplir son cueur entierement,
«De nul desir ny crainte n'a tourment;
«Qui a desir de myeulx et de pis craincte
«N'a jamais eu d'amour la vive attaincte;
«Mais cest amour se peult dire ydolatre,
«Ung mal si grand qu'il n'y a nulle emplastre
«Par qui jamais sceust bien estre guery,
«Ny le plaisir effacé ou pery.
«Vous le sçavez, marché avez ce pas:
«Confessez donc, et ne le cellez pas,
«Que, sans avoir du soleil la lumiere
«Qui vous monstra muable et mensongere
«Celle que tant ten[i]ez loyalle et
        ferme,   Fol. 285 v°
«Jamais n'eussiez sailly hors de ce terme.
«Myeulx vous valust prisonnier estre encores,
«Ainsy qu'estiez, que comme vous voy ores;
«Car excuser nature ne vous peult,
«Mais qui pis est de vous elle se deult,
«Veu qu'en vous n'a nulle inclination
«Qui veoir vous face en la tentation
«Où je vous voy lyé, pris et captif,
«Plus que devant malheureux et chetif.
«Ce vain honneur où vostre cueur aspire
«Est un tirant de tous autres le pire;
«Lyé vous a si fort qu'il vous fait croyre
«Que, pour lesser de vous quelque memoire,
«Fault pourchasser de monter le plus hault
«Que vous pourrez, sans peur de faire ung sault;
«Le bien vous monstre et le mal il vous cache,
«Vous delyant d'un mal il vous attache
«A ung plus grant qui est l'ambition,
«Concupiscence et vayne affection.
«L'honneur est bien digne d'estre estimé,
«Mais s'il est vain, il[doibt]estre blasmé:
«L'honneur est vain s'il n'est au cueur planté
«Et par vertu [engrané et enté,]
«Mais ung desir de vertueux paroistre,
«Et la vertu ne faire en son cueur croistre
«Et demourer au dedans vicieuz,
«Fol glorieux et sot ambitieux;
«Cest honneur là deshonneur se peult dire,
«Qui peu à peu par desir l'homme tire

God has put inside of every creature: 1168
It's a will to self-perpetuation.
But, on seeing for your excitation
And your travail that you could have no more
Than gaze and conversation, as before: 1172
Love of getting more no longer tempted
You; love by itself, all else exempted,
Filled your heart. True-love has such potency
That he who can possess it perfectly   1176
And fill his heart with it to full degree,
From torments of desire and fear is free.
He who has hope for better, fear of worse,
Had never real attack of love to nurse.   1180
But this love can be called idolatrous,
So great a spell there is no drug for us
By which it yet was known to be quite cured,
Its joy obliterated or obscured!   1184
This is the path that you have trod, you know:
Confess it, then; do not conceal what's so:
That, without having had the sun's clear light
To show the constancy and candor slight   1188
In her you'd thought of single heart and
        firm,
You never would have skipped your prison term.
T'were better still the prisoner to be
Just as you were, than such as I now see.   1192
Nature grants you no exoneration;
But, much worse, you bring her desolation
Since there is in you no inclination
To perceive yourself in that temptation   1196
Where I see you trammeled, trapped, and stative,
More than as before a waif and caitiff.
Vainglory that your heart aims toward first
A tyrant is, of all the rest the worst.   1200
It has you so blindfolded you believe:
In order of yourself some fame to leave,
You must climb highest, and must try your best
With ne'er a fear to topple from the crest.   1204
It shows the good and hides the bad from you;
Unbinding from one ill, it bind you to
A greater still, one that's called ambition,
A concupiscence and heart's misprision.   1208
Now, honor is quite worthy of acclaim,
But if it is pretense, it merits blame.
The honor's empty unless it abound
Ingrained by virtue with the heart as ground.   1212
To want, not virtue, but the seeming-so,
And not to cause it in the heart to grow,
Rather inside leaving oneself vicious?
Fool notorious and dunce ambitious!   1216
Such honor a *dishonor* should be called
That bit by bit through lust pulls man enthralled

26

«Et du possible au premier jeu le tempte,	With possibility that it predicts,
Fol. 286	
«De l'impossible à la fin le tourmente,	Then the impossible at last inflicts. 1220
«Car plus son feu fait croistre et augmenter,	As it fans his flame, the burn augmenting,
«Plus fait le cueur bruller et tourmenter;	So his heart's torment grows unrelenting.
«Vous n'avez pas si peu son feu senty	You've not so little felt the fire inside
«Que ne puissiez sçavoir si j'ay menty.	But you can tell I have not falsified? 1224
«Ambition et avarice aussy,	Ambition, yes, and avarice likewise,
«Et le vilain plaisir ord et noircy,	And pleasure vile that people stigmatize,
«Prennent habitz pour couvrir leur laidure,	These choose habits that will cloak their crudeness;
«Car qui soudain pourroit veoir leur ordure	Someone seeing suddenly their lewdness 1228
«Et ce que c'est, en lieu de les ouyr	For what it is, instead of hearing them,
«Les chasseroit et feroit loing fouyr;	Would chase them off, to far exile condemn.
«Mais si bien ont painct et fardé leurs masques	They paint so well the false face they assume,
«Qu'en les voyant,[fust]ce le jour de Pasques,	To look at them it might be Easter's bloom; 1232
«Ainsy que Dieu ilz se font recevoir	The same as God they get themselves received,
«Et par les yeulx font les cueurs decevoir.	And through the eyes cause hearts to be deceived.
«Hypocrisie avez par dehors veue,	You took hypocrisy for what it seemed,
«Que vous avez[par]estime receue	As if it were the thing that you esteemed 1236
«Dessoubz le nom feinct de religion,	Since it bore the false name of "religious,"
«Qui avec soy a une legion	Sheltering a legion of prodigious
«D'espritz malings si couvertz, que l'esleu	Imps, hidden, till immobile and aggrieved
«A peyne fait qu'enfin ne soit deceu.	Is the elect lest he should be deceived. 1240
«Ambition de si mauvais renom	Ambition of such far renowned disgrace,
«Vous embrassez, ayant d'honneur le nom,	Because it sounds like honor, you embrace;
«Mais,[s'elle]estoit devant vos yeulx desclose,	But, if it were disclosed before your eyes,
«Vous trouveriez que le nom et la chose	You would discover that the thing belies 1244
«Sont differentz, et l'honneur tant aymable	Its name: the honor to hold wonderful
«Ne seroit pas orgueil deshonnorable,	Would not be arrogance dishonorable;
«Et[ne]diriez avarice mesnaige	You'd not call greed, 'a household castellan,'
«Ny provoyance, ny acte d'homme saige;	Nor 'foresight,' nor 'an act of prudent man'; 1248
«Mais vous jugez, comme le monde fait,	But you are taking with the world's swift scan,
Fol. 286v°	
«Riche usurier homme de bien parfaict.	The wealthy usurer for perfect man.
«Pareillement, le plaisir de la chair	Likewise, the pleasure that mere flesh can feel
«Se fait si bien soubz beau masque cacher,	'Neath fair masks is so easy to conceal 1252
«Que recevez ce mortel adversaire	That you find a mortal adversary
«Comme ung plaisir utile et necessaire,	To be pleasure 'useful, necessary,'
«Disant qu'il fault, pour mainctenir nature,	Saying one must for the encouragement
«Boire et manger, et force nourriture,	Of nature, drink, eat, take much nourishment 1256
«De jour, de nuict, sans reigle et compas prendre.	And day and night no rule nor compass take.
«Mais tel plaisir fait de luy compte rendre	Such joy asks an accounting one must make
«Avec celluy de la chair dissolue,	Along with that of flesh made dissolute:
«Qui l'ame rend comme le corps polue,	The soul as well as body these pollute; 1260
«Car sans amour ny nulle election,	Lacking love, in ill-considered fashion,
«Puys ça, puys là, suyvant la passion,	Here and there at will pursuing passion,
«L'aveugle fol qui telle vie meyne,	The blinded fools who lead such life unblessed
«Dit la plus layde estre la belle Helene.	May name fair Helen as the ugliest. 1264
«Las! mon enfant, si tu sçavoys la fin	My son, if full outcome were known to you
«Où l'Ennemy tant vieulx, tant faulx, tant fin,	Where man's old enemy, e'er peddling rue,
«Te veult mener, et quelz tourmentz on treuve	Would lead you, what torment one admeausres

«Quand du plaisir l'on a fait longue prevue,
«Tu quitteroys soudain et de bonne heure
«Ce dont il fault que pour jamais l'on pleure,
«De ce jamais dont nul chrestien ne doubte,
«Où le plaisir sans raison l'ame boutte.
«J'en laisseray à voz predicateurs
«Dire le vray, mais fuyez les menteurs;
«Parler n'entendz ny de plus n'ay envie,
«Fors du malheur qui durant ceste vie
«De ces troys vient, et qui les a servis
«Jusques au bout sera de mon advis.
«Duquel feu est, Amy, le cueur espris, Fol. 287
«Qui est des troys tyrans captif et pris;
«Celluy au vray en a la congnoissance
«Qui en a fait la dure experience.
«Au commancer, l'honneur et la richesse
«Font à leurs serfz très plaisante promesse;
«La volupté de la chair les asseure
«De leur donner plaisir oultre mesure,
«Tant que le cueur à ce beau plaisir court,
«Ou a l'honneur ou aux biens de la court,
«Disant en soy: «Quoyqu'il puysse couster,
«De mon desir il fault le fruict gouster».
«Et semble bien à ce desir brullant
«Que le plaisir à venir est trop lent,
«Et que de peu il seroit très contant.
«A il ce peu, soudain en vient autant,
«Et puys d'autant il vient à redoubler
«Mille pour ung,[jusqu'à]faire troubler
«Esprit et corps, qui à concupiscence
«Contre raison portent obeyssance.
«Venons au myeulx qui peult au cueur venir:
«C'est au plaisir qu'il pretend parvenir,
«Où nul ne peult avoir si bonne part,
«Qu'il n'ayt souvent myse en très grand hazart
«Avec les biens sa vie et sa personne.
«Mais des travaulx passez mot je ne sonne:
«Prenons le cas qu'il soit venu au but,
«Le plus heureux que jamais home fut;
«Fortune est tant inconstante et musable
«Que nul estat ne peult estre durable,
«Et ne peult on l'estat heureux changer Fol. 287
«Qu'an malheureux ne se faille renger, v°
«Voire et le riz joyeulx du plus huppé
«Par triste pleur est souvent occupé.
«Le hault estat, quant il en fault descendre,
«Par desespoir fait noyer l'home ou pendre;
«Les biens aquis en peynes et labeurs,
«Quant on les perd, causent tant de douleurs,
«Que le riche homme estant en povreté
«Vouldroit n'avoir jamais si riche esté:
«A peyne peult soustenir l'indigence

After long experience in pleasures, 1268
You would quit at once, long since have foresworn
This thing for which a man must always mourn,
Of which no Christian ever doubts the toll,
Where pleasure without reason routs the soul. 1272
So! I leave it to your preaching pastors
To proclaim the truth. Flee false forecasters!
I then have no more wish nor caveat
Except to speak of harm in this life that 1276
Comes from these three; whoever's served these three
Will, to the end, I'm sure, agree with me.
The stolen heart is dead in him, my friend,
Who by these tyrants has been caught and penned. 1280
The person who has truthful cognizance
Is one who's had the harsh experience.
Wealth and honors do, in the beginning,
Make their slaves a promise that is winning. 1284
Sweetness of the flesh does promise pleasure
To be given them beyond all measure.
Then the heart runs quickly off to savor
Pleasures, honors, coins of courtly favor 1288
Considering: 'Whatever it may waste,
The fruit of my desiring I must taste.'
True, it seems as his desire is burning,
Pleasure lags in answering his yearning, 1292
And merely sampling would make him content.
But, given it? At once the same event
Occurs; the burning proceeds to double
A thousandfold until it will trouble 1296
Both frame and mind, which, to concupiscence,
Against all reason, yield obedience.
Let's take the best that can befall this heart.
Observe: it's pleasure he thinks at the start 1300
To reach, yet none can have so good a part
But he has often placed on risky mart,
Along with goods, his person and his life.
I speak no word of intervening strife. 1304
Let us suppose his goal may have been won
And of all men he's the most happy one.
Still, fortune is so non-assurable
That no condition can be durable; 1308
And since one can not change from happy state
Except to worse he must accommodate,
Indeed, the laughter of the one best-dressed
Contains the tears of woe compactly pressed. 1312
When he must drop from high estate, the pangs
Of grief will drown the man or else he hangs.
The goods acquired with labor and much strain,
When they are lost can cost him so much pain 1316
The rich man fallen upon poverty
Would wish that never so rich had been he:
Almost unable to take indigence

«Qui a vescu toujours en habundance.   Is one who always lived in affluence.   1320
«Quant à la chair, l'homme ebetté et fol,   The carnal brute of no sagacity
«Qui en a prins tant et plus que son soul,   Who's taken more than his capacity
«Enfin dira, s'il ne veult bien mentir,   At length will say, unless he's fraudulent,
«De court plaisir venir long   'From short-lived thrills come long whiles to
   repentir.   repent';   1324
«Le trop qu'il a prins en manger et boire   The excess that he took in meat and drink
«Perdre luy fait la force et la memoyre;   Cost him in strength, ability to think.
«Venus au corps luy donne tremblement   When Venus sets the body quivering
«Pour le meilleur et plus doulx traitement, For sweetest and best treatment she can bring   1328
«Amoindrissant l'esprit, les dentz, la veue; The spirit shrinks, and teeth and vision wane;
«Mais qui l'aura longtemps entretenue,   But he who will such program long sustain,
«En grant sueur se pourra tant chauffer   In great sweat may himself so overheat
«Qu'il sentira quelque peyne d'enfer;   He'll feel the pains of hell he runs to meet.   1332
«Et s'il ne veut suer en telle chambre,   If to sweat in no such room he chooses.
«Il perira perdant membre après membre.   He will die as limb by limb he loses.
«Voilà la fin là où conduict le vice   Behold the end where vice its quarry leads,
«L'aveugle fol qui luy a fait service,   The blind fool who has served it with his deeds,   1336
«Qui bien pensoit, veu le commancement, Who, given the beginning, thought to wend
«De bien en myeulx finer heureusement,   From good to better, happily to end,
«En lieu d'avoir si dure recompense, Fol. 288 Instead of getting such harsh recompense!
«Mais moult remainct de ce que le fol pense. Yet much persists of what the fool invents.   1340
«Si mon parler est difficile à croyre,   If my discourse is too hard to believe,
«Lisez au long une chacune histoire   Do read at length each record we receive
«Des empereurs, des papes et des roys,   Of emperors, of popes and kings; they say
«Qui sont subjectz aussi bien aux desroix   That these are just as subject to the play   1344
«De tous malheurs et d'adverse fortune   Of mishaps and adversities of fate
«Que de plaisir, d'ambition pecune;   As to the joys of surfeiture and spate.
«Serfz se sont faictz, parquoy, selon le maistre According to the lord whose serfs they made
«Qu'ilz ont servy, payez ils doivent   Themselves, whom they have served, they must be
   estre.   paid.   1348
Ilz ont servy le peché à grant tort,   In monstrous error they have courted sin,
«Duquel le fruict est repentance et mort.   Whose fruit is death, repentance, and chagrin.
«O que creulz sont ces troys exacteurs,   Oh, cruel are these three extortioners,
«Ces troys tyrans, importuns tourmenteurs, Tormentors, tyrants, importuning curs,   1352
«Qui en monstrant ung plaisir incertain,   Who, presenting an uncertain pleasure
«Ou la richesse, ou l'honneur qui est vain, That is vain, say honor or say treasure,
«Font par desir perdre boire et manger,   Will cause through lust the loss of food and drink,
«Dormir, repoz jusqu'à mettre en danger   Sleep and repose; they bring to danger's brink   1356
«Vie et santé! Pensant la fin attaindre   Both heath and life! With thought an end to gain
«De ce desir, sans se douloir ny plaindre   Of lust, no more to fret nor to complain
«De froit ny chauld, de mal ny de blesseure, Of cold or heat, of illness or of wound,
«Cuydant trouver la felicité seure   And trusting sure felicity is found   1360
«Et le repoz et le contentement,   Also the repose and satisfaction
«Qu'ilz ont forgé en leur entendement,   That they've pictured in their mind's abstraction,
«Les ignorans suyvant ces troys seigneurs The ignorants who follow these magi
«Ont en leur cueur forgé que les honneurs, Have fabricated in their heart the lie: 1364
«Plaisirs et biens sont la felicité,   Goods, honors, pleasures are the happiness
«Qu'à desirer chacun est incitté;   That each is motivated to possess;
«Et de ces troys seigneurs ont faict ydole, And they have made an idol of these three
«En excusant leur intention folle   To shift the blame for aims of idiocy   1368
«Ou sur le temps ou sur l'occasion,   Upon the times or on expediency,

29

«Estimant sens leur sotte abusion;
«Et par travail n'ont cessé d'aquerir
«Le bien qu'on peult en ce monde querir.
«Si à leur poinct sont venuz à faillir,
«Hors de leurs sens on les a veu saillir,
«En mauldissant l'heure, le temps, le jour
«Qu'aux trois tyrans ont eu foy[et]amour;
«Et si au poinct tant desiré adviennent,
«Craintifz, poureux de le perdre ilz deviennent;
«Songneux, jaloux sont de le conserver,
«Comme songneux furent de le trouver;
«Et s 'ilz n'ont pas plus tost ung bien receu,
«Qu'ung tout nouveau desir ne soit conceu
«Ou d'avoir plus ou myeulx ou autrement.
«Ainsy le cueur de tourment en tourment
«Monte, descend, et de tous costez tourne,
«Tant qu'en ung poinct jamais il ne sejourne;
«Car le desir nouveau qui l'a deceu
«Luy fait trouver fascheux le bien receu,

«Ou s'il est tel qu'à l'heure il s'en contante,
«Crainte l'assault, jalousie le tente,
«Qui sy très fort le viennent martyrer
«Que tout le mal passé du desirer,
«Tout le travail pour aquerir ce bien,
«Estime doulx et quasi moins que rien,
«Accomparé à celluy qu'il endure
«De ceste peur tant effreyable et dure.
«Le hault monté a peur qu'on le desmonte,
«Que l'on l'esloigne ou qu'on luy face honte,
«Et sans cesser il se tient sur sa garde, Fol. 289
«Tousjours pensif, de tous costez regarde,
«Car le pecheur honoré tousjours crainct
«Que l'honneur soit ainsy comme luy fainct.
«Le riche aussy souvent la nuict s'esveille,
«Pour quelque rat grattant soubz son oreille,
«Et son chevet retourne et puys sa couette,
«Jusqu'à la paille où sa bourse ou bougette
«Il a caché, craignant qu'ung desrobeur
«Prenne le bien qu'aveques grand labeur
«Il a aquis; puys s'endort et tressault
«En s'endormant, et se lieve en soursault,
«Prend son espée ou s'en court à la porte
«Tuer celluy qui son tresor emporte;
«Et quand il est à la porte venu,
«N'y trouve nul, fors que luy fol et nu,
«Et voyant l'huys branlant dans l'oustevent,
«Scait qu'il n'y a larron, sinon le vent.
«Ainsy la peur le fait le nuict veiller
«Et tout le jour sans repoz travailler;

Misdeeming sense their stupid fantasy,
And through their work have not ceased to acquire
The worldly goods to which one can aspire.   1372
If, at their peak, it happens that they dip,
The mooring of their senses, too, may slip,
They curse the circumstances, hour, or day
To tyrants they gave faith and love away;   1376
And if they reach the point for which they yearn,
To cringers scared to lose it they then turn
Most careful, as jealous to conserve it
As when getting made their efforts fervid;   1380
No sooner is a benefit received
Than some new target by them is conceived
To get one bigger, better, different.
The heart, from one ache to the subsequent,   1384
May rise and fall, in all directions yearn
So long as at no point it finds sojourn;
For the latest aim that has deceived him
Made the good acquired a thing that peeved him;   1388

Or suppose now no new craving ails him,
Jealousy now tempts him; fear assails him,
Which with such force have come to martyr him
That all the striving, the bad interim,   1392
And all the effort to achieve this gain
He thinks is mild, almost devoid of pain
Compared to that which he now undergoes,
So terror-filled and harsh these horror throes.   1396
Eminence has fear to be demoted
Or removed; his downfall may be voted;
Always he is on his guard, defensive,
Always looks around, e're apprehensive;   1400
For the exalted sinner ever quails
Lest honor be like him, a thing that fails.
Too, often in the night the rich man wakes;
Some scratching rat's beneath his ear; he quakes,   1404
Turns up his mattress, rips the tick until
He comes to straw where petty purse or till
He's hidden, fearing lest some common thief
Take from him all the wealth that with great grief   1408
And labor he's acquired. He goes to sleep
But starts in slumber, springs up with a leap;
He grabs his sword and runs out to the door
To kill the one who'd carry off his store;   1412
But when he's reached the door, he's only found
A naked fool and no one else around;
He sees the hall door shake, his suspects thinned,
And knows there is no robber but the wind.   1416
Thus, fear keeps him on watch; all night awake;
All day at work, no respite can he take;

30

«Mais si par feu, par larrons ou procés,
«Il pert son bien, il tumbe en ung accez
«Pire à porter que fievre continue.
«Car comme il a l'avarice tenue
«Pour son vray bien, duquel depend sa vie.
«Quand l'on luy a son ydole ravye,
«En la perdant, il se veult perdre aussy,
«N'ayant non plus de sa vie soucy
«Que de son ame¡ avoit, en la perdant
«Au feu qui est plus nul autre ardant.
«Et le charnel, qui petit à petit   Fol. 289 verso
«Par gourmander pert goust et appetit
«Et le povoir de femmes festyer,
«Dont le sçait bien vieillesse chastier,
«Luy amenant maladie et foiblesse,
«Et le regret qui plus que tout le blesse
«Des grans plaisirs passez, qui retourner
«Ne pevent plus, quoy qu'on puysse donner:
«Croyez qu'il sent ung cruel purgatoire
«Quand il n'auroit douleur que la memoyre
«Du temps passé, sans les maulx de present,
«Dont son peché en fin luy fait present.
«Ridée il voit sa face et enlaidye;
«Sa santé sent tournée en maladie,
«Force en foiblesse et plaisir en regret,
«Et qu'en nul lieu soit public ou secret
«Ne peult trouver le plaisir qu'il a pris,
«Qu'il devoit bien avoir mys à depris.
«Mais puysqu'il n'a en sa force et vertu
«Par la raison son peché abattu,
«Et l'a porté, soustenu, excusé,
«Estant de luy amoureux, abusé,
«En la vieillesse où laisser le cuydoit,
«L'ayme plus fort sans propoz qu'il ne doit;
«Car en perdant le povoir de jouyr,
«Plus il le cherche et moins le veult fouyr,
«Et plus le temps luy oste la puyssance,
«Plus en delict croist la concupiscence.
«Las! mon amy, qui sont ces troys lyens
«De la prison où vous trouvez tous biens?
«L'un qui vous tient le cueur charnel
  captif;   Fol. 290
«C'est ung lyen qui est faict d'argent vif
«Environné de cent mille beaultez
«Soubz qui pitié couvre ses cruaultez,
«Et si est tant delicat et subtil
«Que vostre cueur, tant soit fort et gentil,
«Rend par foiblesse à terre humilié
«Et à sa chair pris, collé et lyé,
«Si finement que jamais n'apperçoit
«Là où il va jusqu'à ce qu'il y soit;
«Et qui pis est, quant il y est, il pense

But, if by fire, by thieves or court process,
He lose his goods, he falls into access   1420
More ravaging than fever long sustained;
For since it's avarice he has maintained
To be the good on which his life depends,
When someone then his idol apprehends,   1424
On losing it, for loss of self he yearns
As he then has for life no more concerns
Than for his soul he's had, lost as it turns
To fire which more than any other burns.   1428
The carnal disposition, bite by bite,
With gorging ruins the taste and appetite,
With women ruins his chance to titillate —
For these old age knows how to castigate   1432
Him, bringing him disease and weakness, round
Regret for joys once known that gives him wound
More than all else; their pow'r is negative
To come again, despite what he would give: 1436
Trust me, he knows purgatory cruel
If he have but memory to gruel,
Not even counting present pains to shift,
That bygone sin has left as parting gift.   1440
See his face now wrinkled; it displeases
Him to feel his health lost to diseases,
Force to weakness, and pleasure to regret;
And, in no public place nor secret, yet,   1444
Can he be finding pleasure he has prized,
That he should always truly have despised.
And since in time of force and strength he'd not
By reasoning his sinfulness outfought,   1448
He carried it, sustained it and excused
Himself, in love with it, not disabused;
In old age, when to leave it off he thought,
He loves it more, regardless, than he ought,   1452
Because, in losing joy's capacity,
The more he seeks, and less he wants to flee,
The more time takes from him ability;
The more delight grows in cupidity.   1456
Ah, my Friend, what are these three connections
With the prison where you find perfections?
The one that holds your heart in bond to
  flesh
Is link no stronger than quick-silver mesh   1460
Compassed by a hundred thousand splendors;
Sympathy hides cruelties it tenders;
It has so much of tact and subtlety,
However strong and fine your heart may be,   1464
Through weakness it is humbled to the ground,
Inveighed by flesh, entrammeled and fast bound
With such finesse that never does it see
Where he proceeds till there he comes to be;   1468
And what is worse, when he is there, he thinks

31

«Que son malheur ne soit que jeu ou danse,
«Et en crainct rien, sinon le departir
«Du mal auquel il vit joyeulx martir.
«L'autre lyen, qui vous tient par les yeulx,
«Sans vous souffrir de les lever aux cyeulx,
«Il est d'or fin, si bien fait et si riche,
«Que vostre œil plus qu'en ung lieu ne se fiche,
«Soit au prouffit, à la richesse ou gaing,
«Sans regarder ny Dieu ny le prochain.
«Bien que richesse, or et argent, Dieu fist
«Pour en user, et non pour le prouffit
«Particulier; mais, en lieu d'en user,
«Ce fort lyen vous en fait abuser,
«En vous ostant la joye de ce monde,
«Pour ne veoir plus avarice l'immunde.
«Le tiers lyen est tout fait d'escarboucles
«Et de rubiz enchassez dans des boucles
«De fin acier et de très puyssant fer,
«Qu'orgueil a sceu forger et estoffer
«Aveques tant de diverses figures,   Fol. 290v°
«Qu'en ces lyens sont toutes les peinctures
«Qu'au monde on peult et desirer et veoir:
«Royaulme, empire, et leur force et povoir,
«Sceptre, couronne et chapeaux de lyerre,
«Riches trop plus que celluy de sainct Pierre,
«Harnoys, armetz, espées, croix et croces,
«Les uns painctz platz, autres en grosses
       bosses;
«Puys tous honneurs qu'au monde l'on
       demande,
«Tant que la corde est si longue et si grande
«Que vostre corps, teste et piedz, environne,
«En vous servant de manteau, de
       couronne,
«De gandz, souliers; et piedz et mains et teste
«Vout tient lyé, et vous en faictes feste,
«Et l'estimez ung honneur honorable,
«Lequel vous rend à la beste semblable,
«Ayant perdu de conserver l'estude,
«La belle ymaige et la similitude
«De vostre Dieu, pour lequel fustes fait.
«Mais vostre orgueil vous a du tout deffaict
«Pour ces lyens au vray appercevoir.
«Je vous requiers: faictes vostre debvoir
«De livres veoir et tant estudier
«Et requerir, chercher et mandier,
«Que les vertuz qui dedans sont encloses
«Devant voz yeux soient du tout descloses.
«Car en voyant les dictz des philozophes
«Vous en verriez de diverses estoffes
«Et leurs beaulx faictz, et comme desprisé
«Ilz ont le monde et cassé et brisé

His trouble is a dance or some high jinks
And fears for nothing if not parting from
The ill in which he lives glad martyrdom.   1472
The other link, which holds you through the eyes,
Not letting you look up to scan the skies,
Is of fine gold; well made, and so bedecked,
No other place to light can eye detect   1476
But fixes upon profit, wealth, or gain,
With no regard for God nor care humane,
Though wealth, both gold and silver, God has made
To be His useful tool, not profit paid   1480
One man alone. Not being put to use,
This strong attachment brings you its abuse,
Removing joy for you from this world's scene
When you no more see greed to be unclean.   1484
The third's a bond made from carbuncle stones
And rubies mounted on the knuckle bones,
Of iron most powerful and steel most fine
That pride has learned to forge and to design   1488
Such diversity of decoration,
In these bonds is all configuration,
All worldly gains that one could want to see:
The kingdom, empire, force and potency,   1492
The crown and scepter, wreaths of ivy-vine,
Far richer than St. Peter's, and more fine,
With armor, helmet, crozier, cross, and blade,
Here painted flat and there embossed,
       displayed;   1496
All honors that on earth one could
       demand
Until the cord's so long and stout of strand,
It, head and foot, your corpulence surrounds
And serves you as your cloak or makes your
       crowns,   1500
Your gloves and shoes: all, feet and hands and head,
It holds you bound, and in it int'rested;
You deem the honor worthy, as you feast,
That puts you on the level of the beast.   1504
You have forgotten and have not pursued
The fine ideal and the similitude
Of your God, for whom you were created.
But your pride, from all, has isolated   1508
You, even means to apprehend the true.
I pray you: Do the duty yours to do
To look at books, persist in study and
Inquiry, make research, and give command   1512
That virtues which lie in them undisclosed,
Before your eyes in full may be exposed.
For, seeing sayings of philosophers,
You will discover fabrics quite diverse,   1516
Their worthy feats and how they have disdained
The world, how they have broken and restrained

«Tout leur vouloir, n'estimant nulle
   gloire Fol. 291
«Telle qu'avoir de soy mesme victoire.
«Non seulement ilz ont fouy les vices,
«Les grans honneurs mondains, les avarices,
«Mais ont la mort prinse de bon couraige,
«En mesprisant les douleurs du passaige,
«Lisez après les histoires romaynes,
«Greques aussy, et vous verrez les peynes
«Que l'on a[prinses]pour vertu acquerir
«Et pour le vice aussy faire perir:
«La chasteté y verrez adorer
«Et la prudence et la force honorer,
«La charité, la magnanimité,
«La passience et longanimité;
«Les vicieux vous y verrez blasmer.
«Les vertueux en tous lieux estimer.
«Si plus avant voulez faire lecture,
«Prendre vous fault ceste Saincte Escripture,
«Où vous verrez ce qui est commandé
«Et defendu de Dieu et demandé;
«De vertueux le nombre y est bien ample
«Et Jesuchrist y est mys pour exemple.
«Là il vous fault œil et corps arrester,
«Et vostre cueur ouvrir et apprester
«Pour recevoir ceste doctrine saincte.
«Où les vertuz pourrez trouver sans faincte,
«Par qui seront[rompuz] voz vicieux
«Lyens, que tant trouvez delicieux.»
— «Helas! Seigneur, qui tant bien m'aprenez
«Et de mes maulx et vices reprenez,
«Je n'ay povoir de vous dire de non,
«Mais voluntiers je sçauroys vostre
   nom, Fol. 291v°
«Affin d'avoir à jamais la memoire
«De voz bienfaictz, et vous en donner gloire.»
Ainsy luy diz. Lors il me respondist:
«Il sera faict ainsy que tu l'as dict.
«Amy, j'ay nom de science Amateur,
«Je te requiers de m'estre imitateur:
«Tenez, voyez, contemplez et lisez;
«Le mal laissez et le bien eslisez
«Que cy dedans ces livres vous verrez;
«Heureux serez quand mon conseil croyrez.
«Destournez vous du monde et de sa pompe,
«N'endurez plus qu'ainsy vous lie et trompe.»
Moy qui estoys presque à demy gaigné,
En l'escoutant ma veue[n'espargnay]
Et, pour le veoir myeulx à mon gré, m'assis,
En oubliant luy dire: «Granmercis».
Mais plus avant lisoys en chaucun livre,
Plus me trouvoys de mes lyens delivre,

Their total will. No glory, they
   maintained,
Matched having over self the vict'ry gained, 1520
Not only did they flee the viciousness,
Great worldly honors, avariciousness,
But took their death with courage and good heart,
Ignoring throes as they came to depart. 1524
Read afterwards the Roman history,
The Greek also, and in them you will see
The pains men took this virtue to acquire,
And cause a vicious practice to expire; 1528
And chastity you will see there esteemed,
Both force and prudence to be honors deemed,
Like charity and magnanimity,
Firm patience, too, and long-lived constancy. 1532
The vicious there you will see blamed for sin;
The virtuous are widely praised therein.
If you're willing to progress in reading,
Take the Holy Scripture you are needing 1536
Where you'll then see that which is commanded,
What's by God forbidden, what demanded;
Of the virtuous the number's ample,
Jesus Christ is put there as example. 1540
There you must keep eyes and body steady,
Open wide your heart and make it ready
To receive this sacred doctrine, and sense.
Where you can find true virtues, not pretense, 1544
By which will be destroyed meretricious
Bonds you find to such extent delicious."
— "Ah, sir, alas, you who do so well teach
Me and upon my ills and vices preach, 1548
I can't say no to you but, all the same,
I have some eagerness to learn your
   name,
That in my recollection I may store
Your boons, with credit to you evermore," 1552
I said to him. Then he replied to me:
"As you have spoken it, so shall it be.
Friend, I'm known as Learning's Fond Curator.
I beseech you, be my imitator. 1556
Read and observe, deliberate, retain.
Choose good; the evil I pray you disdain.
The good in these books, as you will see.
You will be glad when you have heeded me. 1560
Put the world and worldly pomp behind you;
Suffer it no more to cheat and bind you."
I, who was almost won, if not outright,
While list'ning, was not sparing my eyesight; 1564
To view it as I wished, now took a seat,
Forgetting thanks to him I should repeat,
In every book, the more that I would read,
The more I found myself from shackles freed; 1568

Et me sentoys peu à peu deschargé
Du faix pesant, qui m'avoit submergé
Au plus profond de l'abisme infernalle,
Où mon soleil, ny estoille journalle
N'apparoissoit; mais amour de science
Me fist de moy congnoistre deffiance
Et veoir au clair le vice en sa laideur,
Dont je sentiz telle horreur et hideur
Que m'eust la vie en desespoir osté,
Si apperceu n'eusse d'autre costé
Tant de vertu, tant de vie et honneur,
Que je reprins ma force et ma vigueur, Fol. 292
Et me tournay pour veoir cest home saige,
Et mercier dont par son bon langaige
Avoit tourné d'un tel chemin mes pas;
Mais alentour de moy ne le viz pas.
Si j'en euz dueil, croyre povez que ouy,
Car de sa veue avoys trop peu jouy,
Trop tard l'avoys congneu, trop tost laissé.
Parquoy, le chef à la terre abbessé,
Fiz mes regretz comme du bien perdu,
Par qui mon bien perdu m'estoit rendu.
Lors n'y voyant remede prés ny loing,
Et qu'il m'avoit laissé pour mon besoing
Livres remplis de song saige parler,
En les lisant me prins à consoller;
Et dès ce jour hors de prison sortiz
Et le doulx aer de liberté sentis.
Et moy, qui fuz semblable à cerf ou veau,
Me retrouvay ung homme tout nouveau,
Doulx, passient, sobre, chaste et joyeulx,
Prudent, piteulx, misericordieux,
Et liberal, fidelle, ferme et fort,
Ne me troublant pour vie ne pour mort.
Parquoy mon cueur, qui serf fut detenu,
Estoit contant et libre devenu,
Ne prenant plus plaisir sinon de lire
Cas vertueux, et les faire et les dire;
Qui me povoit trop plus satisfait rendre
Que les plaisirs que le corps sçauroit prendre;
Car il n'y a au monde chose seure,
Fors que tourment, maladie et
    presseure, Fol. 292 v°
Et qui de l'œil interieur verroit
Que c'est de luy, sans regret le lerroit.
Tout tel qu'il est dans les livres le viz:
Plain de pechez, lesquelz j'avois suyvis,
Plain de tourmentz soubz le plaisir cachez,
Et soubz beaultez cueurs vilains et tachez,
Plain de poison soubz viande delicate,
Qui sans eschec le meilleur joueur matte,
Plain d'un espoir joyeux fuyant par pleurs,

And bit by bit I found myself relieved
Of woeful weight that had kept me aggrieved
In bottom depths of the abyss infernal,
Where no sun of mine nor star diurnal   1572
Shone; but dawning love of erudition
Made me party to new self-suspicion,
And clarified vice in its ugliness.
At which I felt such horror and distress,   1576
Despair might then have taken life from me
If, on the other hand, I'd failed to see
Of worth, life, and honor, such a figure
I recaptured all my force and vigor;   1580
I turned myself to view this man so wise
And thank him that the good he would advise
From my old path had turned my steps agley;
But round about me no one did I see.   1584
You can believe I was indeed annoyed
So short a sight of him to have enjoyed!
Too late I'd met him and too soon he'd left.
I sank my head against the earth, bereft;   1588
Like loss of good, his going I deplored,
This man through whom my worth had been restored.
Not seeing near nor far a remedy
But that to meet my need of colloquy   1592
He'd left books of his wise conversation,
Reading them, I grasped at consolation.
And from that day from prison I found vent,
The fresh, sweet air of liberty could scent;   1596
And I, who was then like the calf or hart,
Discovered a new man in every part,
One mild, patient, sober, chaste and joyous,
Prudent and kind, misericordious,   1600
One generous and faithful, firm and strong,
Not fearful of a life or death headlong;
My heart, that slavery had once detained
Had thus become content and unrestrained.   1604
Not taking further pleasure than to read,
Relate, and execute the righteous deed,
That could for me far more contentment make
Than joys in which flesh only would partake;   1608
For there's nothing sure in this world's ration
Except torment, sickness, and frustration;

And he who with the inner eye would see
Its fault, without regret, would leave it be.   1612
All as it is, within the books, I read:
Replete with sins to which I once had sped,
Beneath the pleasure mass of hidden pain,
Beneath the beauties, vicious hearts and stain 1616
And poison 'neath the flesh most delicate
E'er brings the finest player to checkmate,
A flood of joyous hope that ebbs in tears,

D'espines plain couvertes soubz les fleurs,
Plain de chailloux dessoubz peu de tresor,
Qui en bureau convertit le drap d'or,
Plain de tous maulx dessoubz peu de santé,
Desesperant qui plus fut contanté,
Plain de refux après ung long espoir,
Et plain de rien soubz cuyder tout avoir,
Plain de malheur soubz ung heur apparent,
Et plain de mort cuydant vivre en mourant,
Plain d'un enfer monstrant ung paradis,
D'un dyable en lieu de Dieu, et plus n'en dis.
Mais je reviens, Amye, à vous prier
De vous garder de jamais vous fier,
Croyre ou aymer par parolle ne chant,
Present ny don, ce monde trop meschant;
Et si le temps a rompu la prison
Où vous viz prise après la trahyson,
Que pour mon bien en me laissant vous fistes,
Quand de la myenne en me laissant yssistes,
Je vous requiers, gardez vous de ces troys
Cruelz tyrantz, fuyez en tous endroictz Fol. 293
L'occasion de tumber en leurs mains,
Car ilz sont [trois] meurtriers inhumains.
Gardez vous bien de toutes voz puyssances
Des deux premiers, qui sont concupiscences:
L'un, de la chair remply d'ordure et vice,
L'autre, des yeulx apportant avarice,
Le tiers, orgueil de vie, et le plus faulx
De tous les troys, engendrant plus de maulx
Que cueur ne peult penser ne bouche dire.
Parquoy n'en puys assez au vray escrire,
Mais lisez bien livres de toutes sortes:
Vous y verrez leurs tentations fortes,
Où n'ont esté subgectz gens de vertuz,
Qui toutesfoys ont estè combattuz,
Car ilz n'ont point contre celluy povoir
Qui d'aquerir vertu fait son devoir.
Vertu si très loing du vice se tient
Que, cherchant l'un, l'autre lesser convient.
Soyez, Amye, ung petit souvenante
Qu'en vous comptant de [Biétrix et de Dante,]
Je n'oubliay de vous dire que troys bestes
Mettoit au lieu des tyrantz deshonnestes,
C'est assavoir l'onze, lyonne et louve.
Lisez ses chantz, où tant de bien on trouve,
Et vous verrez que ces troys bestes sont
L'empeschement d'aller à ce beau mont.
Dont avoit veu l'espaulle verte et nette,
Vestue jà du ray de la planette,
Qui meyne droit par le royal chemin
L'homme fidelle et saige pelerin.

And underneath the bloom the thorny spears, 1620
Plethora of stones and dearth of nugget
That converts the cloth of gold to drugget,
The host of ills beneath a health but slight
Disheart'ning him who once knew full delight, 1624
Filled with refusals of the hope long sought,
Illusion of possession cloaking naught,
Beneath apparent luck, misfortune lies;
And when one thinks to live, he only dies; 1628
Parading paradise, but full of hell.
A devil in God's place — more I won't tell.
Dear, I return to plead with you — I must —
To guard yourself and never place your trust, 1632
Belief, or love, for sake of word or song
Or gift, this world too bent on doing wrong.
Inasmuch as time has burst the gaöl
Where I saw you caught at the betrayal 1636
You dealt, to my good, in forsaking me
When you quit mine and thereby set me free.
I beg you, do be wary of these three
Mean tyrannies and in all places flee 1640
Occasions into hands of theirs to fall;
For they're three murderers, inhuman all.
Beware! — Use all your strength in your defense —
Of those first two that are concupiscence: 1644
The one, flesh filled with dung and viciousness;
The other, visual avariciousness;
The third, the pride of life, and the most false
Of all the three, engendering more faults 1648
Than heart can think upon or mouth recite.
Of this, enough I can not truly write.
Read books of all the variegations.
You will see therein their strong temptations, 1652
Where the virtuous ones did not succumb —
Though constantly attacked, not overcome.
The three lack final power in dispute
With any virtue-seeker resolute. 1656
As virtue is from vice so widely cleft;
In seeking one, the other must be left.
May you be mindful somewhat still of this:
Telling you of Dante and Beatrice, 1660
I did not fail to tell you he replaced
With three wild beasts the tyrannies debased,
To wit: she-lion, wolf, and leopardess,
To read his cantos full of nobleness, 1664
And you will see that these three beasts account
For hindrance in ascending that fair mount
Whose shoulder draped in verdure fresh and clean
Already, by the sun's ray he had seen 1668
Which by the royal road directly leads
The faithful and wise pilgrim who proceeds.

Je m'en tairay de peur d'estre reprins,
                                        Fol. 293 v°
Comme j'estoys lorsque je vous aprins
Tout le discours de Dante et son histoire:
Impossible est que n'en ayez memoyre.
Mais voulez vous livre plus autantique,
Voyez sainct Jehan, dedans sa canonique,
Commant il dit qu'en la subjection
Des troys puyssans va en perdition
Le monde, et tout ce qu'il enclost et tient;
Car par ces troys sa royaulté mainctient
Et sa grandeur, sa pompe et tirannie,
Ayant Vertu hors de sa court bannie;
Mays, nonobstant qu'au monde n'ayt demeure,
Au ciel se tient attirant à toute heure
Ses serviteurs, ses enfans et amys,
Qui,[là,] fuyant hors du monde, sont mys.
Or suyvez donc, Amye, ceste bende
De vertueux; ce bien je vous demande,
Et ne soyez, je vous prie, esbahye
Si vostre amy qui tant vous suyvye,
Auquel avez fait ung si mauvais tour,
Avant mourir fait devers vous retour.
Las! ce n'est pas pour retourner amant,
Ny amoureux aymant amairement,
Mais ouy bien pour achever mon cours
De vous servir d'aÿde et de secours.
Car Amour veult qu'en tous temps, près et
   loing,
L'amy soit prompt de courir au besoing
De son amye, et ceste amour là mort
N'est point en moy, à qui vous tenez tort.
Il est bien vray qu'il est si fort changé   Fol. 294
Et d'un desir ydolatre estrangé,
[Qu'il] n'est plus tel que le temps passé fut:
A sa folye il a mys fin et but;
Si est il tel envers vous et sera
Que son vouloir jamais ne passera
A souhaitter de vous veoir si remplye
De bonnes meurs, que soyez accomplye.
Vostre salut et vostre bien pourchasse,
Comme autrefoys fist vostre bonne grace;
Rien plus ne veult que vous veoir saige et
   bonne,
Vous asseurant qu'il n'y eut onq personne,
Qui sceust aymer si fort amye ou dame
Qu'aymer vous veult l'amy vray de vostre
   ame.

I shall be silent lest I meet your twit,
Just as I did apprising you of it,   1672
All Dante's discourse and his history —
That you'd forget it is absurdity.
But should you want a more authentic work,
Look in St. John, his canon for the kirk;   1676
Where, he says that it is by submission
To three pow'rs the world goes to perdition —
Worse — taking all that her embrace contains;
Her royalty by these three she maintains: 1680
Pomp, grandeur, and tyrannical rapport;
For she has banished Virtue from her court.
Yet, though among the world good has no bow'r,
In heaven it resides and draws each hour   1684
Its servitors, its children, and its friends
Who are sent there, rescued from this world's ends.
So, follow now, my dear, this goodly band;
This is the boon of you I now demand.   1688
Read on, I beg you; do not be struck mute
If one, your friend who gave you such pursuit,
To whom at last you gave so bad a turn,
Before he dies, to your side makes return.   1692
Oh, it is not as lover to resume,
Nor, loving bitterly, on love presume,
But, mark, to end my charge, to take the chance
To bring you aid and your deliverance: 1696
For True-love wills at all times, near and
   far,
The friend be prompt to rush where her needs are,
His lady's; and that love one must adjudge
A death is not in me, whom you begrudge.   1700
The truth is that, so greatly your friend's changed
And from idolatrous desire estranged,
No longer is he in his former role.
His folly he has given end and goal.   1704
So, he is such toward you and such will be
That his firm will shall never pass, to see
Accomplished in you and so deep-instilled
The goodly ways, that you may be fulfilled.   1708
Your good and your salvation he'd pursue
As in the past he sought good grace from you;
He wants but this: to see you wise and
   good,
Assuring you there ne'er was one who could   1712
So firmly love a lady or love-true
As would this true friend of your soul love
   you.

FIN DU SECOND LIVRE

END OF SECOND CANTO

Fol. 295

Montant plus hault à la perfection,	In climbing higher toward perfection,
Plus je descends à ceste affection	I am more inclined to this affection 1716
Qui est de Dieu très fort recommandée	That by God is heartily mandated,
Et de l'Amour à l'amant demandée,	And to him who loves by Love dictated,
Et plus vertu rend mon esprit contant;	And virtue makes my spirit more content;
Mon desir croist de trop plus ou autant	The same and even more grows my intent 1720
Veoir par vertu contant le vostre esprit:	To see your spirit, too, in good delight.
C'est la raison qui me fait par escript	This is the reason I'm obliged to write,
Continuer de vous faire sçavoir	Still sending you the message vis-à-vis
Tout le discours qu'au monde j'ay peu veoir.	The world that I have been allowed to see. 1724
Or donc, Amie, escoutez ce discours	Listen, Dear, to my deliberation,
Dont les propoz ne peuvent estre courtz,	Matters brooking no abbreviation.
Et si vostre œil jusques icy a leu	Oh, come now, if your eye has so far read
Le bien et mal que j'ay senty et veu	The good and ill I found exhibited 1728
En ma prison, et seconde et premiere,	In my own prison, both cells one and two,
Ne refusez de veoir ceste derniere,	Do not refuse to view this last one, too,
Laquelle faiz et bastys de moy mesmes,	Both planned and built by me, on which I spent
Où je passay mainctz advantz et caresmes,	So many turns of Advent and of Lent. 1732
Jeunant, veillant pour estudier myeulx,	I'd fast, skip sleep, my study maximize
Tant que porter pevent mes povres yeulx;	As long as they could stand it, my poor eyes.
Car tel plaisir ne sçauroit recevoir	No way but through much learning is the mind
L'entendement que de beaucoup sçavoir.	Enabled to have pleasure of this kind. 1736
En ce sçavoir, où tant fort je me fie,	So, of this knowledge where I placed such trust
Une prison bien forte edifie,	I built a prison very strongly trussed
De gros pilliers entour environnée,	With massive pillars cordoned all around
Et d'un chapeau de laurier couronnée,	And with a capital of laurel crowned, 1740
Remply d'honneur: c'estoit la couverture	Imbued with honor; such was cover found
De ma prison, et toute la ceinture Fol. 295v°	On my retreat, and all the girdle round
Estoit de très belle et blanche muraille,	Was handsome, a white wall quite tall in shape,
Bien haulte, affin que personne n'en saille.	Lest one might leap from it to his escape. 1744
Ceste prison par le bas[commançay,]	I undertook this prison at its base;
Et peu à peu pilliers et murs[haulsay]	By bits raised pillars and put walls in place,
Par grand labeur et par long travailler,	With much work and long labor for its sake;
Par mainctes nuitz estudiant veiller;	At study I spent many nights awake. 1748
Tous mes pilliers de beaulx livres je fiz,	Of handsome books I built my every spire
Dont je receuz mainctz plaisirs et prouffitz.	Whence many gems and pleasures I'd acquire
En ung costé mys la philozophie,	And on one hand I placed philosophy,
Où la raison l'ignorance deffie,	Where reason challenges illiteracy. 1752
Qui l'homme fait par sus l'homme priser;	For reason, man above mere man is prized.
Ces livres sont fortz a rompre ou briser,	With difficulty are such works incised;
Ilz sont si[clos] que sans peyne indicible	They are so dense that without untold strain
De les ouvrir ny bien veoir n'est possible;	One can not open them and find them plain; 1756
Et qui les a en grant labeur ouvertz	One who with great labor has uncovered
Et leurs secretz ung petit descouvertz,	Them, their secrets partially discovered,
N'a nul repos, mais tousjours va avant	Can know no rest, but constantly proceeds,
En desirant le sçavoir du [sçavant].	And wishing wisdom of the scholar, reads. 1760
Ce grant monceau de livres sceuz lyer,	This pile of books I thoughtfully combined,
Dont fiz ung grand et très puyssant pillier.	A tall, imposing shaft of them designed.

L'autre d'après fut de la poesie,
Où j'arrestay bien fort ma fantaisie,
Car tant plaisans ces livres sont à veoir
Que j'oublyoys trop plus que mon devoir,
Boire et manger, compaignyes et repoz,
Pour retenir par cueur ces beaulx propoz.
De toutes fleurs chacun livre est couvert,
Faictes d'esmail, sur fondz de veloux verd.
C'est ung plaisir de poesie aprendre,
Mais que le sens l'on puysse bien entendre:

L'entendement n'en est à nul donné, Fol. 296
Fors à celluy qui est poete né.
[J'assemblay] donc ces livres en ung tas,
Dont plusieurs font et moy comme eulx grant
   cas,
Tant qu'ung pillier contremont j'eslevay
Où j'ay souvent mainct passetemps trouvé.
D'autre costé, où gueres je n'alloys,
Je mys à part force livres de loix,
Canons, decretz que sçavoir je vouluz,
Mais par plaisir gueres souvent ne luz.
Couvertz les viz d'une couleur de cendre
Et par dessus, sy je le sçay comprendre,
Force prisons, gibetz, tourmentz, travaulx
Gravé[s] en fer, sans paincture ou esmaulx,
Entremeslez de couronnes luysantes,
Sceptres pesans et citez très plaisantes,
Monstrant povoir les roys faire regner
Et les meschantz à tous tourmentz donner:
Bonne est la loy qui la justice accorde
Au cueur d'un roy avec misericorde.
Ces livres prins et, selon mon possible,
En feiz pillier bien fascheux et penible,
Mais si très fort, qu'il portoit par raison
Et conservoit le faix de la maison;
Car facile est d'abattre l'edifice
Qui n'est pas fait ny conduict par justice.
Puis j'assemblay ces livres fantastiques,
Beaulx et plaisans, où les mathematiques
Lire l'on peult, mais qui bien s'y adonne
La volunté de la chair habandonne,
Car le sçavoir en est si très exquis Fol. 296 verso
Que pour l'avoir tout l'homme y est requis.
Pour y entrer fault passer une haye
Bien espineuse, et qu'a peyne l'on ploye;
Aussy, après ceste fascheuse peyne,
Celluy qui peult courir dedans la pleyne
Du beau verger de ces liberaulx artz,
Ne changeroit au tresor des Cesars,
Ne à leur pompe, où d'honneur[s] sont tous
   yvres.

Next in the sequence was the poetry
Where I would fix my fancy eagerly;   1764
These books look so pleasant, for their beauty
I neglected far beyond my duty
Drinking, eating, rest, and companionship,
To learn by heart fair words of manuscript.   1768
Each book was covered with bouquets, these seen
Enameled on a velvet base of green.
It is a joy of poetry to learn,
But let it have a sense one can discern!   1772

For insight is not given any man
But one a poet since his life began.
These books I grouped anon into a pile
(A number like myself find them
   worthwhile)   1776
Until a soaring pillar I'd compiled,
Where I then often found myself beguiled.
I set apart where I but seldom went
Unnumbered works of legal argument,   1780
The canon and decrees I wished to learn;
But read for pleasure? Seldom would I yearn.
I saw them covered in an ashen blend,
On top, if I know how to comprehend: 1784
Racks, gibbets, gaöl, and works enslaving,
Paint and varnish none, just steel engraving
Mingling crowns, those glinting, royal pretties,
Weighty sceptres, very pleasing cities,   1788
Showing strength enabling monarchs to reign
And yield the wicked to all sorts of pain;
Pity in a king's heart can be blended
Into justice; then the law is splendid.   1792
I took these books, and using all my might,
I made a vexing, difficult upright.
Yes, there with reason was much strength bestowed,
For it must bear intact the structure load   1796
Because the building is with ease destroyed
If judgment in construction's not employed.
I then assembled books fantastical,
Those handsome, pleasing, mathematical.   1800
One can read, but he who grows addicted
Finds himself from will of flesh restricted.
For learning is so truly exquisite
The whole of man is to it requisite.   1804
To enter one must pass a thorny hedge
That he can hardly bend to force a wedge,
But once he has come through this prickly pain,
Our man who can then ride through this domain, 1808
The splendid vineyard of the liberal arts,
Would not for caesar's treasure trade these parts:
Not pomp nor honors whereon men are
   soused

Le grant plaisir qui est dedans ces livres,
Couvertz d'argent, mais j'entendz du plus [vif].
Et par dessus eslevay au naïf
Rondz et carrez, triangles et compas,
Reigles, lignes et sphere, ce que pas
Je n'entreprendz de toutes les nombrer.
Tant y en a, que le seul remembrer
Et les nommer n'est pas en ma puyssance;
Mais il faisoit beau veoir leur ordonnance.
Et du sçavoir qui est encloz dedans,
J'en laisse aux folz craindre les accidens;
Car si, sans plus, n'y avoit que musique
Et ses accordz aveques rethorique,
J'aymeroys myeulx le bien d'un tel sçavoir
Que posseder du monde tout l'avoir.
Des livres fiz ung pillier, et sembloit
Que sa grandeur terre et ciel assembloit.
Ce pillier fait, ung aultre j'en bastiz
De livres grans, et moyens et petis,
De medecine, autant que declarer
Dieu veult en ceulx où il veult esclairer
Par ses reyons les tenebres obscures,
Pour les effectz veoir de ses creatures, Fol. 297
Et pour sçavoir dompter bestes, oyseaulx,
Poissons et tous animaulx, laidz ou beaulx,
Arbres, fleurs, fruictz, herbes et pierres dures,
Tout ce qui est caché en leurs natures,
Et leurs vertuz et leurs complections,
Leurs nourritures et leurs corruptions,
Et de quoy l'un peult à l'autre servir.
Celluy qui veult leur doctrine suyvir
Et parvenir jusqu'au sçavoir parfaict,
Sçaura garder l'homme que Dieu a fait
En la santé en laquelle il est né.
Jusques au jour qu'il est determiné.
Si l'homme est né subject à maladie,
Ceste science voire est bien si hardie
Qu'elle pretend faire mutation
Du mal en bien, et la complexion
Du tout changer par purger et nourrir,
En le saulvant du tout, fors de mourir.
Celluy a bien le poinct caché trouvé,
Par qui l'homme est guery et conservé
Par ung seul simple et sans coust ny despense
Fors le labeur qui ne veult recompense
Que le plaisir d'estre au poinct parvenu
Qu'il recongnoist de Dieu tout seul venu.
Ces livres sont couvertz de quatre sortes:
D'or tout semé de feu et flambes fortes,
D'asur remply de differentz oyseaulx,
D'argent tout plain de poisson[s], de bateaulx,
De vert paré de tous arbres et bestes,

For noble pleasure in these volumes housed, 1812
Enchased with silver; I seek joy most keen.
On top I raised a pyramid gradine
With circles, squares, triangles, arcs, this spire,
With patterns, lines and sphere; I don't desire 1816
To make enumeration of them all.
They are so many that their mere recall
And naming is too much, try as I may.
How fine it was to see their whole array! 1820
Regarding knowledge of the sage contents,
I leave to fools the fear of their accents;
For, if there were but one melodious score
And its accords with rhetoric, naught more, 1824
I should prefer the good of such an art
To having all of this world's goods my part.
I built a shaft where the books resembled
Glory of both sky and earth assembled. 1828
When this was raised, another I then fixed
Of large books, small books, volumes in betwixt,
Of medicine (as much as God would show
In those where He has wish to set aglow 1832
The mystifying shadows with His rays)
To see the issue of His creatures' ways
To learn to tame the beasts, the birds of air,
The fish and fauna, be they foul or fair, 1836
The flowers, trees, fruits, herbs, and stubborn stones,
All that is hidden in their secret zones,
Their virtues and their complex inner folds,
Their food and what corruption each one holds, 1840
And in what way one can the other serve.
The man who would their principles observe
And reach the perfect knowledge of their aid
Will learn to keep that man that God has made 1844
Until the day he's finished and life lorn,
In health like that he had when he was born.
If one is prey to sickness at his birth,
This science is so certain in its worth 1848
It aspires to make a full correction,
Change the sick to well and the complexion
Of all to change by purge and nourishment,
Saving from all save life's relinquishment. 1852
That person has the hidden point observed
If by him man is cured, his health preserved
By one sole herb, no cost and no expense
Save labor that requires no recompense 1856
But joy of having at the point arrived
That he knows all by God alone contrived.
In one of four ways are these volumes bound,
With fire and bright rays sown on golden ground 1860
Or filled with different birds, the cover blue,
Or full of fish and boats, of silver hue;
Or green adorned with trees and quadrupeds

Bien faictz au vif des piedz jusques aux
    testes,   Fol. 297v°
Et les fermans de gommes et racines
Painctes dehors, comme les medecines
Par le dedans l'on pevoit veoir escriptes.
Les medecins qui ne sont hypocrites
Et ne font point de sçavoir le semblant,
Mais le parfaict par labeur vont emblant,
Et quant ilz ont emblé la verité,
En usent bien en vraye charité.
Lors ont escriptz en si très bonne lettre
Que tout à part d'aultres les vouluz mettre,
Et ung pillier en fiz bien autentique.
Mys au milieu de la matematique
Et de celluy de la philozophie,
Bien leur seant je le vous certiffie;
Le medecin est de très bonne estoffe,
Quand d'un costé il est grand philozophe,
De l'autre aussy matematicien:
A tel on doit donner honneur et bien.
D'autre costé, prins plaisir d'amasser,
Où bien souvent vouluz mon temps passer,
Livres de bons et vrays hystoriens,
Où je voyoys les faictz des anciens,
Par quel moyen parvenuz ilz estoient
Et quels labeurs pour parvenir mettoient,
Les faitz aussy de fortune diverse,
Prospere aux uns et aux autres adverse.
Les faictz passez à les veoir font entendre
Qu'on ne se doit à la fortune attendre,
Ny son esprit en ce monde arrester,
Mais à vertu recevoir l'apprester; Fol. 298
Que l'on ne doit en la prosperité
Se resjouyr, ny en l'adversité
Desesperer, prenant exemple à ceulx
Qui aux vertuz n'ont esté paresseux,
A ceulx aussy que l'on a veu tumber
Pour se laisser aux vices succumber.
Les faictz passez sont maistres des presens,
Desquelz nous font ces beaulx livres presens;
«Qui par autruy se chastye il est saige»:
Ce proverbe est bien en commun usaige.
Ces livres sont à ouvrir bien faciles,
Mais à suyvir les vertuz difficiles;
Ilz sont couvertz d'or et dessus taillez
Force chappeaux tous de vert esmaillez;
Les autres sont de poignantes espines
Pour les meschantz, et honneurs pour les
    dignes.
Ung pillier fiz de livres beaulx et grans,
Lesquelz je sceuz bien loger en leurs rengs.
Ung autre après je mys de bons aucteurs,

Well-drawn, lifelike from feet up to the
    heads;   1864
The bindings made with gums and roots applied
Outside resembled medicines inside
That one could see described within these writs.
The doctors who are not pure hypocrites   1868
And do not feign some learning à la mode,
But labor the perfection to decode,
And having grasped the truth with clarity,
Make use of it with valid charity.   1872
Since in such goodly letter they have traced,
I, wanting them apart from others placed,
Raised a post authentic, emblematic,
Set between the subjects mathematic   1876
And the spot where philosophy would lie,
Their proper place, to you I certify.
The doctor is of very worthy brand
Be he philosopher upon one hand   1880
And, on the other, a mathematician:
One should give him wealth and high position.
I took great pleasure making volumes climb,
Across where I should wish to spend my time,   1884
Mid books of good historians who've told
The truth, where I'd see deeds of men of old
And by what means they had achieved success,
What labors they did that they might progress,   1888
The facts, as well, of fortune the perverse,
Enriching some and to the rest adverse.
One understands from facts passed in review
That one should not expect a fortune due,   1892
Nor fix upon this world his total wit
But lend his mind to virtue, to have it;
That one should not in his prosperity
Be prideful; nor, in his adversity,   1896
Despair; adopting as example those
Who at the virtues were not indisposed,
And those, also, whom we have seen to come
Descending, since to vice these did succumb;   1900
For past events are teachers for today,
Of which these fine books give us a display.
A common proverb is that, "He is wise,
One whom the fate of others doth chastise."   1904
These volumes can be opened with great ease;
Their virtues are more difficult to seize.
With gold they're covered; etched on top are seen
Full many crowns, enameled all in green,   1908
While others, of sharp thorns, are for serving
Wicked folk, and honors for
    deserving.
I raised a shaft of fine books that impose,
That I'd learned how to place in their own rows; 1912
I raised a shaft from authors the most choice

Par lesquels mainctz se sont faictz orateurs;
J'en recueilliz de tous pays et langues,
Plains d'oraisons et de belles harangues,
Par qui le droict peult estre conservé
Et l'inocent de la mort preservé,
Par qui le cueur des Roys est amoly,
Tant le langaige est plaisant et poly,
Par qui doulceur en colere est tournée
Et la colere en doulceur retournée;
Par quy bon droit au besoing trouve [ung]
  ayde,
Et mauvais droit bien souvent bon remede.
Fol. 298v°
Car l'orateur par son prudent parler
Fait comme il veult le droict ou tort aller,
Et doit l'on bien l'horateur honorer,
Quant nul propoz il ne peult ignorer;
Et double honneur il a bien meritté.
Quand il soustient le droict et verité.
Ces livres sont couvertz de satin blanc,
Semez dessus de parolles par rang,
Toutes sortans d'une vermeille bouche,
Où la parole en saillant point ne touche,
Mais par chesnons d'argent fin à merveilles
Sont doulcement portées aux oreilles,
Qui font le bort des livres à l'entour,
Tirant les cueurs par plaisir et amour;
Car bien parler si très fort l'homme attire
Qu'il veult souffrir joyeusement martyre.
Ainsi posay ce beau pillier antique
De ceste tant aymée rethorique,
Auprès duquel mys la theologie,
Où je gastay mainct flambeau de bougye,
Lisant de nuict docteurs irrefragables,
Docteurs subtilz, serafiques, amables,
Les anciens, les moyens, les modernes,
Que l'on congnoist par leurs œuvres externes.

Leurs bons espritz aux livres on voit myeulx
Qu'onques leurs corps l'on ne congneult aux
  yeulx;
Et qui les a bien leuz et bien sondez,
Il pourra veoir qu'ils sont très bien fundez
De declairer l'Escripture très saincte
Selon leur sens, et n'ont usé de faincte, Fol. 299
Bien que les uns l'ont au vray entendue,
Les autres non, mais obscure rendue.
Les uns n'ont fait que des translations
Pour les montrer à toutes nations;
Autres ont prins labeur à l'exposer,
A la notter ou bien à la gloser,
Paraphraser ou aditionner;

Where many orators have found their voice;
I gathered some from every land and tongue,
Full of orations and fine pleas among   1916
Them, by which the legal right is conserved,
The innocent from death can be preserved,
By which the hearts of monarchs can be warmed,
So pleasing is the language, nicely formed,   1920
By which a gentleness to anger's churned,
Or anger back to sweetness is returned,
Thereby good law at need can find an
  aid
And remedy for bad law oft be made.   1924

The orator by prudent speech and heed
Helps, as he wills, the right or wrong proceed;
And one should show the orator respect,
Since no contingency he may neglect;   1928
A double honor is his certain due
Whenever he sustains the right and true.
These books are covered with a satin, white,
Spread on the top with words aligned aright,   1932
All coming from a mouth vermillion red,
But no word makes contact while being said;
By chains of silver wondrously refined
They're gradually borne to ears, designed   1936
To border these books all the way around,
Attaching hearts through love and joy there found;
Because good speech so strongly bids one come
That he will gladly suffer martyrdom.   1940
So I set up this fine shaft, antique brick,
Of that skill so beloved, the rhetoric,
Alongside which I put theology,
Where many candle wicks were burned by me   1944
In reading doctors one can not dispute,
The affable, seraphic, and astute,
The old, the medieval, up to date,
Whom one knows by their works that
  demonstrate.   1948
One sees their good minds better in their books
Than ever eye can gauge them by their looks;

He who has read them, and deeply sounded,
Can discern that they are quite well founded   1952
To make clear the most sacred text in style
Matched to their meaning and have used no guile;
Though certain ones have seized the truth, I'm sure,
While others failed and made it more obscure.   1956
Some have made straight foreign tongue translations
Purposing to show them to all nations;
And some have taken trouble to explain,
To add some notes or gloss, or to make plain   1960
By some paraphrase or fresh addition;

41

Autres luy ont bien sçeu le nez tourner,
La voulant rendre à leurs humeurs subjecte:
Ce sont ceulx là que Moÿse rejecte,
Qui font raison contre la foy jouster,
Quant ont voulu oster ou adjouster

Quoyque ce soit à la saincte parolle,
En aprenant au Saint Esprit son roolle.
[Mais cet esprit, qui n'est de nul contrainct,]
Monstre l'esprit, auquel il a emprainct
Son feu très cler qui ne se peult celler,
Mais par escript il se fait reveler:
Celluy auquel habitte tel esprit
L'on voit aussy en lisant son escript.
A retourner ces livres m'arrestay,
Mais les lisant bien peu me contentay,
Voyant en eulx si forte difference
Que par les uns me croissoit l'esperance,
Et desespoir par les autres venoit;
Leur different en herreur me tenoit,
Ung jour joyeulx, ravy jusques au cyeulx,
L'autre damné, fascheux et soucieux.
Mais, pour le bien que j'y povoys cueillir,
Je ne craignoys tous livres accueillir, Fol. 299v°
Dont fiz pillier plaisant et agreable.
Et tout en hault mys la Bible admirable
Comme le but où tous les autres tendent,
Dont les plus près sont ceulx qui myeux
    l'entendent,
Car ceulx du temps des apostres premiers,
Qui de les suyvre estoient coustumiers
En leur vertu, doctrine et saincte vie,
Mys au plus hault, car j'avoys bien envie
De leur garder reng selon les espritz
Que je sentoys en leurs divins escriptz.
Plus bas, je mys les livres qui plus bas
Ont leur esprit et dont faiz moins de cas,
Bien qu'il n'y a nul si plain d'ignorance
Que l'on n'y trouve une bonne sentence:
L'homme qui est du Saint Esprit apris
Fait son prouffit et du vert et du gris.
Couvertz ilz sont de diverses couleurs,
Selon qu'ilz sont faictz de divers docteurs,
Et d'or très pur mille estoilles luysantes,
Mises parmy des nues fort nuysantes,
Bien richement sur le fons eslevées,
Qui de plusieurs sont fort belles trouvées,
Du livre sainct qu'au plus hault j'avoys mys
Souvent m'estoys à le lire soubzmys,
En regardant la lettre et la figure
Où je prenoys souvent en ce pasture;
Couvert estoit de la peau d'un aigneau,

Others tilt their noses at it, wishing
To make the Scripture subject to their whim;   1964
Such were the ones that Moses cast from him,
Who tilts of faith and reason do arrange
When they would add, subtract, or somewhat
    change
No matter what upon the holy scroll,
They try to teach the Holy Ghost its role.   1968
This Spirit, though, that is by none constrained
Marks the spirit in which is diaphaned
Its most clear light, which can not be concealed
But in a writing comes to be revealed.   1972
One in whom such Spirit dwells, enlighting,
One sees, therefore, when one reads his writing.
I lingered turning through each document,
But reading them I scarcely felt content: 1976
I saw in them a difference of scope
That, while some authors brought increase of hope,
Thanks to some others a despair arose,
Their quarrel gripping me in error's throes   1980
One day delighted, wafted to the skies,
The next day damned, perplexed, and exercised,
But since I there could reap some benefit,
There was no book that I feared to admit;   1984
Withal I raised a welcome, pleasant spire.
Topmost I put the Bible to admire,
As the goal tow'rd which all others tend
The nearest are those that best comprehend
                                                    1988
It. Apostles, men contemporary—
Since these were adherents customary
In their virtue, creed, and consecration—
I shelved highest, wanting their location   1992
To keep their rank according to the mind
That in their sacred writings I divined.
I placed the books some lower that reflect
With less insight, to show them less respect;   1996
Though there is none so full of ignorance
But one finds there good culled experience:
The man who's taught by Holy Spirit may
Derive his profit both from green and gray.   2000
The books were covered in a different tint
According as the authors left imprint:
A thousand shining stars of purest gold,
Where noxious storm clouds threatened to enfold, 2004
Were set with richness, raised upon the base,
Admired by many for their pretty face.
I, with the sacred book I'd honored most,
Observing form and letter, was engrossed,   2008
And thus to read it I was often led.
And I was often on this pasture fed;
Its cover was a lamb's skin taking hue

42

Gouttes de sang très vermeil et nouveau,	From drops of blood of deep vermillion, new, 2012
De sept fermans fermé lequel encores	With seven clasps; and closed it still remains
A l'ignorant qui le dedans ignore. Fol. 300	To one not knowing what the book contains.
Là je tenoys de grace la vigueur	There it was I learned of grace's vigor
Et de la loy l'importable rigueur,	And, as well, of law's unswerving rigor 2016
Qui du pecheur requiert si grosse amende	Which asks the sinner such a heaping fine
Que, si bientost du vice ne s'amende,	That if from vice he does not soon resign,
Payer luy fault, car il y est tenu	He will be made to pay (for there is due)
Plus que ne vault son bien et revenu.	More than he has in goods and revenue. 2020
Ce costé là de satisfaction	Methods of obtaining satisfaction
Me donnoit peyne et desolation;	Brought me pain and comfortless distraction.
Et si ne fust la très seure promesse	And if there were no promise without fail
Que Dieu donra par travail et tristesse,	That God will grant through sorrow and travail, 2024
Douleur, tourment, son royaulme agreable,	Through pain and torment, His beguiling realm,
Je trouvoys trop penitence importable.	I would find penitence to overwhelm.
Mais pour avoir telle possession	But to have such fine anticipation
Et ne tumber en la damnation,	And not have to plunge into damnation, 2028
Jeuner, veiller et pleurer et prier,	Then, to fast, stay watchful, pray, and implore,
Et en mon cueur louer et adorer	And in my heart give praises and adore
Dieu tout puyssant, et, pour luy obeyr,	Omnipotence in God, and to obey
Suyvre le bien et tout peché fuyr	Him, seek the good, from evil turn away, 2032
M'estoit plaisant et facile à porter.	All these were easy, pleasing to sustain
Car j'estimoys pour me reconforter	For I think I'll be comforted again.
Que par labeur long repoz aquerroys,	Through labor, long repose I should obtain,
Et qu'à la fin parvenir je pourroys	And, in the end, admittance I should gain 2036
En une paix et ung contentement	Into a peace and state of full content
Par la vertu frequenter seulement,	If I chose virtue only, to frequent,
Qui l'homme rend sans faincte et sans envie,	Which frees a man from pretense and desire
Ny passion, tant comme il est en vie,	As long as he's alive—from passion's fire; 2040
Et après mort reçoit une couronne	And after death he has a coronet
De ses bienfaitz que le Puyssant luy donne.	Of benefits that God will round him set.
Voilà commant enfermé dans la lettre	Imprisoned in the letter thus, you see,
En liberté je pensoys du tout estre. Fol. 300 v°	I thought myself with all, at liberty. 2044
J'environnay de ces pilliers ma tour,	My tower I enclosed with pillars tall,
Où de papiers fiz ung mur alentour	Of papers made an all-encircling wall,
Et de cahyers et d'œuvres amassées:	Including notebooks and the works amassed
Tant de ce temps que des choses passées;	From modern times as well as from things past; 2048
Le fundement fut d'a b c petits.	The a, b, c's in small size alphabet
Pour incitter ung peu les appetiz	Composed the base. The taste somewhat to whet
Des plus petis, ces livres sont tout plains	Of youth, these books are filled and they assail
D'or et d'asur, de sainctes et de sainctz:	With gold and blue, with saints female and male. 2052
Ceulx qui moins sont de lire diligens	Some folk, who show less reading diligence
Disent que sont livres à povres gens.	Declare such books should go to indigents.
Aveques eulx je meslay la grammaire;	I intermingled them with grammar stacks.
Pour faire brief et venir au sommaire,	To make this brief and come to its climax, 2056
De livres fiz si beau et fort circuit	With books I made so fine and strong a ring
Qu'il me sembloit, veillant toute la nuict,	It seemed to me, awake all evening,
N'ayant lumiere autre que de chandelles,	That, having only candles for a light,
Car le soleil, la lune et les estoilles	For sun and moon and stars gave me no sight — 2060
Ne m'esclairoient, ce qui ne povoit estre,	A thing that could not be for me, bereft
Car je n'avoys laissé nulle fenestre	In that I had not any window left
Pour veoir dehors, que, lisant à par[t] moy,	To see outside — I read apart yet saw

Tout le dehors, tout le monde et sa loy
Voyoys plus cler, et myeulx le congnoissoys
Que grand myeulx veoir à cler je le pensoys.
Car, estant pris de leurs tentations,
Ne povoys veoir leurs imperfections,
Et en lisant povoys appercevoir
Le monde myeulx que quand le cuydoys veoir;
De terre et cieulx l'œil ne voit la nature,
En les voyant, si bien qu'en l'escripture.
Ainsy encloz, cuydant le tout enclorre,
Puys çà, puys là, par les livres me fourre,
   fourre, Fol. 301
Et me sembloit que j'estoys bien au large,
Ayant perdu d'ignorance la charge.
Je m'envoloys par la philozophie
Par tous les cyeulx, puys la cosmographie
Qui me monstroit la terre et sa grandeur,
Faisant mon cueur courir de grand ardeur
Parmy l'Europe et l'Afrique et l'Asie,
Où sans cesser couroys par fantasie,
Car, de mon corps, il ne bougeoit d'un lieu.
Theologie aussi jusques à Dieu
Dressoit mon vol par ses subjestions,
Me proumenant en mille questions;
Et d'un costé en l'autre me tournoys
Et en ung poinct jamais ne me tenoys,
Car le desir d'aprendre me poussoit
Et le cuyder de sçavoir me haulsoit.
L'une me faisoit courir et tost aller,
L'autre sur [mer] et jusqu'aux cyeulx voller;
Cuyder faisoit mon labeur sembler moindre
Pour parvenir où je vouloys attaindre:
C'estoit d'avoir sur tout honneur, louanges,
Ou [d']estre mys desjà au reng des anges,
Rendant mon corps par vertu impassible,
Comme estant chose à ceste chair possible.
Je desiroys le plaisant fruict manger
De tout sçavoir, sans craindre le danger,
Pour parvenir à cestuy là de vie
Où l'ame en Dieu sans mourir est ravie.
Vous qui lisez l'estat auquels j'estoys,
Où tout ennuy de moy je
   rejectoys, Fol. 301v°
Pas n'eussiez dit qu'une telle maison,
Si belle à veoir, eust esté ma prison;
Et me voyant tant aller et venir,
Et par plaisir lisant, entretenir
Tous ceulx qui sont très savantz estimez,
Dont les sçavoirs sont veuz et enfermez
En leurs escriptz, ne m'eussiez reputé
Pour prisonnier, car, tout bien disputé,
Failloit juger ma vie très heureuse

The universe, the world and all its law,   2064
More clearly, knew it with more lucid light
Than when I thought to see it fully bright.
Being caught myself by their temptations,
Nowise could I see their limitations.   2068
While reading, I could better comprehend
The world than when on sighting I'd depend.
Eye sees neither earth nor skies by sighting
Half so well as it sees these in writing.   2072
Thus, thinking to enclose all, while enclosed,
First here then there, through all the books I nosed.

In learning's wondrous wake I seemed to be,
Discharged of ignorance, in open sea.   2076
I took a flight throughout philosophy,
Cruised all the heavens, then cosmography,
Which showed me earth and all her great expanse
And caused my heart with ardor to advance   2080
Through Europe, Africa, Asian nations,
Where, in fancy, I would launch invasions;
For with my body, I'd not quit the spot.
Theology, as well, clear up to God   2084
Prepared my flight, thanks to its suggestions
Leading me into a thousand questions;
First one way, then another, I revolved
And never on a single point resolved: 2088
By the desire to learn I was propelled
And by my faith in learning was upheld.
The one caused me to go faster than before;
The other, over sea to heavens soar.   2092
Illusion made my labor seem the less
To get where I was going with success,
Which was to have first honor, to be praised,
Or to the rank of angels to be raised,   2096
Finding passive body through virtue kept,
A thing the flesh can possibly accept.
I wished to eat but of the pleasant fruit,
All knowledge, and no danger fear en route;   2100
Quick, not dead, to come to that position
Where the soul is borne to God's fruition.
You who read of my condition now where
I kept on driving from me every care   2104

Would not have said such house, so fair to see,
Were nothing but a prison house for me.
And seeing me so often come and go
And read for pleasure that I came to know   2108
All those who have the scholar's fame deserved,
Whose findings in their writings are preserved,
No name of "prisoner" had you inveighed;
Because, when all the benefits were weighed,   2112
One had to judge a benedicity

44

Et moy vivant en liberté joyeuse.
Tel l'on m'eust dit et tel je m'estimoys,
Dont mon estat et moy mesme j'aymoys,
En louant Dieu qui m'avoit delivré
De ma prison où par vous fuz livré,
Puys des tyrans de la prison seconde,
De l'ignorance et des vices du monde,
Et que n'estoys plus tel que le povre homme
Que publiquain ou grand pecheur [on] nomme,
Larron, meurtrier, faulx tesmoing, adultere;
Et mes bienfaictz ne luy vouloys pas taire:
Que je jeusnoys et donnoys grande aulmosne,
Souvent j'estoys à sermon, messe ou prosne,
Tousjours lisant, escrivant, prouffitant;
Voire et pensoys que nul n'en fist autant,
Car de bien peu ou point me voyoys suyvre
Pour avoir pris l'extremité de vivre.
Ung tel estat jamais n'eusse laissé,
Si le Très Hault ne se fust abessé
Ainsy qu'il fist, quand Adan regarda,
Qui au beau fruict sa main trop hazarda.

Fol. 302

Et me voyant au milieu des delices
D'un paradis, ce sembloit loing de vices
Dont ne vouloys ny ne povoys vuyder,
Pris et lyé finement d'un cuyder
Faulx et menteur, contraire à verité.
Il ne fut pas contre moy irrité,
Ainsy [qu'il] fut descendant en Sodosme,
Après qu'il eut veu le peché de l'homme;
Il descendit et veid bien le peché
Où j'estoys plus que jamais empesché,
Car plus peché ressemble à la vertu
Et plus il est de ses habitz vestu,
Plus dangereux il est à decevoir,
Car pour vertu il se fait recevoir.
Il vid le mal que je ne congnoissoys,
Mais, qui plus est, très grand bien le pensoys;
Luy, qui du cueur est le vray congnoisseur,
Congneut l'estat que je tenoys très seur
Estre le plus des autres dommageable.
O la bonté très grande et admirable,
Qui ne voulut la terre faire ouvrir
Pour m'engloutir et mon peché couvrir,
Comme à Dathan et Abiron advint!
Ny contre moy ung Pinées ne vint,
Pour me tuer comme vray zelateur
En mon cuyder, dont j'estoys amateur,
Le deffaisant et moy par une mort;
Il ne transmist aussy Sanson le fort
Pour mes pilliers abattre et ruyner,
En me faisant dans ma prison

My life in freedom and felicity,
These are the words you'd have—I, too,—employed.
My status and myself, then, I enjoyed   2116
Praising God who'd brought me liberation,
Freed, through you, from my incarceration,
From ignorance and worldly infamy,
The second prison of the tyranny;   2120
And that I was no more like one, poor man,
Who's called "grand rascal" or a "publican,
Crook, thug, adulterer," or "thief of name."
I could not wait my blessings to proclaim   2124
To him, to fast, make gifts to charity,
Frequenting mass and prone and homily,
Forever reading, writing, as I'd clutch,
And truly thought no other did so much;   2128
I, little, if at all, could see the link:
To get a prize, I chased it to life's brink.
Never such a state might I have ended
Had not The Most High himself descended   2132
Precisely as when Adam was observed
Whose hand had too much to the fair fruit swerved.

And seeing I was in a paradise
Mid such delights; it seemed remote from vice,   2136
A place I neither would nor could avoid:
Caught, I was slyly bound by faith alloyed
With falseness that honest truths negated,
Not with me was He so irritated   2140
As once He was when His descent began
On Sodom when He'd seen the sin of man;
But come he did and saw the sin that soiled
My life wherein I was the more embroiled   2144
Because, as sin looks like its opposite
And wears a garment like in cut and fit,
The greater is one's chance to be deceived.
Disguised as good, vice is within received.   2148
God saw the vice I failed to recognize
And, what's more, took to be the finest prize.
The one who is the true heart's connoisseur
Would recognize the state I thought quite sure   2152
To be, of all the rest, maleficent.
Praiseworthy goodness most beneficent,
Who was unwilling earth should open wide
To swallow me and my transgression hide   2156
As Dathan and Abiram were interred!
No Phinehas against me would be stirred
To kill me as a proof of his great zeal
Against my cult and love that I did feel,   2160
Expunging by one death both me and wrong;
God sent to me likewise no Samson strong
To make my pillars crumble and descend
And in my prison bring my days to end;

Ny Samuel ne luy pleut m'envoyer	Nor Samuel would send me, to upbraid,
Comme à Saül, qui vint à devoyer	As came to Saul who happened to have strayed
De la foy ferme et par ung sacrifice	From law established, and by sacrifice
Voulut couvrir son infidelle office,	Had tried to cover his misdeeds, entice 2168
Faisant une œuvre apparentement bonne,	By doing work of seeming good renown,
Dont il perdit l'honneur de la couronne;	Through which he lost the honor of his crown;
Car Dieu, qui void le cœur de l'hypocrite,	God, seeing hearts, is more incensed to see
Plus fait de bien et plus contre s'irrite.	A hypocrite do acts of piety. 2172
Il ne print pas de Jupiter la fouldre	He did not take from Jove the lightning thrust
Pour mon cuyder et moy bouter en pouldre.	To bring my vain belief and me to dust,
Mais par doulceur, qui est son vray cousteau,	But with His kindness, His true armament,
Glesve trenchant, flamboyant, clair et beau,	His gleaming, trenchant blade magnificent, 2176
Par cest esprit esgu, fort et puyssant,	Made by this spirit powerful and keen
Mamelle et chair et os departissant,	Till breast and flesh and bone it can trephine,
Qui mect à rien ce cuyder vain et sot	That sets at naught this fantasy absurd
De tout sçavoir, sans plus, par ung seul mot:	Of learning all: with not more than one word, 2180
Mot prononcé et digne d'estre ouy,	The word pronounced and worthy to be heard,
Mot par qui est tout le ciel resjouy,	That Word by which all sky with joy is stirred,
Mot apportant aux mortz vie eternelle,	That brings the life eternal to the dead,
Innominable à la bouche charnelle,	Word that by carnal mouth can not be said, 2184
Mis sur la terre et pour nous abregé,	But put on earth as our epitome,
Mot par qui est le monde soulagé,	The Word sent as world comforter to be,
L'enfer rompu, peché mort et mort morte,	Through whom are hell and sin and death erased,
Cousteau pierreux ayant puyssance forte,	The stone knife that, with mighty power graced, 2188
Par qui sont tous imparfaictz circonciz,	Can all the imperfections circumcise,
Et les vivantz en chair mortelle occiz.	The living mortal flesh bring to demise;
Par ce très fort glaive de Josué,	By this strong sword of Joshua, who knew
Qui a peché et le pecheur tué.	Which man had sinned and the wrongdoer slew. 2192
De tel cousteau tuant non punissant,	With merciful, clean-killing instrument,
Très doulcement adonques le Puyssant, Fol. 303	Most quietly, the Lord omnipotent,
Qui droict au cueur par l'œil tant soudain entre,	Who, through eye to heart so swiftly enters,
[Frappe] le myen, au plus profond du centre;	Struck mine to the heart where its depth centers 2196
Et la façon fut en lisant ung texte	In this fashion: As I was reading text
Où Jesuchrist sa bonté manifeste,	Where Jesus, manifesting goodness, next
Disant à Dieu: «Pere, je te rendz graces,	Tells God, "My Father, thanks I give to thee,
«Qui aux petis et à personnes basses	Who to the small and those of low degree 2200
«As revelé tes tresors et secretz,	Thy treasures and thy secrets hast revealed
«Et aux sçavans, gentz doctes et discretz,	And from the learnéd these things hast concealed;
«Les as cachez: tel est ton bon plaisir.»	For such is the bounty that doth please thee."
Lisant ce mot, soudain me vint saisir	With this word at once there came to seize me 2204
Une clarté plaisante à veoir et belle,	A thrilling radiance fair to behold
Mais sa lumiere et vertu estoit telle	Its blaze and strength such power did unfold
Que l'œil charnel la trouva importable,	As feeble eyes of flesh could not sustain
Pour estre trop luysante et agreable;	Because excessive blaze and charm ask strain; 2208
Ce feu, par qui tout mal est consummé,	This fire wherein evil is cremated
Pour mon œil cloz, ne fut moins alumé	Through closed eyes no less illuminated,
Dedans mon cueur, qui [de] luy fut espris	Sparkling in my heart, which was enraptured
Avant que l'oeil l'eust conceu ne compris.	Ere the eyes had aught perceived or captured 2212
Et tout ainsy que fouldre ne s'arreste,	And, quite as if the lightning never flared
Sinon à ce qui contre elle s'appreste,	To strike a thing unless it had prepared
De resister, brisant les os d'un corps	Resistance, breaking body's bones with spark

Sans que la chair en ayt marque au dehors,	Without the flesh's showing any mark, 2216
Brullant l'espée et laissant le foureau,	To burn the sword but not disturb the sheath,
En desprisant le foible, tendre et beau;	Scorn weak and fair and tender, strike beneath,
Ainsy ce feu en mon œil foible et tendre	This fire scorned feeble, tender eyes of mine;
Ne deigna pas si grand vertu estendre,	It would not there such wondrous force assign 2220
Mais, en passant oultre ce foible mur,	But went beyond this shallow wall with shock
Vint en mon cueur trop plus qu'un rocher dur.	To strike my heart far harder than hard rock
Qui contre luy voulut s'esvertuer	That every effort in protest would make
Ne se voulant pour riens laisser tuer.	Before allowing its defense to break. 2224

Fol. 303 v°

Bien longuement ceste lutte dura	For some time had the struggle been played out
Entre nous deux, dont mon cueur endura,	Between us two, in which my heart held stout
Par maincte année et longue experience,	Through long experience and many years,
Par mainct tourment et maincte impassience,	Through frequent torment and frustrations's tears, 2228
Tant de douleurs, qu'à la fin se rendit,	So many pains that it at length concurred
Quand dans ce feu une voix entendit.	When, in this light, a unique voice it heard.
C'est ceste voix qui au buysson ardant	Voice that, in the burning bush, [his sextant,]
Fist au pasteur, qui estoit attendant,	Told the shepherd, come to learn, expectant 2232
De son sainct nom la verité sçavoir:	Of truth regarding its most holy name,
«Je suys qui suys qu'œil vivant ne peult veoir».	"I am who am unseen by eyes." The same,
Ceste voix là, ceste parolle vive,	That very voice, that Living Word [of yore,]
Où nostre chair ne congnoist fondz ne rive,	Of which our flesh knows not the depth nor shore 2236
Me print, tua et changea si soudain	Invaded, slew, remade me; move so deft
Que je perdis mon cuyder faulx et vain.	That of vain, false belief I was bereft.
Car, en disant: «Je suys qui suys», tel maistre	As "I am who am" it was decreeing,
M'aprint alors lequel estoit mon estre;	Such a master taught as *was* my being. 2240
S'il est qui Est, hors de luy je ne puys	If He's what is, then I can but insist:
Dire de moy sinon que je ne suys.	Outside Him I myself do not exist.
Si rien ne suis, las! où est ma fiance,	If I am nothing, where can be my pledge
Vertu, bonté et droicte conscience?	Of virtue, goodness, conscience's straightedge? 2244
Or suis je riens, s'il est Celluy qui Est?	Am I then nothing since He is who is?
Voylà comment quelquefoys j'estoys prest	See how sometimes I showed propensities
De me vouloir aveques luy debattre.	And willingness to give Him argument!
Mais Verité qui sçait Cuyder abattre,	But truth, which knows how to divest dissent, 2248
Disant: «Je suys,» le mist à la renverse,	In saying, "I Am," caused my creed's reverse,
Comme avoit fait la cohorte perverse.	As once had done the old cohort perverse.
Ce mot: «Je suys qui parle aveques toy»	This word, His "I am He that speaks with thee,"
Gaigna le cueur par amour et par foy	Won a heart to love and fidelity 2252
De ceste là qui ne le voulut croyre,	She did not wish to entertain belief
Ne aussy peu donner de l'eau à boire; Fol. 304	Nor give Him water for His thirst's relief.
Mais quand ce mot en son cueur fist sentir,	But He caused her heart to feel this sentence,
Luy engendra ung ferme repentir.	And engendered there a firm repentance. 2256
Moy, travaillant à ce très parfond puys	I, toiling at this excess pedantry,
De trop sçavoir, oyant dire: «Je suys»,	A fount most deep, heard I Am call to me.
Et ensuyvant ceste Samaritaine,	Like that Samaritaine of whom they tell,
Laissay mon seau aveques la fontaine,	I also left my pitcher with the well. 2260
Où tous les jours ne faisoys que puyser	Everyday I drew but did not finish,
Et ne povoys ma soif amenuyser	Helpless there my great thirst to diminish
Quand ce mot là dans mon cueur fut venu,	Until my heart allowed this Word incised.
Le Messias au vray y fut congneu,	The true Messiah there was recognized 2264
Et d'autre part mon peché clerement,	And then, by contrast, sin was evident

47

Toute ma vie et mon gouvernement.
Mais pour avoir des vices congnoissance
Cela n'est pas vraye resipicence,
Car le peché et le vice est si laid
Qu'en le voyant tel qu'il est, il desplaist.
Qui peché void sans masque ou faulx visaige
Le chassera bien tost de son couraige,
Car se puante et orde vilennie
Le faict bannir de toute compaignye,
Tant qu'il n'y a ny larron ny meurtrier
Qui n'en voulust renoncer le mestier,
Si de plaisir ou prouffit couverture
Peché n'avoit pour couvrir sa laidure.
Mais le regret d'avoir peché commis
Pour à telz cas vilains estre soubzmis,
Ou bien le dueil d'avoir commis telz faictz
Pour estre mys au rang des imparfaictz,
En se cherchant et se voulant parfaire:
Ce desplaisir n'est pas le salutaire,   Fol. 304v°
Pour ce qu'il [vient] de nostre terre impure
Dont il ne peult saillir que toute ordure.
Mais ce beau mot, qui procede d'en hault,
Venant en nous monstre nostre deffault
Aussy à clair qu'ung livre où chacun lit,
Et le monstrant aussitost l'abolit;
Et de là vient vraye contrition
Quand on sent bien ceste abolition;
Ce mot: «Je suys qui les pechez pardonne»
Plus de regret par amour au cueur donne
Que du peché la honte ou le malheur,
Ny de l'enfer l'eternelle douleur.
Amour luy fait oublier sa deffaulte
Et de peché fait qu'à la grace il saulte;
Et plus de grace il se trouve asseuré,
Plus son peché il void desmesuré;
Car qui n'a veu lumiere lumineuse
Ne peult juger tenebre tenebreuse,
Mais qui peult veoir lumiere sans nuée,
L'obscurité en clarté voyt muée,
Car la clarté à tenebre est contraire:
L'une venant, l'autre convient retraire.
Peché au vray ne peult peché paroistre
Si Dieu en soy ne le nous fait congnoistre,
Peché en Dieu n'est pas, mais il s'y voit
Car, hors de Dieu où il est, nous deçoit
Tant que nul œil ne le peult veoir en chair
Tel comme il est; mais qui peult aprocher
Par vive foy dedans ceste lumiere,
Il void peché, sa source et sa matiere; Fol. 305
Mais, quand tout tel comme il est il appert,
Ceste clarté qui le monstre, le pert.
Ce mot: «Je suys» est de telle efficace,

Through all my life and in my government.
Now, mere taking mental note of vices
Lacks return to goodness that suffices;   2268
For the sin, also the vice, is so lewd
It brings distaste when it is frankly viewed.
He who sees his sin unmasked, lacking art,
Will drive it forthwith from him with good heart 2272
Because its stink and dirty villainy
Would banish it from every company
Until there were no thief nor murderer
But to renounce his calling would prefer   2276
If sin would clothe no more its ugliness
In profit and in pleasures to impress;
And, if regret for having sinned is loosed
Because to ugly ranks one is reduced,   2280
Or if one sorrows to have done such deeds,
For ranking with defectives no one heeds,
Or in searching self sees imperfection,
This displeasure does not bring correction;   2284
Because it comes from earth, our own and soiled,
It can but issue from it wholly spoiled.
But this fair Word that comes from the On High,
In coming, shows us where our defects lie,   2288
As clearly as a book where one may read
Abolishes while pointing out the need.
From its coming springs the true contrition
When one truly feels sin's abolition.   2292
This Word, this "I am He who pardons sins,"
Brings to the heart regret through love that wins
Ahead of shame or sin's unhappiness
Or an eternity of hell's distress.   2296
Love helps one to forget his compromise;
From bygone sin to grace, effects his rise.
The more one finds himself assured of grace
The more he sees his sin is out of place.   2300
He who has never seen the gleaming light
Can nowise judge the dark of gloomy night.
He who sees the light of clouds denuded
Sees the darkness into light transmuted   2304
Because the light to darkness is opposed:
One forthright, one to make retreat disposed.
And sin, in truth, can not appear as such
If God to us does not reveal as much.   2308
Now sin is not in God, but in His light
Is seen; for, God lacking sin deceives our sight
So much that eye in flesh can not perceive
It as it is; while he who can believe,   2312
Examining in light of deity
Beholds sin, source and corporeity;
When all such sin is shown quite unalloyed,
By clarity it is forthwith destroyed.   2316
The Word, I Am, has such capacity

48

Vertu, povoir et puyssance et audace,
Qu'aux ennemys donne espouvantement
Et aux amys, au milieu du tourment,
Donne repoz, et les plus agittez
Dans ceste mer sont par ce mot jettez
Hors de peril, et menez au seur port.
Car ce mot là leur est force et support,

Rendant le cueur avec la mer tranquille.
Mot vertueux! O parolle gentille,
Qui par puyssance ennemys faict tumber,
En relevant ceulx que voys succumber;
D'un mesme mot les faiz vivre et mourir,
Ung mesme mot peult blesser et guerir;
Ce mot: «Je suys» ung amy ressuscite,
Et l'ennemy à cruelle mort cite.
Quand Joseph dist à ses freres: «Je suys»,
Ils furent tous en grande craincte induictz,
Car leur peché devant leurs yeulx revint,
Tant que nul d'eux ne sçeut lors qu'il devint,
Fors Benjamin, [que ce mot consola.]
Le plus petit voyant son frere là,
Frere et amy il sentoit Joseph estre,
Mais l'œil des grans le voyoit juge et maistre:
L'un regardoit son frere sans contraincte,
Et de le veoir les autres avoient craincte.
Donques ce mot: «Je suys Celluy qui est»,
Tel que l'homme est, le monstre sans
    arrest,   Fol. 305v°
Ce mot là, c'est ung glaive qui revelle
Le fondz des cueurs par façon non nouvelle,
Et qui en a l'ame bien transpercée
Feindre ne peult ne couvrir sa pensée.
Ce mot: «Je suys» l'hypocrisie chasse,
Et le cuyder pert son lieu et la place;
Ce mot icy l'infidele endurcit
Et le fidele abat et adoulcit.
En lisant donc ce passage devot,
Viz la lumiere et entendiz ce mot:
«Je suys qui suys», qui si très hault tonna
Que tous mes sens et force[s] estonna,
En me faisant veoir le sens de la lettre:
C'est qu'il luy plaist aux cueurs des petis mettre
Son Sainct Esprit, par lequel reveler
Se faict en eulx pour les renouveler
Au jeune estat de la pure innocence,
Tant seulement par ceste congnoissance;
Et les prudentz sçavantz et grans docteurs
Laisse dedans leur vieille peau, doubteux,
Sans s'asseurer, mais vont vacilant, comme
En nuict obscure on void vaciller l'homme
Qui bas et hault de baston et mains taste

For virtue, power, and audacity
It gives His enemies embarrassment;
While to His friends, amid their harrassment,   2320
It brings repose; and those at sea who quail
Are given instant help to set the sail
Away from peril, led to certain port;
That Word becomes their strength and their
    support;   2324
It calms the heart and brings a tranquil sea.
O Word of virtue, Word of sympathy
That make all enemies perforce succumb,
Relieving those whom You see overcome!   2328
With this same word You help them die and live:
The same word can both wound and healing give.
This word, I Am, resuscitates a friend
And cites the enemy to cruel end.   2332
When to his brothers Joseph said, "I am,"
They were afraid because they knew their sham,
Because their sin before their eyes returned
Till none knew then what he became or earned   2336
But Benjamin, one whom this word consoled.
The youngest there his brother did behold
And felt that Joseph was compassionate;
The grown ones viewed him as a magistrate,   2340
Not being innocent like Benjamin
But fearful of this victim of their sin.
So "I Am He that Is," word summary,
Reveals man as he is eternally;   2344

This word is sword or lancet that lays bare
The bottoms of the hearts (stroke nowise rare),
And one who has his soul pierced by this lance
Can not pretend nor hide his thought nor stance.   2348
The Word, "I Am," dispels hypocrisy,
Displaces credulous autocracy;
This Word can turn the faithless to a stone;
The faithful, chastened, to his knees is thrown.   2352
As I read this line I became devout,
I saw the light and heard this Word ring out;
"I Am Who Am!" So loudly it thundered
That my force and senses all were sundered,   2356
Causing me thus to see the letters' sense.
He plants in hearts of insignificants
His Holy Spirit, the revelation
Of Himself in them, their restoration   2360
To innocence of youthful purity,
And all uniquely through this surety.
The great doctors and savants studious
It leaves in their old shells, still dubious,   2364
In darkness, never reassured. One can
Observe them vascillating like a man
Who, high and low, cane in hand is feeling

Où c'est qu'il est, et tumbe s'il se haste.
Ceste clarté me vint lors esclairer,
Et ceste voix les secretz declairer,
Et la chaleur du feu me penetra
Tant que petit et plus rien me monstra;
Et quant en riens par luy fuz parvenu,
Celluy qui est le vray Tout fut congneu, Fol. 306
Et me monstra que toute mon estude
Plus que jamais c'estoit ma servitude.
Ce feu divin en ma prison ouvrant
Brulla le hault, et en la descouvrant
Mist le chapeau de laurier tout en cendre,
Remply d'honneur, où tout grand cueur doit
    tendre.
Tous mes pilliers pilliers ne furent plus,
Et ne fuz plus en leurs vertuz recluz;
Mais toutesfoys les livres des pilliers
Viz sans nul mal à terre tous entiers,
Subjectz à moy, abbattuz à l'envers,
Sans nulz fermantz deslyez et ouvertz.
Mais toutesfoys rien qu'ung mot je ne viz,
Bien qu'il y eust de differentz devis;
Ce mot: «Je suys» partout j'y retrouvay,
Tout le surplus fut de moy reprouvé.
Ce mot icy je congneuz en Hermès
Plus clairement qu'en [nul] si ne nul mais,
L'on ne sçauroit Pere et Filz demander
Ne Sainct Esprit plus clair qu'en Pimander;
Or n'estoit il de nation juïfve,
Mais il avoit congnoissance naïfve,
Par cest esprit, qui tout homme illumine
Venant au monde et qui çà bas chemine,
De Cil qui Est, duquel l'election
L'avoit tiré à la perfection
De ce sçavoir qui n'est par l'homme aquis,
Et qui seul est à l'homme bien requis.
Job n'estoit il pas prince oriental
Suyvant le bien et delaissant le mal Fol. 306v°
Et non subject à circoncision?
Il a congneu la resurrection
Et en a dit trop myeulx et plus avant
Que nul qui ayt escript, tant soit sçavant.
Celluy qui Est sans doubte il congnoissoit
Et à luy seul sa complaincte adressoit,
Illuminé de ceste charitable
Clarté de Dieu, c'est l'esprit veritable.
Ceste lumiere a Socrates receue
Quant doulcement accepta la cigüe,
Croyant si bien que l'ame est immortelle
Que pour avoir ceste vie eternelle
La mort receut comme en alant aux nopces,
En oubliant ces mondaines negoces,

For his path, and haste would send him reeling. 2368
This clarity then came to light my way;
This voice came, all the secrets to display;
The heat of flame now pierced me to the core,
Reducing me to nothing more and more. 2372
And when, through Him, to Nothing I had come,
The One who is true-All was known, The Sum.
He showed me all my study could be viewed
To be, now more than ever, servitude. 2376
This fire divine, prison walls expanding
Burnt the roof, and, as it was disbanding,
The laurel chaplet brought to ashen end,
The honored crown for which great hearts
    contend! 2380
My columns were no longer pillars wreathed;
I was no longer in their virtue sheathed;
I saw the pillar books, though, without strain,
All of them, all upon an earthly plane, 2384
Now subject to me, fallen, overthrown,
Devoid of binders, open, come unsewn.
Lo, I saw a lone Word in their matter,
Though they compassed different kind of chatter. 2388
This I Am in all I recollected;
All the surplus words I then rejected.
This same Word in Hermes I recognized
More clearly than in "if's" and "but's" disguised. 2392
One could not ask for Father, Son more clear,
Nor Holy Ghost, than in *Pimander's* sphere.
Though not of Israel nor its tradition,
He still had a native intuition 2396
Through the Spirit that lights every man
Who comes among the earthly caravan
From Him Who Is, Him by whose election
Man was first attracted to perfection 2400
Of wisdom that is not through man acquired,
And is the only good by man required.
Now, was not Job an oriental prince
Pursuing good and shunning evil's hints, 2404
One not subject to the circumcision?
Yet of resurrection he had vision,
Spoke of it ahead and even better
Than the wisest devotee of letter. 2408
To Him Who Is, no doubt, Job did attest,
And to that One alone his plaint addressed,
Illuminated by God's kindly light
That is true spirit, essence of God's might; 2412
This is the light that Socrates once knew,
When meekly he accepted hemlock brew,
So firmly trusting in the deathless soul
To have this life eternal he paid toll 2416
In death, but went as to a bridal feast,
Like one for whom all mundane traffic ceased,

Disant le corps lequel devoit perir	Declaring that the shell that atrophies
N'estre pas luy qui ne povoit mourir,	Was not himself, someone who always is, 2420
Mais qu'il estoit celeste auquel la Mort	But that he was divine, one whom Death's arm
Ne peult toucher ne luy faire aucun tort;	Can neither touch nor bring to any harm;
Nature en luy estoit illuminée	For nature in him was aglow like morn
D'une clarté qui du hault ciel est née.	With light that of the upper realm was born. 2424
Platon très bien a suyvi sa doctrine,	And Plato followed doctrine it designed
Qui est si très subtile et si trés fine	Which is so very subtle and refined
Que l'on voyt bien, et de tous ses semblables,	One sees it well, and from his counterparts
Par leurs escriptz tant grans et admirables,	Whose writings show such great and wondrous arts 2428
Que chair et sang ne les ont pas apris,	As flesh and blood could not suffice to train;
Mais ung esprit seul parle en leurs espritz;	A single spirit speaks in each one's brain.
Et cest esprit en moy si bien ouvra	As this spirit in me operated,
Que tout mon cueur des livres delivra,	Soon my heart from subtle books was liberated. 2432
Ne regardant en tous qu'ung seul acteur	The single mover in them all I seek
Qui fait parler philozophe et aucteur. Fol. 307	Who makes philosophers and authors speak.
La medecine à terre viz espandre,	I saw the medicine on earth expand
Dont ce clair feu me fist le sens entendre:	Whose meaning bright fire let me understand: 2436
C'est qu'honorer le medecin il fault,	It is the doctor we must dignify
Car son sçavoir est venu de là hault:	Because his knowledge comes here from on high;
Ministre il est du grand vouloir divin:	He is a minister of will divine
S'il fait jeusner ou qu'il oste le vin,	Prescribing fasting or proscribing wine 2440
Ou saigement vienne les corps purger,	Or wisely come to purge anatomies.
Nous luy devons obeyr et juger	We must obey him and must judge that he's
Qu'il est de Dieu moyen à ce commis,	God's means and by God to this committed:
Et n'estre à luy comme à l'homme soubzmis;	Not be, as to man, to him submitted. 2444
Car qui en l'hom[m]e a fiance, il est dit	For one who has his trust in man, it's said,
Qu'il est de Dieu reprouvé et mauldit.	By God will be reproved, accurst, gainsaid.
Par cest esprit congneuz qu'il n'y a rien	This Spirit taught me: nothing in the scenes
Creé çà bas qui ne nous soit moyen	Of earth exists but may for us be means 2448
Pour eslever en hault nostre penser;	To raise our thoughts on high and God extol.
De les nommer je ne veulx commancer,	I will not undertake to call the roll,
Mais tant y a que toute creature	But many as there are of God's design,
Du Createur est belle creature.	Each creature the Creator made is fine. 2452
L'œil charnel rien que le dehors ne voit,	The carnal eye sees only the outside;
Et c'est le mal qui l'aveugle deçoyt,	By like disease the blind man is denied,
Car il croit estre en l'herbe la vertu,	For he thinks, "In the herb the virtue lies,"
Sans veoir que Dieu est d'elle revestu	Not seeing God has donned it as disguise 2456
Pour aveugler celluy qui cuyde veoir	To blind the one who thinks he can perceive
Et le dedans ne peult appercevoir,	Although the inside he does not receive,
Mais le dehors travaille de congnoistre,	But works to know the shell—one not seeing
Sans regarder dont la vertu prent estre.	Any source whence virtue gets its being. 2460
C'est ce qui fait demourer ignor[a]nt	This is the cause he can not see his mark,
Le medecin en tenebre courant.	The doctor operating in the dark.
Et quand ce mot: «Je suys qui suys» se monstre	But when this Word 'I Am' is manifest
En son esprit, ô l'heureuse rencontre!	Within his spirit, Oh, what meeting blest! 2464
Fol. 307 v°	
Alors du pain void la vie et sustance	He sees then life and substance of the bread
Estre Dieu seul, où gist la susistance	Are God alone, by whom all things are fed
De tous vivantz, d'arbres et d'animaulx,	That live, the animals and trees survive;
Et qui garder veult homes et chevaulx.	God wants to keep both man and horse alive. 2468

51

Celluy qui dit: «Je voys», et ne se boutte
Qu'à regarder le dehors, ne void goutte;
Mais qui ce mot: «Je suys» [trouve] partout,
Le vray sçavoir a congneu jusqu'au bout;
Des medecins et de medecine use,
Mais au dehors toutesfoys ne s'abuse;
L'homme il reçoyt ainsy qu'a Dieu servant,
Sa medecine il congnoist si avant
Qu'il n'y voit rien que la vertu divine.
Ainsy voyant dedans la medecine
Très clairement le Createur ouvrer,
Par cest esprit [qui] me fist recouvrer
L'intelligence et le sens trop caché,
Je ne fuz plus des livres empesché.
D'autre part, viz tumber mes livres beaulx;
Où sont comprins les sept artz liberaulx;
Ce feu les a de tresbuscher hastez,
Mais toutefoys ne les a pas gastez,
Car j'apperceuz que leur beaulté premiere
Croissoit tant plus recevoit de lumiere,
Dont je congneuz que Dieu, à ceste foys,
Qui par raison, par mesure, par poix,
Son œuvre faict, a par sa sapience
Luy seul en l'homme ennenté la science;
Car luy seul est raison, poix et mesure,
Qui fait trouver la science très seure. Fol. 308
Las! tant me fut ce sçavoir difficile,
Quand de mon œil charnel et imbecile
Je regardoys les figures portraictes
Que les sçavantz aux livres ont retraictes!
Sans grant labeur des escriptz anciens
Ne se font pas mathematiciens;
Mais quand l'esprit par terre les ouvrant
Fut entre tous ung seul mot descouvrant,
Tout mon travail fut tourné en repoz,
Quant ce beau mot trouvay en tous propoz:
«Je suys qui suys fin et commencement,
«Le seul motif d'un chacun element,
«Auquel tout est et a vie et se meult,
«Celluy qui est fait du tout, ce qu'il veult,
«Du cercle rond sans la circunference,
«Par tous costez egal sans difference!
«Commancement ne fin ne s'y retrouve,
«Et n'y a chose estant ou vieille ou veufve
«Qui de ce rond n'ayt pris creation
«Et nourriture et conservation.
«Du monde tiens multitude et grandeur
«Dans ma divine eternelle rondeur;
«La ligne suys, le chemin et la voye
«Par qui nully jamais ne se forvoye;
«D'exterieur en l'interieur entre
«Qui va par moy, et au milieu du centre

He who says, "I see," while non-commital,
Seeing outside solely, sees but little.
The one who finds I Am thoughout the whole
Has found authentic learning's final goal,   2472
Uses doctors, medicines, and science;
On externals, though, puts scant reliance;
The man he greets as servant of the Lord.
His medicine he grasps with view so forw'd   2476
He sees no virtue not divine therein.
Thus I could now behold in medicine
The Great Creator plainly, as He worked.
Through this new spirit where the secrets lurked   2480
I could recover sense most deeply hid,
And lofty books no longer could forbid.
Another place I saw my fine books fall
Comprising seven liberal arts in all;   2484
The fire had hastened their disruptive chute
But not laid waste to them, nor left them mute;
For, their primary beauty, I perceived,
Increased according to the light achieved,   2488
In which I recognized the Master there
Who does His work with reasoning and care,
Weights and measures, wisdom His affiance,
God alone in man implanted science.   2492
The Lord alone is reason, weight and length
Which gave to science certainty and strength.
How difficult this knowledge was for me
When, like an imbecile, I looked to see   2496
With eyes of flesh the figures there portrayed
Within the books that learnéd men had made!
Lacking search of ancient erudition
One is not a learnéd mathematician;   2500
But when the spirit spread them on the ground,
Among all was this single message found;
All my work was made a recreation
When I found this in each dissertation: 2504
'The End and the Beginning, I prevail,
The sole motif of every small detail
Made from the All according to His will
In Whom all is that life and motion fill,   2508
The circle round without circumference,
At all points equal without difference;
In Whom is no beginning and no end,
And no things old or new but that extend   2512
From this circle where they knew creation,
Nourishment, and likewise conservation.
I hold earth's multitude in supernal
Cycle vast, divine, and sempiternal;   2516
I am line of reference, path, and way
Through which no person ever goes astray.
From outside to inside let him enter
Who proceeds by me, and at mid-center   2520

«Me trouvera qui suys le poinct unique,
«La fin, le but de la mathematique;
«Le cercle suys dont toute chose vient,
«Le poinct où tout retourne et se
    mainctient.   Fol. 308 v°.
«Je suys qui suys triangle très parfaict,
«Le tout puyssant, saige et bon en effaict,
«Qui fut, qui suys et seray à jamais,
[«L'eternel Dieu où n'y a si ne mais,]
«Pere puyssant du monde createur,
«Très saige Filz du monde redempteur,
«Esprit très sainct le monde illuminant,
«Divinité les troys en ung tenant;
«Brief, aux neuf cieulx ne se voit nul aspect
«Qui n'ayt à moy sa fin et son respect.
«En ces papiers et livres n'a figure
«Qui ne soit veu trop myeulx qu'en
    l'escripture;
«Je suys qui suys, mais que l'espesse toille
«De l'ignorent et trop aveugle voille
«Soit mys à riens aveques son venin
«Par mon clair feu et mon esprit divin.»
O combien fuz resjouy doublement
Quand j'entend[i]z ces mots si clairement,
Et le secret d'un sçavoir si subtil
M'estoit monstré par cest esprit gentil,
Qui me tournoit la peyne que longtemps
J'avoys portée en plaisant passetemps!
Car puysqu'ung seul est la fin de la peyne
De tous sçavantz, ô bonté souveraine,
Qui a trouvé ce but il se repose,
Car qui a tout ne veult plus nulle chose.
Ce fort esprit aveuglant les voyans,
Illuminant les aveugles croyans,
Monstre qu'ung seul estre et vie à tous donne:
Tout vient de luy et tout à luy retourne. Fol. 309
La poesie aussy jetta par terre,
La descouvrant, ce doulx feu sans tonnerre;
Moy, par qui sont ces livres revestuz
Et tant aymez, les voyant abattuz,
Ung bientost pris et l'ayant relevé
Tout plain d'esprit et clarté le [trouvay;]
La fiction, faicte subtilement,
Ne me donnoit plus vray l'empeschement;
Lors je congneuz que les poetes tous
Ont très bien dit de dire «Dieu en nous»,
Car Dieu en eulx leur a fait souvent dire
Ce que jamais par ouyr ne par lire
N'avoient congneu. O povoir autentique
Qui les [a] fait par fureur poetique,
Le temps futur predire clerement,
Et le passé monstrer couvertement,

He will find me point of hieratics;
I am end and aim of mathematics.
I am the circle from which all things come,
Where all is kept and it returns in sum.
I'm I Am, that triangle all correct,
Almighty, good and wise in my effect,
Who was, who am, and ever more shall be,
Eternal God, the seat of certainty,   2528
The Father of the World, the Mighty One,
Redeemer of the world, enlightened Son,
Holy Spirit, world's illumination,
Holy Three in one incorporation;   2532
Briefly, no aspect of the heavens nine
Fails to respect me, for its aims are mine.
There is no figure in the writings here
But elsewhere than in writ would seem more
    clear;   2536
I'm the I Am, so let the matted pall
Of every ignorant, the blinding caul,
Be destroyed with all its supuration
By my Holy Spirit's conflagration."   2540
How my joy was multiplied sincerely
When I understood the words so clearly!
The secret of a wisdom so refined
Had been revealed me by this gentle mind   2544
It turned the hurt by which I'd long been pained
To pleasure by which I would be sustained!
Since it's for Oneness that all savants strive,
(Oh sovereign good!) where all seek to arrive,   2548
Whoever finds this end may find new ease.
If one has All, no further thing will tease.
This Great Spirit blinding to the sighted—
By whom blind believers are yet lighted—   2552
Gives proof that One alone gives life to all:
Each comes from Him and may expect recall.
The poetry was cast upon the ground,
Sweet light exposing it without great sound.   2556
I, whose hand the bindings had selected
And so loved, on seeing them ejected,
Quickly picked one up and in raising it
Fast found it full of clarity and wit;   2560
The fiction wrought with subtle argument
No longer offered me impediment
When I could see that bards unanimous
Had spoken well to speak of "God in us."   2564
For God in them has often made them say
What they have not learned any other way,
Not heard nor read. Oh, authenticity!
Bard-fury born of His complicity,   2568
Of future time to tell with clarity,
Of past with covert similarity

Soubz fiction la vertié rendue,
Qui n'estoit point de leurs sens entendue.
Car si le vray, lequel est contenu
En leurs escriptz, fust à leurs cueurs venu,
Il y eust eu autant de bons prophetes
Qu'il y a eu d'agreables poetes;
Et si n'y a prophete qui ne soit
Poete vray, qui bien les apperçoyt.
Ce mot: «Je suys qui suys» en leurs devis
Plus clairement qu'aux troys autres je viz,
Tant qu'il n'y a dans la methamorfose
Qui sçeust trouver de la lettre la glose,
Où Cestuy là qui Est l'on apperçoyve,
Mais que le vray la[fable]ne deçoive. Fol. 309 v°
C'est luy qui fist la terre et le deluge
Là où trouva Deucalion refuge;
C'est luy qui fut destructeur des Géens
Qui furent faictz des serpentines dentz.
Celuy qui Est: c'est le très fort Athlas
Et le sçavoir de la sage Palas;
C'est Jupiter les geantz fouldroyant,
Et le cuyder et l'orgueil pouldroyant
Qui, dans la tour dont Danes fut concierge,
Par pluye d'or rendit grosse la vierge;
C'est luy duquel l'ignorante Semelle
Ne peut souffrir la divine estincelle;
Divinité fait, plus que nulle fouldre,
L'ame charnelle en son neant resouldre.
Lors mise à riens et convertye en cendre,
Nouvelle vie en les deux œufs vint prendre,
Qui, en passant par ces [mers] tant nuysantes,
Après au ciel sont estoilles luysantes;
C'est Acteon qui cerf est devenu,
Portant chapeau d'espines tout cornu,
Par trop aymer ceste nature humaine,
Dont par ses chiens il mourut en grant peyne;
C'est Leanter qui pour Hero passa
Ceste grand mer, là où il trepassa,
Et par sa mort à soy tyra s'amye,
Qui par mort fut en l'amy endormie;
Brief, il n'y a d'amour nulle figure,
Où je ne trouve au vif la portraicture
Du vray amant et seul amour parfaict,
Par qui tout est pensé et dit et faict. Fol. 310
Et s'il y a quelque chose lacive,
Là se peult veoir la folie naïfve
Et le malheur qui vient de trop aymer,
Que verité nous contrainct de blasmer.
D'autre costé, en regardant Penye,
Qui est de tous et fouye et bannie,
Qui de Procus enyvrée engrossa,
Car l'un le vin l'autre la faim pressa,

Where, masked in fiction, truth is projected,
That their minds had not at all suspected! 2572
For, if the truth, the one that is contained
Within their writs, had been through hearts obtained,
As many authors had been prophetic
As were pleasant poets homiletic. 2576
There is no single prophet who is not
True poet and the bard's compatriot.
I saw Him Who Is in their invention
Better than in three paid more attention: 2580
There's no reader of *Metamorphoses*
Who, reading letters, knowing how to seize
The gloss where One who Is comes into view
But says: "The fable does not lack the true." 2584
'Tis He that made the earth and the deluge
From which Deucalion later took refuge;
He was the killer of offspring Gaean
Sprouted from the dragon's teeth protean. 2588
He Who Is was one with Atlas's might
And equally Athena's keen insight,
Jove felling giants with his flaming thrust,
Pretense and pride reducing to mere dust, 2592
Who bred Danae, keeper of the tower,
Raining gold upon the virgin's bower;
It was he when Semele, unaware
Of his goldhead, did not survive the flare. 2596
Divinity, beyond what bolts are dealt,
Makes carnal soul into its nothing melt.
When set at nothing, merest ash of strife,
Inside two eggs He came to seek new life, 2600
Which, having crossed such hostile seas as these,
Rose to become the bright Dioscures.
He is Acteon, changling stag, adorned
As if with crown of thorns his head were horned; 2604
For, loving human nature far too well,
He died in pain as to his dogs he fell;
Leander, who, in love with Hero, swam
The sea and drowned, was also the I Am; 2608
And by his death drew to him into sleep
His loved one, who, like him, embraced the deep.
No image of true love appears to me
But there a lifelike portraiture I see 2612
Of the True Lover and sole perfect Love:
Each thought, each word, and deed from Him above.
And if some act appear lascivious,
There's seen the foolishness oblivious 2616
And mishap that from too much love must come;
The truth impels us to opprobrium.
Take Penye, if a moment we diverge,
Whose conduct met with banishment and scrouge: 2620
She by Procus was made drunk and vanquished,
Man by wine and girl by hunger anguished,

54

Et, bien que l'un fust à l'autre contraire,
Necessité les sceut si bien attraire
[Que] des deux vint Amour, le vray moyen
Que l'homme est homme et sans lequel n'est rien:
Celluy qui Est en cest amour je voy,
Il est qui Est, et a son estre en soy,
Bien qu'il soit filz du grant Dieu d'habundance,
Ayant pris chair subjecte à indigence;
Son povoir vient de la divinité
Et son tourment de nostre humanité,
Dont sort Amour, ce divin feu brullant,
Qui va tout autre amour anichilant.
Celuy qui Est, à qui bien l'ymagine,
Se voit aussy dedans ceste Androgine,
Qui sa moictié ne cesse de cercher,
Ne la trouvant ne se fait que fascher:
Ce feu brullant, ceste amour vehemente,
Qui met en l'ame une divine attente
De recouvrer sa part et sa moictié,
Ne [souffrera] qu'elle prenne amytié.
En autre lieu, car rien que son semblable
Ne lui sçauroit jamais estre agreable.
Joseph voulut ses freres recevoir Fol. 310 v°
Quand son semblable aveques luy peut veoir,
Ou autrement n'eussent point veu sa face.
Jà n'est besoing que si long discours face,
Il me suffit de vous monstrer cest Ung,
Celluy qui Est, que je trouve en chacun
Livre plaisant de ceste poesie,
Dont mon ame est plus que jamais saisie;
Car si en eulx le mensonge m'a pleu
Las! mainctenant qu'au descouvert j'ay veu
La verité, Celluy qui Est sans doubte,
Et la doulceur dedans l'amer je gouste,
Lessant l'escorce et prenant la mouëlle,
Plus que jamais voy poesie belle,
Ne m'arrestant au parler ny au chant,
Mais plus avant dedans je voys marchant;
Car le dehors, ainsy qu'il souloit faire,
Ne me tient plus lyé par trop me plaire.
En regardant ce pillier poetique,
Par terre viz celluy de rethorique,
Je viz soudain par ce feu abattant,
Et tant s'en fault qu'il allast rien gastant,
Que sa clarté, qui tout illuminoit,
Double beaulté à tous livres donnoit,
Où l'escripture et l'art estoit gardé;
Mais clairement y estoit regardé
Celuy qui est de [l'orateur] la grace,
Lequel jamais d'ouyr on ne se lasse:
Celluy qui Est de l'orateur est langue,

Though they were two quite opposite. In fact,
Necessity made opposites attract   2624
And generated love through them, the means
That man is man, without which none advenes.
That One Who Is in this love I behold:
He is What Is, his own life does enfold;   2628
And though son of Him, God of abundance,
He took flesh and poverty's encumbrance.
His power comes from His divinity,
His torment, from our own humanity,   2632
From which comes Love, the brilliant fire divine
Which causes every other love's decline.
The One Who Is, to one who sees within
Is seen also within the Androgyne   2636
Compelled to seek the other half it knew,
Whose grief, not finding it, can but accrue:
This burning fire, this love-born veh'mency
That gives the soul divine expectancy   2640
That it will find its part and hemisphere,
Will not permit its forming friendship here,
Another sphere; for, nothing but its own
Could ever be to it the pleasure known.   2644
Joseph wanted to receive his brothers
When he knew them for his own; for, others
Were not to be allowed to see his face.
There is no need such long discourse to trace;   2648
It is enough that I show you this One
That I find One Who Is in books—I'm done—
In poetry in which I am much pleased,
By which my soul is more than ever seized;   2652
If I was thrilled before by mascarade,
With this discovery that I have made
Of Truth, The One That Is, beyond all doubt,
The sweetness in the bitter I've found out,   2656
I will now leave the shell and take the meat
And more than ever find the poem sweet,
Not hesitating at the words or song;
But, penetrating deeper, march along.   2660
Exteriors, which once brought happiness,
No longer bind by pleasing to excess.
In looking where the poets' post was found,
I saw the rhetoric's upon the ground   2664
There, all at once, by this reductive light.
So far was it from introducing blight,
Its brilliance, that on ev'ryhand was shed,
Gave double beauty as its colors bled   2668
To all the books where writ and art were kept.
But clearly there He was beheld, adept,
The One Who Is, who is that speaker's grace
That never tired an audience apace.   2672
The One Who Is is every speaker's tongue

55

Celluy qui Est forge en luy la harangue,
Celluy qui Est est son sens, sa raison, Fol. 311
Et inventeur de toute l'oraison;
Celluy qui Est est la vraye eloquence,
Sa grande audace et sa bonne audience,
Puysque sans luy l'homme ne peult rien faire,
Ny commencer, moyenner ny parfaire,
Et que de tout est l'estre et le facteur.
Celluy qui Est est le seul orateur:
Si l'orateur par son orgueil s'avance
Et ce don là de luy seul venir pense,
Il est larron desrobant à son maistre
Son sens, sa force, et sa vie et son estre.
Donques voyant Celluy qui Est partout
Es oraisons plus que jamais prent goust,
Voyant Celluy dont la parolle vient,
Qui le bon droict de l'inocent soustient
Ou le fait perdre, exerçant passience
En ses esleuz qui ont en luy fiance.
Plus n'admiray la beaulté de langaige,
L'invention, l'art, la reigle et l'usaige
Que je trouvoys difficile à suyvir,
Car Celluy seul auquel tout doit servir
Ne se voulut dans ces livres celler,
Mais par ce feu clairment reveller,
Comme l'esprit de tout entendement,
Parolle et voix et vie et mouvement.
En ce penser n'estoys fasché ny las,
Quand le pillier plus prés viz cheoir à bas
Des livres vieulz, des antiques histoires,
Trèstous ouvers, mais leurs lettres très noires,
Que j'avoys veu par vieillesse effacées,
Fol. 311v°
Rememorant mainctes choses passées,
Renouveler leur vie [en] ce feu cler,
Trop plus soudain et beau que nul escler,
Qui les monstra claires et reluysantes,
Et les me fist trouver trop plus plaisantes
Que ne souloys, ce seul Ung retrouvant
En chacun livre où le feu est ouvrant.
Tout empereur ou roy, duquel l'histoire
Je regardoys, me donnoit la memoyre
De ce grand roy, plain d'admiration,
Constitué sur le mont de Syon;
Celluy qui seul conduict la monarchie,
La fait asseoir sur toute hierarchie.
Donné luy a les gentz pour heritaige,
Le terre aussy jusqu'au dernier rivaige;
Sceptre puyssant luy a voulu donner
Pour chastier les siens et gouverner:
Bien heureux est qui le peult appaiser
Par ung très humble et amoureux baiser.

Who forges arguments in him, unsung;
He Who Is provides him sense and reason,
Author of the speech for every season. 2676
For He Who Is is the true eloquence,
The speaker's daring, his good audience,
Without Him there is nothing man can do:
Begin, produce the half, nor see it through. 2680
That I Am is the mover of the whole.
The I Am is the orator, the sole.
If, through his pride, an orator advance
And think his gift to be his own, by chance, 2684
He is a thief who robs his Lord, of course,
Whence comes his sense and being, life and force.
So everywhere the I Am meets my sight;
In speeches now I find increased delight; 2688
I see Him from whom advenes the Word;
The good right of the innocent is heard
Or brought to loss by Him, patiently august
With chosen ones who place in Him their trust. 2692
I'll no more admire fine words, abusage
Where invention, art, the rules, and usage
Cause only difficulties to pursuit
Because the One alone whom all must suit 2696
Did not wish in these books to be concealed,
But by this fire, with clarity, revealed
To be the spirit's elucidation,
Voice and word, its life and animation. 2700
In this concept I was not vexed nor floored
To see the nearest pillar past me lowered:
The old books, antique history and fact
Completely open, but their letters black, 2704
Perserving many things by time erased
That I had seen before by age effaced,
Their life renewed in fresh effulgence there,
More fair and startling than a lightning flare, 2708
Which showed them to me clear and doubly bright;
It let me find them more intense delight
Than once I did, this unique One disclosed
In each book where the fire left it exposed. 2712
Emperors and kings, upon inspection
Of all history, brought recollection
Of that great king filled with adoration,
Vested on Mount Zion with his station, 2716
The one who led the Jewish monarchy
To place it over all the hierarchy
And gave it tribes to keep forever more,
The land also, down to the final shore; 2720
A mighty rod he tried to leave therein
To give his people rule and discipline.
Quite blessèd is the one who can appease,
With humble, loving kiss set all at ease. 2724

Ainsy lisant d'empereurs, roys et princes,
Qui ont conquis royaulmes et provinces,
De leurs bons duqs et chefz et capitaines,
Qui ont l'honnuer achapté de leurs peines,
Le seul qui Est dedans leur hardiesse
Voyoys à clair, car il est la noblesse
Qui hors du cueur dechasse villennie
Et qui l'entrée à vice et à peur nye.
C'est luy qui est le cueur de tous les cueurs
Et la victoire aussi de tous vainqueurs,
C'est luy qui est prudence militaire, Fol. 312
Qui fait tirer la flesche au sagitaire,
Qui fait la lance et l'espée offenser
Quelque orgueilleux qui se cuyde offenser;
Luy seul qui Est est Dieu de la bataille
Sans qui ne fait l'homme chose qui vaille.
Celluy qui Est je trouvoys en Cartaige,
Qui ont apris, fuyant guerre ou dommaige,
Pour appaiser du Dieu tout puyssant l'ire,
Sacrifier à mort ou à martire
Quelqu'un d'entre eulx, et lors me souvenoit
De Celluy seul qui pour tous mort prenoit.
Celluy qui est en celluy se monstra
Qui toute armé dedans le gouffre entra,
Lequel sembla si contant d'un seul chef
Qu'il se ferma sans [s']ouvrir derechef:
Le povoys veoir enfer pour nous fermé
Quand le puyssant y entra tout armé.
Pour n'alonger propoz, je ne povoys
Histoire veoir sans luy que je trouvoys
Par tous costez, mesmes jusques aux fables:
Tant fut caché soubz propoz agreables
Le grand povoir de Dieu et sa main forte.
Lisant des roys et d'empereurs la sorte,
Je contemploys qui vainquent et combatent,
Et les palais et les hommes abattent,
Edifient et levent d'autre part
Qui de leur grace ont aquis quelque part;
En ceulx qu'à tort ilz ont à mort offert,
Qui leurs tourmentz doulcement ont souffert,
Du corps de Christ l'ymaige j'en remembre,
Qui a souffert et souffre en chascun
   membre   Fol. 312 v°
Depuys le temps de l'inocent Abel,
Et souffrira jusqu'qu dernier mortel
Juste ou esleu; mais quand au divin corps
Seront uniz tous les membres, alors
Royaulme, empire et papal cessera,
Car Dieu seul [roy] et grand prestre sera.
Déjà l'est il, mais il est incongneu,
Et le sera jusqu'à ce que venu
Soit sur son arc triomphant et celeste;

I read of emperors, kings at the helm,
The conquerors of provinces and realm,
Good dukes and chiefs and captains in their lead,
Who captured honor for some daring deed,   2728
But clearly in the daring I would see
Sole Being, for He is nobility
Who from the heart rules out the villain smear
And bars the entry to all vice and fear;   2732
And He it is, the heart of every heart,
Of all the victors, the victorious part,
Courage of the military marcher
Guiding each shaft shot by every archer,   2736
Wielding lance and sword in battle blended
When a proud one thinks himself offended;
Sole God of every battle on this earth,
Without Him man can do no deed of worth.   2740
I found I Am in Carthage; for men there
Learned how, for fleeing war or its despair,
Almighty God's great wrath to overcome:
To sacrifice to death or martyrdom   2744
One of their number, which made me recall
The One Alone who took on death for all.
The One Who Is revealed Himself in him
Who, fully armed, went off the crevice rim,   2748
Which gulf then seemed contented by this chief
And closed for good; it gave the rest relief.
I could envision hell as barred to us
Because the strong one had once entered thus.   2752
In brief, lest I too much elaborate:
Without I Am I could not contemplate
History! Him I found on every hand,
In fables even. So much hidden stand   2756
God's force and hand beneath beguiling things.
In reading fates of emperors and kings,
I studied conquerers that warring go
That palaces and men may be brought low,   2760
But civilize and raise another place
The ones who somewhere have acquired their grace.
In those to whom death was dealt in error,
Humble sufferers of pain and terror,   2764
I could see Christ's body and remember:
He has suffered always in each member

Since Abel's time when innocence was slain,
And with the final mortal will know pain   2768
(One righteous or elect); but when again
All members join in the divine corps, then
Realm, papacy and empire will have ceased,
For God alone will be both king and priest.   2772
He is so now, except He stands unknown
Until the time He be returned and shown
Upon His arc as Lord of Heaven dressed.

Celuy qui est sera lors manifeste,	The One Who Is will then be manifest; 2776
Bons et mauvais triumpher le verront,	The good and bad alike will see Him win;
Les uns cryront et les autres riront;	And some will cry as some raise merry din.
Et qui aura çà bas l'homme adoré	Whoever will have worshipped man on earth
Et Dieu en luy estre tout ignoré.	And in him scorned God as the total worth 2780
Se trouvera de son labeur confuz,	Will find himself embarrassed at his task
En recevant du repoz le refuz;	And that he is refused what rest he ask;
Mais l'œil qui est par la foy inspiré	Whereas the eye that was by faith inspired,
Et qui au blanc a visé et a tiré,	That boldly took its aim point blank and fired, 2784
Ne regardant qu'ung seul en toute chose,	Did see but One in all phenomena
Aura repoz et desjà se repose.	Which is to peace the prolegomena.
Ce propoz là je pensoys, et aloys	I scanned the whole while pondering this thought
Tout regardant, quant le pillier des loix	And saw the pillar of the law now brought 2788
Viz à mes piedz aveques les canons	To rest completely at my feet and near
Et les decretz, que si cher nous tenons.	The canon and decrees that we hold dear.
Le feu brulla des loix l'obscurité	The fire burned through the laws' obscurity
Et me monstra du sens la pureté,	And showed me their intentions' purity: 2792
Non pour debattre et vouloir contester	Not mere debate in effort to disprove
Qu'il seroit bon de plusieurs loix oster,	It would be good a few laws to remove,
Ou moderer, accorder, exposer,	Or harmonize, interpret, make a change
Ou rabiller et si bien disposer Fol. 313	In some, amend so well as to arrange 2796
Qu'il n'y eust loy qui fust desrogative	That there were no law that would derogate
De ceste loy naturelle et naïfve,	This law that is of nature and innate,
Que Dieu planta au cueur du premier homme,	That God sowed in the heart of that first man
Depuys qu'il eut transgressé par la pomme:	When through the apple human sin began. 2800
C'est ceste loy dont les justes vesquirent,	The righteous ones lived by the holy law,
Qui Dieu partout en toutes choses virent;	And God in all things, everywhere, they saw.
Ce n'est aussy pour dire que la loy	This does not say as well that law as found
Escripte soit de si très bon aloy	Be written of such excellent compound 2804
Qu'elle suffit quant à la punitive	It satisfies all justice punitive
Justice, aussy à la distributive,	As well as justice termed distributive;
Ny dire aussi que ceste loy de grace	Nor does it say, what's more, that law of grace
La loy humaine abolit ou efface.	Will human law abolish or erase; 2808
Ma fin n'est pas de reprendre ou de mordre,	To undermine, malign, fault or amend
De rabiller ou de confondre l'ordre,	The present order is nowise my end.
Mais ouy bien comme ce feu entendre	Mark how this fire had helped me grasp the law
Me fist la loy, et comme on la doit prendre:	And how one should interpret law he saw: 2812
Ceste clarté, ce veritable feu	This veritable fire, lucidity,
Me fist Celluy qui Est veoir au milieu	Made Him Who Is quite visible to me
De toutes loix, tant que les plus rebelles,	Mid laws of every kind, to such extent
En le voyant parmy, je [trouvay] belles.	I could admire the most recalcitrant, 2816
Ce clair esprit les yeulx illumina	Beholding Him. This same Spirit's vision
De Socrates, quand il determina	Lighted Socrates in his decision
D'endurer mort pour obeyr aux loix	To take death, obedient to the voice
De son pays, combien qu'il eust le choix	Of his own country, though he had the choice 2820
Pour ce coup là d'endurer le danger	To risk this stroke and settle Athens' broil
Et se saulver en pays estranger.	Or save his life by flight to foreign soil.
Je ne craindz point de dire sa response	I'm not afraid to say his countermand
Estre de Dieu, par son esprit, semonce:	Had come by way of Spirit, God's command 2824
«Les loix, dist-il, en terres differentes	Thus: "In various countries, discipline
«Des loix d'en hault sont et seurs et parentes.	To laws on high is sister or close kin;
Fol. 313 v°	

«Que tout arrest des seurs au ciel donné
«Est par les seurs de la terre ordonné,
«Je m'enfuys de celles de ma terre,
«Je n'auray moins aux estrangeres guerre.
«Si j'ay de mort par le ciel ma sentence,
«Avoir ne puys de la terre dispense,
«Car tous pays luy sont obeyssans;
«Parquoy plustost à mourir me consens
«En ce pays, par ses loix, dont le soing
«J'ay tousjours eu, que de mourir plus loing,
«Sachant très bien que si le ciel à mort
«Ne m'a livré, nul ne peult tenir tort
«A son povoir ny à mon innocence;
«Donq à ses loys feray l'obeyssance.»
Ce philozophe, en si saige oraison,
A surmonté toute humaine raison.
O chrestiens, qui la foy catholique
Pensez avoir, regardez ceste etnique,
Au moins tel est de l'Eglise tenu,
Voyez à quel sçavoir il est venu:
De Celluy seul qui Est a eu science,
Car autrement n'auroit eu passience.
Nous, ignorans, craignons les loix civiles,
Papes et roys, et parlemens de villes,
Tourmentz, gibetz et chaynes et prisons,
Tant que par peur souvent le vray taisons;
Regardons hault à nostre election,
Nous ne craindrons la condamnation
Que contre nous l'homme peult decretter;
Mort ne tourment ne vouldrons
    rejecter,   Fol. 314
Sachant qu'ung Dieu—[c']est Celluy seul qui
    Est—
A contre nous de mort donné l'arrest,
Lequel devons aussy doulcement prendre
Que si sa voix vive povions entendre,
Croyant qu'il est des hommes le povoir
Et que rien n'est fait que par son vouloir.
Donques, voyant le povoir evident
De ce grand roy et premier president,
La loy que tant j'avoys tenue obscure
M'estoit très claire, et doulce la plus dure,
Veu qu'il n'y a qu'ung seul legislateur
Qui de justice est le vray zelateur,
Qui fait escrire aux empereurs et roys,
Jurisconsultes et papes, tous leurs droictz:
Qui les regarde, il perit soubz leur faix,
Mais qui void Dieu en eulx, il vit en paix.
Ces livres là des loix je regardoys
Et à ce seul que j'y vis j'entendoys,
Mais contrainct fuz de regarder derriere,
Car de ce feu la puyssance et lumiere

Each decree in heaven instituted,
Through the laws of earth is executed.   2828
If I escape the laws of my own land,
I am no less at odds on foreign strand.
If, to die, God sent my condemnation,
None on earth could grant me dispensation.   2832
All nations are to Him obedient.
So I must rather to my death consent
In this, my land, and by its laws, whose cause
I always served than die by foreign laws.   2836
If heav'n my death warrant has commuted,
No one can exist who can refute it,
Deny its power nor my innocence;
So, to its laws I'll give obedience."   2840
This friend of wisdom in this speech so wise
Surpassed what human reason can devise.
Christians, you folk who think that you excel
In Catholic faith, behold this "infidel";   2844
At least such stamp is by the church maintained.
Behold the wisdom that he had attained,
Receiving knowledge from The One Who Is.
Such patience had not otherwise been his.   2848
We ignorants are cowed by law in gowns,
By popes and kings and parlements of towns,
By laws and torments, gibbets, jails, and chain
Until we hush the truth, oft fearing pain.   2852
Let us look on high for our election:
We'll not fear society's rejection;
Whate'er decree against us man may use,
Our death and torment we will not refuse,   2856

Well-knowing that one God, the One Who Is,

Has ordered death for us; command is His.
We should as meekly give in to man's choice
As if we listened to God's living voice.   2860
Believing that He rules through people still
And nothing can be done but by His will.
Then, seeing here the power evident
In this great King and foremost president,   2864
The law that I'd quite thought obscurity
Was clear, and kind was harsh security,
Given there is but one legislator
Who of justice is true perpetrator.   2868
The kings and emperors have Him as cause,
Like popes and lawyers, when they write their laws.
One falls beneath their weight who studies these,
But, seeing God in them, one lives at ease.   2872
I saw this single figure as I scanned
Those books of laws and came to understand,
But had to look away because there came
Both light and power from this single flame;   2876

59

Avoit jetté par terre le pillier
Que j'avoys sceu plus fort edifier,
Voire et ouvrir par milles et par cens
Les livres cloz en me monstrant leur sens:
Theologie alors viz sans obstacle
Que je trouvoys difficile miracle,
Car leurs ergotz et leurs distinctions,
Assavoir mon et contradictions,
N'ont resisté qu'à travers leur escorce
Celluy qui Est ne se monstre en sa
        force;   Fol 314 v°
Luy qui le ciel jusqu'à la terre abesse,
Qui fist parler myeulx que l'homme l'anesse,
Fait parler ceulx qui n'ont langue ne bouche,

Et des parleurs si fort la gorge bousche
Que seulement la voix n'en peult sortir.
C'est Celluy seul qui sçait bien assortir
Les instrumens pour sa volunté faire,
C'est luy qui sçait à luy mesmes complaire;
Par luy aussy à luy nous complaisons,
Par luy en nous tout son vouloir faisons.
Docteur n'y a qui sur papier sçeust mettre
Ung tout seul mot ny escrire une lettre,
Si la vertu de Dieu ne luy permet,
Qui plume et encre et force en sa main met;
Mais s'il advient que ce docteur abuze,
Cuydant sçavoir sans ceste grace infuse,
Et qu'il se vueille à escrire ingerer
Sans que l'Esprit luy vienne suggerer
Des sainctz escriptz la vraye intelligence,
Il ne sçauroit, par nulle diligence
De son sçavoir aquis fresle et humain,
Faire ung bon traict de sa mortelle main;
Mais ceulx qui sont du Sainct Esprit conduictz
Ne sont jamais seducteurs ne seduictz.
Celuy qui Est se voit en ces deux sortes:
Car, en lisant des uns les œuvres mortes,
L'on void Dieu seul aveuglissant les yeulx
De ceulx qui sont plains de leur Adam vieulx,
De leur cuyder et de leur vaine gloire, Fol. 315.
Lesquelz auront horrible purgatoire,
Changeant le mal en bien, le bien en mal,
Voire et en lieu de monter, tout aval
Vont mener ceulx en une basse fosse
Qui les ont creuz; ainsy l'aveugle pousse
L'aveugle au lieu où l'on brulle et l'on tremble,
Pour cheminer d'une doctrine ensemble.
La verité a dit: «Laissez-les là»:
Laissons les donc, mais voyons par cela

Que Dieu n'est moins en eulx très glorieux,

It brought to earth the very strongest post,
The one I had elaborated most,
To open books by thousands, tomes most dense,
Revealing to me their once hidden sense.   2880
Theology I saw empirical,
That I had found a deadlocked miracle.
Not their quiblings neither their distinctions,
Affirmations nor their contradictions   2884
E'er could prevent but that behind their shell
The One Who Is, with all His force, should well.

He who brings heaven down where earth can see
And Balaam's ass to speak more sense than he   2888
Gives those that have not mouth nor tongue clear
    speech,
And chokes the throats of shouters till the breach
Will not allow the voice to pass its gate.
He is the only one to designate   2892
The instruments to carry out His will,
He is the one who can His wish fulfill
And through Him also we His purpose suit;
Through Him in us we follow His pursuit,   2896
There is no doctor who could understand
Enough to write a jot by his own hand
Had he not God's virtue animating
Him, pen, ink, and strength articulating.   2900
And if it chance this doctor, out of place,
Takes knowledge to be less than dint of grace
And tries to undertake the writing feat
Without the Spirit's coming there with mete   2904
Suggestions, messages of Holy Writ;
By no amount of diligence at wit,
Nor human knowledge, frail and second-hand,
Could he make one good stroke of writing hand; 2908
Those that are by Holy Mind conducted
Never are seducers nor corrupted.
He Who Is is beheld in these two kinds;
For, reading morbid works of certain minds,   2912
We see God only making blind the eyes
Of those whom their old Adam occupies
With their false belief and their vainglory;
They will know horrendous purgatory,   2916
Exchanging ill for good and good for ill.
And, yea, instead of climbing, down the hill
Proceed to lead into the pit of hell
Their followers. The blindmen thus compel   2920
More blindmen to proceed where they must burn
And for their doctrine tremble in their turn.
The Holy Writ has told us, "Leave them there,"
Let's leave them, then, but learn from their
    despair: 2924
God in them is not less efficacious,

Les aveuglant, que bon et gracieux
Se monstre en ceulx qui n'ont d'eulx nulle estime,
Qui prennent Dieu pour la force et la lyme
De leur sçavoir et leur simple parler,
Dont humblement se sont voulu meller,
Ne s'estimant, je dy le plus sçavant,
Fors que la plume au leger escrivant,
Du Sainct Esprit l'instrument imparfaict,
Sans lequel n'est ung seul bon livre fait.
O que celluy qui a l'experience
Du Saint Esprit voit bien la difference
Des escrivans, car en ung purement
Trouve Celluy qui Est tant clairement,
[Qu'il] peult juger l'esprit evangelique
Parler dedans ce docteur autantique;
En l'autre non, mais ung cuyder haultain
De trop sçavoir conduysant plume et main.
Mais pour juger des mauvais et des bons
Ce qui en est, fault que nous regardons
Qui le plus près de l'Escripture touche,
Car l'Evangile est la pierre de touche Fol. 315 v°
Où du bon or se congnoist la valeur
Et du plus bas la foiblesse et paleur.
Tout bon docteur en ses escritz cherchant
De descouvrir le cueur lasche et meschant
Du vieil Adam et sa condition,
Plain de peché et de damnation,
En le mettant à riens et mort et cendre,
Qui, d'autre part, s'efforce à faire entendre
Que Dieu est tout estre, bonté, sçavoir,
Vertié, vie et puyssance et povoir,
Auquel nous tous vivons, mouvons et sommes,
Qui a porté de noz pechez les sommes,
Et sur la croix par dure passion
En a pour nous fait satisfaction,
Et qu'a luy seul et en luy devons croire,
En luy rendant louange, honneur et gloire,
En reverant et craingnant sa puyssance,
Et s'asseurer en ceste congnoissance
Du seul vray Dieu, createur et bon pere,
Et de Jesus, que pour nous estre frere
Et redempteur a çà bas envoyé,
Nous rachaptant du monde desvoyé,
N'ayant desdaing de nostre chair mortelle:
En ces deux poinctz gist la vie eternelle.
Ce docteur là, qui telle verité
Par escript mect, a très bien meritté
D'estre estié sçavant et veritable.
L'autre, duquel la doctrine est doubtable,
C'est cestuy là qui l'homme enorgueillit
Et qui l'excuse encores qu'il faillist, Fol. 316

Blinding them, than when benign and gracious.
He shows himself in those less arrogant
Who own Him force and honing instrument   2928
For them, their thought and simple speech—and those,
The folk humbly wish to interpose
And deem, while ledger writing's in pursuit,
They are but pens (though I say most astute,)   2932
The faulty tools of Holy Consciousness—
Without whom not a book can find success.
Oh, how the one who has experience
With Holy Spirit sees the difference   2936
In scribes! In one he is obliged to find
That He Who Is has been so well defined
That one may judge evangelicity
To mark that doctor's authenticity;   2940
While in another, arch opinions brand
As pedantry his guide of pen and hand.
To judge the good from those that give offense
Indeed, we must decide by evidence   2944
Which ones come closer to the gospel pure,
Because the Gospel is the touchstone sure
Whereby the value of good gold is known
And, in base ore, wan hue and weakness shown.   2948
Each honest doctor struggling in his writs
To show the truant heart and evil wits
Of ancient Adam and his condition
To be full of sin that courts perdition;   2952
By dealing death and dust to him makes good.
Likewise, he tries to make it understood:
God is goodness, knowledge, and all being,
Truth, life, and strength and power decreeing;   2956
We live, move, and have our being within
Him, who assumed the burdens of our sin
And, by suff'ring on the cross dire passion,
For ourselves gave final satisfaction;   2960
It is upon Him only that we must,
Bestowing honor, glory, praise, and trust,
And holding His strength one that we must fear,
Be certain through the knowledge given here   2964
Of true God, good Father, and Creator,
And of Jesus, brother, liberator,
One sent to us that we should be bought back
From bondage from this world gone off its track   2968
In its failure to scorn flesh that's mortal:
Here on these two points rests life immortal.
The doctor who records such verity
Has well deserved for his asperity   2972
To be known as learnéd and veracious;
But the one whose doctrine is fallacious
Is one who pumps man full of silly pride,
Excusing him more than is justified,   2976

61

En luy donnant povoir, sçavoir, bonté,
Et que par luy peult bien estre dumpté
Le peché joinct à nostre chair humaine,
Voire effacé par son labeur et peyne;
Ainsy le fait confier en son œuvre
Et son enfer en son neant luy cœuvre
D'une si povre et foible couverture
Que, s'arrestant trop à la creature,
Du Createur la confiance il pert,
Ne le voyant aux livres en appert;
Mais loing de luy, comme ung juge effroyable,
[Est] Jesus Christ à demy secourable,
Comme n'ayant entierement parfaict
Nostre salut ainsy comme il a fait.
En ces deux poinctz gist la damnation:
D'attribuer nostre salvation,
Redemption, aux hommes en partie,
Et de luy seul dont la vie est partie
Ne croyre pas que du tout dependons,
Affin qu'honneur à luy seul nous rendons.
Ces livres là diminuant l'honneur,
Gloire et vertu qu'au souverain seigneur,
En le louant, devons attribuer,
Qui nostre foy en doubte [font] muer,
Qui arrester nous [font] en mille sortes
Et confier aux creatures mortes:
Ces escriptz là, tant soient ilz devotz,
Bien painctz, bien dictz et rempliz de beaulx
    motz,
Ils sont suspectz et leur [doctrine] aussy.
Mais les premiers, qui suyvent sans nul
    si   Fol. 316 v°
L'intention de la Bible sacrée,
—Ceste doctrine au cueur doibt estre ancrée
Pour tirer hors nostre nef du naufrage,
Où rien ne sert, aviron ne cordage,—
Mais cest esprit dans la parolle encloz,
Quand il luy plaist, myeulx [qu'à] fer ou à cloux,
Celluy qui Est en nostre cueur imprime,
Et ce beau mot, qui descend de la cime
Du ciel très hault et du cein paternel,
Engrave en nous, dont le povoir est tel
Que nostre nef, d'espoir desemparée,
A sa venue est du tout reparée,
L'unde abattue et rompu le vent fort,
Tant qu'elle vient à son desiré port:
Ces livres là partout se doivent lire,
Et cestuy là les sçaura bien eslire
Qui a toujours son sens exercité
En l'Escripture, et qui est excité
De cest esprit divin, qui est aucteur
De Verité contre l'esprit menteur.

Attributing good, thought, and strength to man
To overcome that which no human can:
Sin that's with the human flesh connected,
Claiming that man's work the purge effected.   2980
He has man trust his own productiveness
And hides from him his hell in nothingness
With covering so poor and far from strong
That, dwelling on the creature overlong,   2984
Man neglects the faith in the Creator,
Who's not seen in books [of such a traitor.]
Oft pictured wrongly as a frightful judge
Is Jesus Christ, one who must half begrudge   2988
His help, one having not entirely earned
Salvation for us, as He did, [we learned.]
These two points determine our damnation:
That we grant the chance of our salvation,   2992
Our redemption, in part to mortal man:
On Him through whom we know that life began
Not to believe that we depend for all
So that our honors must upon Him fall.   2996
Those books, by lessening, distributing
The honor we should be attributing,
The praise, and virtue due the sov'reign Lord,
Which change our faith to doubt and disaccord   3000
That give us pause a thousand different ways,
Conferring on dead creatures trust and praise:
Such books as those, devout as they may be,
Well pictured, well-phrased, filled with melody,   3004
Are all suspect, like their doctrine, subtle.
But the former that make no rebuttal

To what the Holy Bible would impart—
Their doctrine must be anchored in the heart,   3008
In case our ship wrecks, to be of avail
When nothing else will serve, not oar nor sail—
But that one spirit that the word engrails.
When He wills, better than with iron or nails,   3012
The one Who Is into our hearts is pressed;
And this fair Word that comes down from the crest
Of highest heaven and the Father's heart,
Brings balance, and such power can impart   3016
That our poor ship, abandoned to despair,
When He has come, is put into repair;
The wind is harnessed and the wave is smoothed
Till she come to her wished-for harbor, soothed: 3020
Those are the good books everywhere to use,
And he will know that these are books to choose
Whose sense and practice e'er were united
With the Writ and one who is excited   3024
By God's Spirit, which for this believer
Is Truth's Author, fighting the deceiver.

Ces livres donc clairement j'advisoys
Et en mon cueur de chascun divisoys,
Mais entre tous j'en viz ung d'une femme,
Depuys cent ans escript, remply de flamme
De charité, si très ardentement
Que rien qu'amour n'estoit son argument,
Commancement et fin de son parler,
Que l'on sentoit, en le lisant, bruller
Dedans le cueur ung cuyder faulx et vain,
[Par] cest amour, qui brulle si soudain
Que du rocher il fait saillir l'eau vive. Fol. 317
O qu'elle estoit ceste femme ententive
A recevoir cest amour qui brulloit
Son cueur et ceulx ausquelz elle parloit!
Bien congnoissoit par cest esprit subtil
Le vray amy qu'elle nommoit Gentil
Et son Loing Près. O que c'est bien nommer
Celluy qui doit par sus tous estre aymé!
Le Gentil n'est subject à servitude,
Mais par amour prend la solicitude
De declarer sa grande bonté haulte,
Où de bonté et d'amour y a faulte;
Il donne et mect là où il n'y a riens
Et par amour communique ses biens;
Il est gentil, et par sa gentillesse
Gentille fait et plaine de noblesse
L'ame charnelle, et qui est si très orde
Qu'elle n'a rien meritté que la corde,
Pour la trainer en l'eternel supplice,
Tant est vilaine et plaine de malice!
Mais ce Gentil sa gentillesse espand
Sur la vilaine, et point ne s'en repent.
Car de noblesse il ne pert ung seul poinct
En la donnant où n'y en avoit point,
Mais anoblit par gentillesse l'ame,
Que de vilaine il fait devenir dame;
Il est gentil et gentillement ouvre
En l'humble cueur auquel il se descouvre.
Loing se peult dire en voyant sa haultesse
Tant differente à nostre petitesse; Fol. 317 v°
Le ciel est loing d'enfer, divinité
Loing de la chair de nostre humanité,
Le bien du mal, et la vertu du vice.
Mais vraye amour usant de son office,
Ce Dieu, tant loing qu'il ne se laissoit veoir,
A rendu près de nous; par son povoir
Ce Loing est Près, et le ciel [à la] terre
Amour fait joindre, mettant fin à la guerre
D'entre le Loing et Près, par tel accord
Que le très Loing, vaincu par une mort,
Est près de nous, mais je vous dy si près
Que je ne puys trouver termes exprès

So I judged these books with penetration
And gave each my heart's consideration.   3028
I saw a book that bore a maiden's name.
Composed a hundred years ago, aflame
With kindness and with warmth to the extent
That loving was her total argument,   3032
Commencement and the end; all else she spurned.
One felt, in reading it, that there was burned
From out her heart a vain creed, one corrupt,
By this love, that thus sending spark abrupt   3036
Makes living water from the boulder spring.
Oh, eager was this lady for one thing:
To have this love that let her heart convoke
As well the hearts of those to whom she spoke, 3040
And she knew through this subtle turn of mind
The True Friend whom she gave the name of "kind"
And her "One distant-present." How well-named
The One whose love is foremost to be claimed!   3044
Not subject is the Kind to servitude;
Through love He takes on the solicitude
To manifest His goodness here on earth,
Here where of love and goodness is a dearth.   3048
He furnishes supply where there is lack;
Through love he gives the goods from His own back.
He is refined, and through gentility
Of His, lends kindness and nobility   3052
To carnal soul that in the mire would grope
Until it merit nothing but the rope
That leads to hell endless and supplicious,
So malign is it and so malicious.   3056
Unstinting of Himself, the Kind One spent
His kindness on the woman miscreant.
Nobility He loses not one jot
In giving it where erstwhile it was not,   3060
Enobling through nobility her soul.
What errants He converts to lady's role!
He gently works since He is one genteel,
In humble hearts His presence to reveal.   3064
In view of His exaltedness you'd call
Him "distant," diff'rent from ourselves, the small,
As heaven is from hell, divinity
Is far from flesh of our humanity,   3068
As good from evil, virtue far from vice.
Yet True-Love, making its own sacrifice,
Has changed God's inaccessibility
And placed Him close to us; Love's potency   3072
Brought distance near; and Love, compositor
Of earth and heaven, puts an end to war
Between the Far and Near by such accord
As for the death of Christ is the reward.   3076
The Most Remote is here, but I affirm
That, ready-made, I find no fitting term

63

Pour declairer comme est près ce très Loing.
Mais qui a veu, par extresme besoing,
Combien de mal vient du Loing purement
Qui a perdu du Près le sentement,
Dira le Près nous estre en tout affaire
Comme la vie et l'estre necessaire.
Gentil Loing Près! et que ce nom est beau!
Il est puyssant pour faire du tumbeau
Saillir le mort, car, où ce Loing Près vient,
Mort ny enfer le pecheur ne detient.
Gentil Loing Près! celle qui t'appella
Par ung tel nom, à mon gré, myeulx parla
Que maint docteur qui tant a travaillé
D'estudier, dont je [m'esmerveillay]
Comme ung esprit d'une vierge si basse
Fut si remply de la divine grace;
Car ceulx, qui ont bien longuement apris,
De leur travail doivent avoir le pris,
Estans louez d'avoir fait leur devoir Fol. 318
Pour aquerir ung si divin sçavoir;
Mais ceste-cy, remplye d'ignorance,
Qui n'avoit point des lettres apparence
Et qui n'avoit frequenté nulle escolle,
Fors de l'Esprit qui tout esprit console:
En l'escoutant parler clair comme ung ange,
Je n'en sçauroys donner nulle louange
A ceste là qui est de sçavoir plaine
Sans son labeur, son estude ou sa peyne;
Mais à Celluy duquel elle est aymée
Et par amour toute en luy transformée
En fault donner l'honneur entierement.
Car il en est fin et commacement,
Et se voit myeulx sa puyssance divine,
Où moyns reluyt science femenine;
Dont ce gentil Loing Près est honoré,
Voyant qu'il a haultement labouré.
Et par amour l'ignorance subtile
Rendue il a et sçavante et gentille;
Car tel qu'il est sa bonté sans meritte
Rend le vaisseau où par grâce il habitte.
Je sçay très bien que le docteur sçavant,
Qui est à Dieu par son labeur servant,
Et qui nous rend l'Escripture evidente
Où sa peyne est à l'esperit aydante,
Estant par foy uny au Createur,
Lequel le prend pour cooperateur
De son ouvraige, ouvraige salutaire:
C'est, sans cesser, arracher et retraire
De l'ignorance et de la main du diable Fol. 318v°
L'ame, que Dieu a faicte à son semblable.
Ces bons docteurs, où l'on se doit mirer,
Assez ne puys louer ny admirer,

To say how near the Distant comes to be.
One who has seen in his extremity   3080
What great harm comes purely from estrangement,
From lost sense of Presence, what derangement,
Will declare the Presence necessary
To all deeds and life's own corollary.   3084
Kind Far-Near One! A name so sweet can stir
The dead to rise from out his sepulchre;
Because wherever Distant-Near obtains,
Not death nor hell the sinful man restrains. 3088
Kind Far-Near One, the girl who summoned you
By such a name spoke better, in my view,
Than many doctors who have spent their days
In study. I was filled with great amaze—   3092
That the spirit of a maid so lowly
Welled with the exalted grace most holy!
For those who have with lengthy labor learned
Are due the prize that their long work has earned, 3096
Praise for having made due inquisition
In pursuit of perfect erudition.
This girl lacking every look of letters,
Filled with ignorance, [unlike her betters,]   3100
Had not frequented any school or rolls
Except that of the spirit that consoles
All minds. She speaks. I hear an angel's phrase.
And though I could not give the slightest praise 3104
To one who is with understanding filled
And has no fields of study ever tilled,
Unto the One by whose love she is warmed
And through it wholly into Him transformed   3108
I give it, and there all the honor pin.
He is the end of it and origin.
His potency divine is better seen
When women's learning less displays its sheen; 3112
Thus this kind Distant-Presence is made known
Through what He has magnanimously sown.
Through love He's made ignorance discerning,
Gentle, knowing, as if filled with learning;   3116
He's such His goodness turns to naught, through grace,
The vessel where He finds His dwelling place.
I well know the scholar is deserving,
One who, through his labor, is God-serving,   3120
Making Scripture easier to find,
Wherein his work is helpful to the mind,
He's joined by his faith to the Creator,
Who accepts him as collaborator   3124
In His work. A most salutary task
Is e'er from ignorance to rip the mask,
And from the devil's grasp the soul retrieve,
That God in His own image did conceive.   3128
Good doctors, on whom one ought to reflect
I can not give enough praise or respect

Ny n'ay sçavoir pour leur esprit comprendre,	I lack the knowledge to take in their wit
Ny de leurs faictz digne louange rendre;	To render to their work praise due to it. 3132
Mais seulement de celle m'esmerveille	But I marvel at this girl, their sequel;
Dont je n'ay veu escripture pareille,	Of her writings I've not seen the equal
Et qui n'a eu pour maistre et precepteur	Though she had for master and deviser
Qu'Amour tout seul de soymesme inventeur.	Love alone, which was its own adviser. 3136
Ainsy tournant ces livres et virant,	While turning through those books to change my course
Que tant je fuz de sçavoir desirant,	I wanted to learn much from their discourse.
Je congneuz bien que [de] tout leur possible	I recognized that each, as best he could
Chacun tendoit de declairer la Bible,	Would try to make the Bible understood, 3140
Qui de science est le vray fundememt,	Which is fundamental to all learning,
Ce que nul œil ne peult veoir clairement	And no eye could ever be discerning
Sans la clarté de l'esprit veritable.	Without the brillance of true spirit's light.
Ceste clarté me fut tant secourable	Such help to me was this intense insight 3144
Que le seul ung Celluy qui Est me monstre	I saw that only He Who Is would greet
En chascune lettre où mon œil se rencontre;	Me in each letter that my eye would meet.
Et, nonobstant qu'en tous livres il soit,	Although He'd be in all books—provided
Si l'œil de chair la lettre ne deçoit,	By the letter eye were not misguided— 3148
En cestuy cy, où n'y a mot ny tiltre	In this no point of writing anywhere
Que le divin esprit n'ayt voulu tistre,	Appears but Holy Spirit wove it there;
Très clairement se peult veoir et aprandre,	Quite clearly He can be discerned and traced,
Gouster, sçavoir, incorporer et prandre.	Explored and learned, embodied and embraced. 3152
Ce livre icy est escript du grant doigt	This book is writing of that great index,
Donnant povoir au porteur de la Loy,	Granting God's law-bringer strong effects
Dont il vainquit tous les magiciens	To overcome the Pharoah's magic men
De Pharaon et leurs artz anciens.	With all their ancient magic arts and ken. 3156
C'est ce doigt là qui escrivit les tables Fol. 319	It's the finger that inscribed the table
Dessus le mont des [mandemens] notables,	Of great laws, upon the mount; unable
Dont le peché rendit le peuple indigne	Was the tribe, made unworthy due to sin
De regarder ceste lettre benigne;	To view the blessèd writing carved therein, 3160
Car l'œil lisant la lettre en vain labeure,	Because an eye becomes incompetent
Si le peché en son cueur fait demeure;	If sin within the heart is resident.
Le doigt de Dieu a le peché prescript	God's finger has for us the sin proscribed
Dedans le cueur là où il a escript	Within the heart wherein He has inscribed 3164
Son sainct vouloir, sa juste intention,	His sacred will, His precise intention;
Et sa vertu fait une motion	His strength causes motion, an extension
Par charité, qui n'est plustost sortie	Of love. As soon as is the motion flown
Du doigt de Dieu qu'elle ne soit sentye;	From God's own finger, its effect is known. 3168
Ce puyssant doigt escript, meult et reforme	This potent finger writes, moves, and reforms
Le cueur de chair, et par nouvelle forme	The carnal heart, and, through a change of norms,
Le fait divin, luy qui estoit charnel,	What is carnal He then makes supernal,
En le rendant par la mort eternel;	Rendering the same, through death, eternal. 3172
Ce doigt de Dieu nous monstre l'amytié	God's own finger shows His love paternal,
Du pere à nous, non point par la moictié	For us not to be half-strength or vernal,
Mais toute entiere et telle qu'il la pense,	But full strength and consistent with His thought,
Dont par escript nous donne congnoissance;	Through Scripture is our knowledge of it brought; 3176
Par ce doigt là chascun peult recevoir	Through the finger, each can be recipient
Le necessaire et suffisant sçavoir.	Of the knowledge needed and sufficient.
O livre escript de la divine main,	O Book by hand divine inscribed [to feed
Manne très doulce et necessaire pain,	Us] manna sweet and bread that we most need, 3180
Sans lequel est nostre ame pis que morte,	For lack of which one's soul is worse than dead,

Bien heureux est qui en la main te porte
Et en son sain comme ung tresor te garde,
Et plus heureux qui te lit et regarde
Et par plaisir avecques toy confere;
Mais très heureux celluy qui te préfère
A tous les biens que le monde luy
    donne,   Fol. 319 v°
Lesquelz pour toy sans regret habandonne,
Duquel le cueur est librairie faicte
Pour reposer de ce très grand prophete
Le livre saint, l'Escripture immortelle,
Où gist la Loy tousjours vieille et nouvelle:
Vieille, faisant sentir Adan le vieulx
De tout malfait sans cesser envieux,
Vieille, en monstrant nostre creation,
Nostre neant, nostre dejection,
Vieille en rigueur d'aspre commandement
Que l'on ne peult accomplir nullement,
Quoy qu'elle dye ou commande ou exorte,
Qui n'est porté d'une vertu plus forte;
Car rendre à Dieu ce qui luy appartient,
Le cueur de l'homme ung tel povoir ne tient:
Parquoy elle est loy vieille et de rigueur,
Puys loy nouvelle est de telle vigueur
Que l'homme peult de mort ressusciter
Et le pecheur à bien faire [exciter;]
Loy de doulceur, de bonté et de grace,
Qui la rigueur de la premiere efface,
En effaçant le peché du pecheur,
Loy, que partout doit porter le prescheur,
Loy aportant la très bonne nouvelle
Du vray salut, qui l'homme renouvelle,
Loy par qui est le malade guery,
Où le povoir estoit mort et pery
De faire bien. O loy qui veult donner
Telle vertu que tu faiz retourner
Le vieil Adam en premiere jeunesse Fol. 320
Et le vilain en parfaicte noblesse,
Loy qui luy metz en main force et vertu,
Loy par laquelle il est si revestu
De Jesuchrist, que luy abhominable
A l'œil de Dieu est fait très agreable
Par ceste peau et très puyssante escorce,
Dedans laquelle il reprent telle force
Qu'il peult la loy de rigueur observer,
Et de peché aussy se preserver;
Car ceste peau de [l'agneau] triumphant
Le fait de Dieu devenir vray enfant,
Par l'union du Filz du Pere aymé,
Pour lequel est filz adoptif nommé;
Et si le Filz son nom luy communique,
De ses vertuz luy donne la pratique:

The one who bears you in his hand unread
Thrives, guarding you like treasure in his heart;
More blest is he who reads what you impart   3184
And likes to talk with you in conference;
Most blest is he who shows a preference
For you above all goods the world returns;

Which goods, for you, without regret he spurns; 3188
His heart is made library for the book,
Repository wherein one may look
To find the prophet's text, the Scripture true,
Where lie both laws: the old, the ever new.   3192
The old makes primal Adam clear to us,
At every misdeed ever mischievous.
And it describes creation, our first phase,
Our nothingness and the outcasts' malaise,   3196
Quaint with the sternness of its harsh command,
A law one can not execute as planned—
Whatever it may say, dictate, or urge—
Unless supporting, stronger force emerge;   3200
For, giving God that which is His, not ours,
The feeble, human heart has no such pow'rs.
Such law is obsolete, one based on force.
Then comes new law, such vigor in its course,   3204
From very death it can the man revive,
And rouse the sinner tow'rd good deeds to strive.
This law of kindness, goodness, and of grace
The sternness of the former can erase   3208
For it can sinful man from sin divide.
This law the preacher must take far and wide,
A law that excellent good news conveys
Of true salvation that renews man's ways.   3212
The law that brings the curing of the ill
In whom the power had been dead and nil
For doing good. Law that would delegate
Such virtue that you move to reinstate   3216
The jaded Adam in his former youth,
Vest with nobility the once uncouth,
Who put both strength and virtue at his side,
O Law, through which he is redignified   3220
By Jesus Christ! Once unacceptable
In God's sight, he is made receptible
Thanks to this fleece and potent vestiture,
In which he gains such power to endure   3224
That he is able to observe the law
With strictness, to preserve himself from flaw
Because this fleece of the triumphant lamb
Lets him become the true child of I Am   3228
Through union with the Father's much loved Son;
Thereby the name "Adopted Son" is won.
And if to him the Son pass on his name,
To him likewise come virtues of the same: 3232

66

Parquoy, uny à ce parfaict amant,
Peult accomplir la Loy entierement.
Ceste Loy donq de rigueur tant noircie
Est par la loy de la grace adoulcie,
Par qui l'amour en nostre cueur opere;
Et cest amour satisfaict Dieu le pere,
Car Jesuchrist, faisant en nous sejour,
En nous la Loy acomplit par amour:
La fin, le but de toutes ces deux loix,
C'est Jesuchrist, qu'ignorer je souloys
Pour m'arrester à ceste lettre escripte,
Où est la mort au vif paincte et descripte.
Longtemps m'en suys contanté et repeu,
Car pas n'estoit le voille en moy rompu:
Mais, par ce feu et lumiere eclairante,

Fol. 320 v°

Qui le secret du livre est declairante,
Celluy qui Est je viz clair sans obstacle
Et dans ce feu, ô merveilleux miracle!
L'esprit divin, qui livres et papiers
Et fundement et [muraille] et pilliers
Avoit jetté par terre doulcement,
Et les faisoit servir de pavement
Par où povoys en liberté marcher,
Sans plus m'enclorre en eulx ny m'y cacher.
Cest Esprit là des livres me fist maistre,
Qui serf en fuz, à dextre et[à]senestre
Me fut decloz, ouvert et delié
Le sens qui trop m'avoit esté lyé,
Couvert, caché, [me liant] et couvrant
Par ignorance, où m'aloys enyvrant;
[Par]le desir de sçavoir je beuvoys
Jusques à trop, combien que n'y trouvoys
Contantement ny satisfaction,
Ny à ma soif desalteration.
De ces desirs à miliers et à cens,
Tous mes espritz, mes forces et mes sens
Furent liez si bien et finement,
Que mon vouloir et mon entendement
Par ung cuyder, aveques ma raison,
Dedans mon cueur forgèrent ma prison:
Ce qu'au dehors en mon corps je sentoys,
Tant que jamais de prison ne sortoys
Car, quand le cueur est pris, le corps n'est pas
En liberté de faire ung tout seul pas.
Mais cest Esprit, qui au cueur frappe
    droit,   Fol. 321
Rompt le lyen qui le tient en destroict,
Et quand cuyder d'estre chose qui vaille
Et le desir ont perdu la bataille
Contre l'Esprit, lequel monstre combien
Peu de chose est ung homme et moins que rien,

Once united with this lover holy,
Lo, the law he can accomplish wholly.
Old law, therefore, for sternness so bewrayed
Is by the law of holy grace allayed;   3236
In our hearts, thus, love is operative;
This love, God the Father takes as sative.
Jesus Christ who is in us residing
Fulfills law in us through love abiding;   3240
The end and aim of both aforesaid laws
Is Christ, with whom I never used to pause,
But on the written letter often dwelled
Where death is vividly described and spelled;   3244
A long time I was happy and content,
Because the veil in me was not yet rent;
But by this flame, light illuminating

Him, the secret of the scripture stating: 3248
I saw Who Is without impediment
And in this flame—Oh, marvelous event—
The Spirit that books and dissertation,
Wall and pillar, even the foundation,   3252
Along the ground had quietly bestrewn
And turned them to my use as paving stone
To freedom, whence I could advance with stride
But no more close myself in them to hide;   3256
This spirit acted to give me command
Of books, me, once their serf. On every hand
Was now disclosed, unbound, and open wide,
The meaning that they had been wont to hide   3260
When I was bound, lost in delitescence,
Drunk on ignorance's effervescence.
Through thirst for knowledge, excess I imbibed,
Not finding, though, contentments as prescribed; 3264
Although I drank [till I was drunk and drenched,]
I found this merely left my thirst unquenched.
In these desires a thousandfold intense
I sank my wits and strength, and every sense   3268
Was bound so fast, bound with such invention
That my will and erring comprehension,
Through false credo and with reasoning art
Had forged a prison for me in my heart   3272
That outwardly in body I so felt,
I never left the prison where I dwelt;
For, when the heart is snared, the frame is not
At liberty to step beyond that spot.   3276
But Spirit, which strikes straight into the core

Can break the line that moors the ship to shore.
And when illusion as to one's own worth
And one's desire for mastery of earth   3280
Have lost the battle to the Spirit's light—
Which shows a man to be a thing but slight

67

Et que ce Rien vient[à]estre agreable,
Plus que l'honneur plaisant et proffitable,
Les livres sont ouvertz, decloz, patens,
Et les labeurs tournez en passetemps.
Ainsy fut fait, car ce feu combatit
Mon cueur, et moy vainquit et abattit
Tant que je fuz très clairement voyant
Que mon cuyder et moy estions noyant;
Et quand ce Rien de bon cueur j'euz receu,
Celluy qui Est fut soudain apperceu
Dans chascun livre et papier et volume
Par cest Esprit, dont la clarté alume
Toute tenebre, et toute prison rompt,
Poulsé d'amour qui le rend fort et prompt.
Or fuz je donc par ce feu mys au large,
Qui d'ignorance et cuyder me descharge,
Et ma prison en liberté muée.
Voire en repoz ma peine commuée.
Tous mes lyens, par qui fuz empesché
D'aller avant: j'en fuz bien detaché,
Et qui plus est me servirent de corde
Pour me tirer à la misericorde.
Ainsy deffaict de tous empeschemens,
M'assis pour veoir ces deux beaux testamens,
M'arrestant là, ainsi qu'au but final, Fol. 321 v°
Cause de bien, destruction de mal;
Ces instrumens n'ayans qu'un seul respect
Par union d'amour d'un trive aspect.
L'un regardait vers l'autre à luy contraire,
Couvrant tous deux le propiciatoire,
Ainsy que deux cherubins très ardans,
Qui tous deux sont en ung poinct pretendans:
C'est d'accorder leur different langaige
A monstrer ung seul bon, puyssant et saige.
Moy regardant ceste figure estrange,
Considerant de l'un et de l'autre ange
Le doulx regard et façon admirable
Du beau milieu de la dorée table
Mise sur l'arche, où la manne est enclose.
Il me sembla que j'ouÿs quelque chose,
Non come ung vent de la terre partant,
Ny comme ung feu ses flammes departant,
Mais comme ung vent gracieux et plaisant,
Très doulx et souef, lequel m'alloit disant
Par ung parler d'esprit et de feu plain
Que je ne peuz veoir ny entendre à plain,
Car si remply je fuz de ceste gloire
Que ce qui est possible à ma memoire
D'en retenir est moins que rien, au pris
Du très grand bien dont je fuz tout espris.
Le son fut doulx, mais si très vehement
Qu'il estourdit mes sens [entierement;]

And how this Nothingness is prizable,
Above all honors most advisable—   3284
The books are open, spread out, on display;
The studies undertaken, turned to play.
And so it was; for lo! this fire attacked
My heart, and by it I was beaten, wracked   3288
Till I could clearly see that, as for me
And my illusions, we were quite at sea.
When nothingness I willingly received,
The One Who Is was all at once perceived   3292
In every book and paper, thick or slight,
Through Spirit, whose great clarity can light
All shadow, also every prison rift,
Impelled by love that makes it strong and swift. 3296
This fire now set me at full liberty;
From ignorance and falsehood rescued me;
My prison into liberty was changed,
My difficulty for repose exchanged.   3300
Gone the bonds by which I was impeded!
I was quite detached and thence proceeded.
And what is more, they served me as lifeline
To draw me unto mercy, grace divine.   3304
Divested thus of all impediments,
I sat to view these two fine testaments,
I halted there as if I'd reached my goal:
The cause of good, o'er evil the control.   3308
These instruments with single reference,
In love combining triple referents,
Faced each other, two sides of the story,
As they covered the propitiatory;   3312
Like two cherubim, glowing with much light,
Both looking to one point, there to unite
Their different languages, to harmonize,
To show a single One, good, strong, and wise.   3316
I let my eyes from this to that one range
Tracing the angels of this figure strange—
Their winsome look, execution able
At true center of the golden table   3320
Where, in the Ark, the manna would repose.
Then to my ear it seemed some sound arose,
Not like a windblast from earth departing,
Nor a fire, its forkéd lances darting,   3324
Rather like a gracious wind appeasing.
Then there came to speak to me a pleasing
Speech of spirit, soft, bearing such a light
That I could neither see nor hear aright   3328
Because I was so greatly filled with awe
And what I could recall of what I saw
Was less than naught against the total ground
Of this vast good that I, enthralled, now found. 3332
The sound was soft but forceful, so intense
It left me giddy and devoid of sense.

Et si j'avoys eu le cueur esjouy,
Quand, en lisant, premierement j'ouÿ
Celluy qui Est se declairer sans faincte Fol. 322
En toute lettre et escripture maincte,
Dont contanter assez je me devoys,
Ceste seconde insupportable voix
Me [resjouyt] et m'attyra à soy
En me faisant passer par dessus moy.
Mais je ne peuz du très grand bien jouyr
De la parolle en ceste voix ouyr
Toute par rang, car elle fut si prompte
Qu'impossible est que je le vous racompte;
Impossible est qu'une mortelle aureille
Sceust distinguer ceste voix non pareille,
Ny la memoyre en donner souvenir,
Ny que le cueur la sceust bien retenir.
Mais de son prompt passaige ne me plains,
Car en passant laissa[mes]sens si plains
De sa vertu, où toute force habunde,
De son sçavoir et doctrine parfunde,
De son amour et feu vivifiant,
De sa bonté les siens bonifiant,
Que si la voix en moy eust fait demeure
Tant seulement une minute d'heure,
Si doulce estoit qu'elle eust esté suyvie
De ma povre ame estant d'amour ravie;
Car sans regret elle eust lessé mon corps
Pour estre unye à ses divins accordz.
Ce n'estoit pas ceste voix effreyable
De Dieu, qui fut à son peuple importable
Disant: «Elle est de telle pesanteur
«Que myeulx aymons parler au serviteur.»
Pas n'est la voix pour laquelle Caïn Fol. 322 v°
Mist son esprit et salut en dedaing;
Pas n'est la voix qui si avant chercha
Le cueur d'Adam que d'elle il se cacha;
Pas n'est la voix qu'Abraham proposa
Au malheureux qui requerir l'oza
De bien peu d'eau dont avoit fait refuz,
Mais il en fut par ce pere confuz:
Las! c'est la voix qui à Noé promist,
Quand hors de l'eau et de la mort le mist,
Que jamais plus ce monde grand par eau
Ne destruyroit, et, pour mettre le sceau
A sa promesse, l'arc luy monstra aux cyeulx,
Dont en repoz mist ce bon homme vieulx;

C'est ceste voix qui, par bonté immense,
Promist donner à son juste semense,
Lorsque d'enfans avoit perdu l'espoir,
Mais contre espoir son espoir eut povoir;
Ceste voix là sa promesse adjousta

If I thought my joy of heart exceeding
When first I heard Him, as I was reading, 3336
Declare Himself the One Who Is, all told,
In every jot and writing manifold,
With that I should have been quite well content;
This second voice, unbearable event, 3340
Delighted me and drew me to its zone
By causing me to pass above my own.
I was not to have the special favor
From this voice of hearing words, nor savor 3344
Them in order; for they were far too swift.
So I can not convey to you this gift.
It is impossible that mortal ear
Detect this voice that is without a peer, 3348
Or memory achieve of it recall,
Or that the heart know how to hold it all.
At its swift passage I make no protest
Because it left my senses so impressed 3352
With force that it possessed where strengths abound
In wisdom and in doctrine all-profound—
With His love and flame exhilerating,
In His people, His good generating— 3356
If then the voice had entered me to stay
So much as one whole minute of that day,
It must have been, close on leaving, followed
By my soul, in love completely swallowed 3360
And joyfully vacating my remains
To be united with those holy strains.
'Twas not that voice of God's so terrible
His people found its ring unbearable 3364
And said: "Such heaviness is in His voice
That speaking with the servant is our choice."
Nor was this voice the one for which son Cain
Would place his soul and safety in disdain, 3368
Nor that which probed so deeply Adam's heart
That Adam sought to place himself apart,
And not the voice that Abraham advanced
To that one, anxious, who entreaty chanced, 3372
But by this patriarch was then decried
Because the slightest water he'd denied.
This is the voice that unto Noah vowed—
When rescue from death's waters was allowed— 3376
Not to destroy this earth again by wave,
And, as the seal upon His promise, gave
The rainbow, hung for him amid the skies,
With which He calmed this old man good [and
wise.] 3380
It is this voice, through goodness wide indeed,
That promised to His righteous to give seed;
When he had lost his hope of having heirs,
God's will prevailed against hopes like despairs. 3384
That voice gave Jacob promise he'd be blest

A son Jocob, quand contre luy jousta:
L'ange par l'homme à l'heure fut vaincu,
Lequel n'avoit que la foy pour escu;
C'est ceste voix que l'on luy apporta,
Estant bien vieulx, dont se reconforta,
Quand on luy dist que son Joseph vivoit
En tel honneur qu'Egipte luy servoit;
C'est ceste voix qui Moÿse appella
Dans le buisson, et puys à luy parla,
En luy donnant povoir de retirer
Ceulx que vouloit Pharaon martirer;
C'est ceste voix disant de son David, Fol. 323
Qui le vouloir de Dieu par foy suyvit,
Qu'ung homme avoit trouvé selon son cueur,
Dont le peché ne vainquit la faveur
Que luy avoit pour l'advenir promise;
C'est ceste voix qui par l'Esprit est mise
Au cueur de tout patriarche et prophete
Disant du Christ chose encore non faicte;
C'est ceste voix que Saint Jehan se dit estre,
Car la parolle il laissa à son maistre,
Et par sa voix il nous monstra l'aigneau,
Le portefaix de tout nostre fardeau;
C'est ceste voix qui, en tant de façons
De temps et lieux, de personnes et sons,
S'est faicte ouyr par doulceur et rudesse,
Et par menasse et par doulce promesse,
Pour attirer au ciel ce monde bas,
Et de tristesse en l'eternel soulas,
Dont bien petis en furent les prouffitz:
Mais à la fin ceste voix par le Filz
S'est faicte ouyr, en s'escriant si hault
Que croyre, aymer et confesser le fault.
C'est ceste voix qui dist: «Venez trestous
«A moy qui suys tant amyable et doulx.»
Ceste voix dist: «Retournez, retournez,
«O Sunamitte, et à moy seul venez.»
Puys dist: «Venez, faictes de voz cueurs seaux,
«Tous ayans soif puyser des vives eaux.»
Ceste voix là l'amy ressuscita
Lorsqu'à pleurer vraye amour l'incita,
Ceste voix là par son puyssant effort, Fol. 323 v°
N'estimant rien le povoir de la mort,
D'entre ses dentz en a plusieurs tirez,
Que pourrez veoir quand l'escript saint lirez;
Ceste voix là, tant admirable et digne,
Nous a monstré la volunté divine
Parlant, preschant en tous lieux et au temple,
La confirmant de miracle et d'exemple;
Et pour la fin, c'est la voix qui pria
Pour les pecheurs, et qui si hault cria
Qu'elle perça oreilles et entrailles

When, wrestling with the angel, Jacob pressed;
And straightway was the angel forced to yield,
Though Jacob, mere man, had but faith as shield. 3388
This voice they brought to Jacob, then grown old,
And by it he was comforted when told
His Joseph was still living and deserved
Such honors that by Egypt he was served! 3392
It spoke to Moses whom it called by name,
In the fire bush; this was the voice, the same.
It gave him power [in viaticum]
To save those Pharoah marked for martyrdom. 3396
This is the voice that gave to David fame,
That one who, through his faith, pursued God's aim;
It said He'd found "one after His own heart";
Nor did a sin deprive him of that part 3400
Of favor God had promised, yet to come.
This voice the Spirit sent to hearts of some;
It went to every patriarch and seer
To speak of Christ, events yet to appear. 3404
This voice Saint John declared himself to be,
Because the Word would be his Lord, said he;
And through his voice to us this prophet showed
The Lamb to be the bearer of our load. 3408
This is the voice that in so many ways,
So many persons, places, sounds, and days
Made itself heard, with gentleness, with edge,
As much with menace as with dulcet pledge, 3412
Drawing heavenward this people lowly,
From their sadness unto solace holy,
A world for whom the profits were quite small
Till, through the Son, this voice at last would call 3416
With such great exhaltation it inspired
Faith and confession, and their love acquired.
The voice said, "Come to me, every nation.
I am love and comfort, your oblation." 3420
Said this voice, "Come, return; you must return,
O Shunammite, To me alone, come turn!
Come make your heart a vessel from whose lip
The thirsting can the living waters sip." 3424
That very voice indeed revived the friend
When love called forth their mourning for his end;
Voice exerting force of special power,
Deeming death no reason one should cower. 3428
It pulled a number from the monster's maw—
As you can see when you read holy law;
That Voice worthy of our admiration
Showed to us God's will and true dictation, 3432
In the temple and all places preaching
God, by marvel and example teaching.
And finally, it is the Voice that prayed
For sinners; and so strong a plea it made, 3436
The entrails then of Justice and the ears

De la justice et du Dieu des batailles,	Of Him the God of battles, it would pierce,
Qui du peché soudain prenoit vengeance,	God wont with swiftness to avenge a sin.
Fut exaulcé[e] apportant indulgence	The voice was raised to bring indulgence in 3440
Que jamais nul n'avoit sceu aquerir	That none had ever learned how to acquire
Par son prier, pleurer ou requerir;	By chanted pleas, requests or wailing dire.
C'est ceste voix de Jacob qui supplante	This is the voice of Jacob, who supplants
Du frere grand le bien, car il se plante	His elder brother Esau, to advance 3444
Devant le pere, où benediction	Himself before their father who will bless
Receut estant couvert de passion,	Him; where, when vested, Jacob finds distress
Que merittoit le peché qu'il portoit	The more intense because he wears the skin
Par ceste peau qui nous representoit;	That symbolizes his and our own sin. 3448
C'est ceste voix par laquelle derive	And by this voice from God does word arrive
De Dieu à nous ceste parolle vive,	Among us in a form that is alive.
Qui tant et tant de bons motz a chanté	So many precepts has this voice extolled
Qu'il n'y a cueur qui n'en soit contanté:	There is no heart but by it is consoled. 3452
Quand est du mien, s'il n'en est satisfaict	If mine is not entirely satisfied,
Entierement, il est très imparfaict,	The fact is that it is unqualified;
Car rocher n'est si dur qui n'en fendist,	There is no rock so hard that it's not split;
Ou qui de l'eau en l'oyant ne rendist.	Or hearing, lets no water come from it. 3456
Ung mot sans plus d'elle j'ay retenu, Fol. 324.	The Word, the essence of it, I retain.
Qui est souvent devant mes yeulx venu:	What's often come before my eyes is plain:
«Où est l'Esprit là est la liberté».	"Where Spirit is, there, too, is liberty."
Et me donna ce mot la seureté	This motto brought me the security 3460
Qu'ayant receu cest esprit veritable,	That, once I had attained true spirit light,
Plus ne seroys prisonnier miserable,	No more was mine the prison wretch's plight.
Car cest Esprit, qui tout m'aneantit	For, this same Spirit, one which had annulled
Et mon cuyder et desir amortit,	My last delusions, and desire has lulled, 3464
Me sçait et peult en ung Rien transformer;	Soon can have me into Nothing moulded;
Et ce Rien là ne se peult enfermer,	And that Nothing can not be enfolded,
Car Rien ne crainct prison ne porte close;	Not fearing any cell nor gate on earth;
Ilz n'ont povoir sinon sur quelque chose;	For doors rule only things of worldly worth; 3468
Mais où cuyder d'estre est entretenu,	But where false thought of being is maintained,
Tant soit petit, peult estre retenu;	However small, one still can be restrained;
Et quand ce Riens à son Tout est uny,	And when this Nothing with His All is plunged
Et le cuyder en luy mort et puny,	And all false credence in it dead, expunged, 3472
C'est liberté plaisante, pure et plaine,	Comes pleasant liberty, quite pure and plain,
Contantement et joye souveraine.	And in it joy and sweet contentment reign.
Tout le malheur que l'homme peult patir	With all the suffering that man can deal,
Ne se sçauroit de Rien faire sentir,	He is unable to make Nothing feel. 3476
Et de tout bien qui l'homme en orgueil monte	Of all those goods that cause man's pride to mount
Celuy qui est mis à Riens ne tient compte,	The one reduced to Nothing takes no count;
Car Tout, auquel inseparablement	Feeling that he is with All united
Il est uny, est son seul sentement;	Is the sole sense that can be excited. 3480
Et ce Tout là ne sçauroit estre pris,	The All is such that it could not be snared,
Car tout le monde est dedans luy compris.	For all the world and goods in it are shared.
Ce Tout est tel qu'on ne le peult comprendre,	The All is such it can not be interned
Et tout comprent, de nul ne peult aprendre	Yet includes all; by none can it be learned 3484
Et tout aprent, tout le monde environne	Yet learns of all, encompassing the rest,
Ce Tout qui est de ses œuvres couronne;	This All that is of all His works the crest.
Et tout l'honneur à luy seul appartient, 324 v°	To Him all honor, love, and glory fall
Gloire et amour, comme à celuy dont vient	As to the One who is the source of all: 3488
Tout; ce qu'il fait est et sera à naistre,	What He has made and what is yet to be,

Car par ce Tout et en ce Tout ont estre,
Il les enclost par grandeur indicible
Et vit en eulx par façon invisible;
Par le dehors toutes choses contient
Et par dedans en les tenant se tient.
Qui pourra donc ce Tout emprisonner?
Nul, car sur tous a povoir d'ordonner.
Et cestuy là qui ce Tout a congneu
Tant qu'il est Rien en son sens devenu,
Ne se sentant plus estre ne plus vivre,
Et ce cuyder, qui les mondains enyvre,
Il voit deffaict, et la verité prendre
Son lieu au cueur, en luy faisant entendre
Que Celluy seul qui Est est de tous maistre,
Et qu'il est Tout en tous, la vie et l'estre;
La verité monstrant ce Tout parfaict
Rend le cuyder [de] l'homme tout deffaict,
Car hors du Tout n'est habitation
Où l'homme puysse aquerir station;
Si par cuyder quelque chose il se pense,
De son seul Tout s'eslongne et [desavance,]
Mescongnoissant son estre tel qu'il est,
D'estre à son Tout uny il n'est pas prest;
Mais quand son Rien il voit et tel se sent,
Il vient petit, povre, nud, innocent,
Et si petit qu'estre en luy ne sejorne,
Mais en son Tout le voit et le retourne.
Car puysqu'au Tout son estre voit et
    veult   Fol. 325
Qu'en luy seul soit, son Rien à l'heure peult;
Et ce Tout là, où son seul estre il croit
S'incorporer et retourner tout droit,
C'est le chef d'œuvre et de foy et d'amour
Par qui au Tout le Rien fait son retour.
Qui prendra donc ce Rien qui est vollé
Jusqu'à Tout, auquel est si collé
Que la haulteur du ciel, ny le profond,
Empeschement à l'union ne font?
Mort ny peché, douleur ny passion
N'en feront point la separation,
Car cest amour de Dieu est invincible,
Et tout luy est et facile et possible;
Parquoy tenir ne peult prison ne corde
Celluy qui est par la misericorde
De ce grand Tout, par vive congnoissance,
Mis tout à Rien, ainsi qu'à sa naissance,
Et si petit qu'il ne se peult congnoistre
Fors seulement en sa vie et son estre,
[Qu'il] recongnoist en son Tout seulement,
Et de ton Dieu les bienfaictz contemplant
Parquoy ce Riens n'a peur de nul tourment.
En luy est bien la liberté libere,

Have being through and in totality,
Enclosed in wideness we can not define;
In them All lives by means eye can't divine,   3492
And from outside He holds all things contained;
And holding them, inside is thus restrained.
Who will be able, then, All to detain?
No one, for over all All can ordain.   3496
That one by whom the total has been seen
Until he knows how little he can mean,
No longer feels his is the vital state,
Sees error serving to inebriate,   3500
The worldly ones defeated: truth assumes
Its place within the heart. The truth then looms:
I Am is the master overseeing;
He is All in every life and being;   3504
This perfect whole that truth bids us inspect
Reveals man's credo to be in defect.
Outside All there is no habitation
Where a man can have a separate station.   3508
If he has some size in his opinion,
From his wholeness he subtracts dominion.
Failing to appraise his situation,
He's not ready for his integration;   3512
When he sees and feels himself nothingness,
He shrinks, is poor, dull, and lacks even dress,
So small that life-force in him won't sojourn,
Seeing life in All brings him its return.   3516
For since he wants his life-force in All's throng,

His nothingness can instantly belong.
The All, where his sole being he believes
To be incorporated and reweaves,   3520
Is faith's chief work and love's own masterpiece
In which to All the Null gives up its lease.
Who then shall take the Nothing from the vast,
Its own, where it has flown and sticks so fast   3524
No height of sky nor any depth of sea
Is able to prevent their unity?
Not sin nor death, pain nor agitation
Can at all effect a separation: 3528
This love of God's can not be overthrown,
Whose ease and potency in all is known.
Never rope nor jail of any fashion
Binds the One Who Is, thanks to compassion   3532
Of the All, and by His fresh perception
He is naught, as at His fresh conception,
So very small that he can ne'er be known
Except in life and being He be shown   3536
Where one may see Him in Totality.
Contemplating your God's benefactions,
This Nothing thus fears no brutality.
In Him, indeed, is freedom consummate:

Car ce qu'il veult et ce qu'il delibere
Il sçait et peult faire à sa volunté.
Et nul vivant n'est franc ny exempté
De son povoir et feu inevitable;
Parquoy il est à soy mesme agreable,
De soy contant, satisfaict et joyeulx,
Car il est Tout, qui la terre et les
   cyeulx   Fol. 325 v°
En ses braz tient et les tourne et demayne,
Comme il luy plaist, et dedans se promaine.
Mais sa bonté, qui jamais n'est oyseuse,
Qui de sa gloire est tousjours amoureuse,
A fait le ciel à force d'amour fendre
Et son seul filz çà bas à nous descendre,
Pour nous tirer de prison orde et salle
Où le cuyder, plain d'invention malle,
Nous retenoit, et faisoit apparoistre
Que chacun doit penser quelque chose estre;
Et puys desir d'estre et valoir beaucoup
Suyvoit cuyder, et plaisir tout à coup
Après les deux venoit le cueur lyer,
En lui donnant de peynes ung milier.
Las! myeulx vauldroit à l'homme n'estre né
Que par cuyder estre ainsy proumené
De Dieu, de soy de son estre et naissance:
Cuyder le fait perdre la congnoissance;
Mais par ce Filz, transmis à nous çà bas,
Sont appaisez ces differentz debatz,
Car nostre chair il a prise et l'a mise
Du Tout à Rien: là gist nostre franchise.
Et ce Rien là il voulut esprouver,
Quand sur la croix se monstra estre ung ver
Et homme non, en s'aneantissant
Et nostre Rien de cuyder nettissant.
Lors, quand à Rien eut mys Adam charnel,
Il le tira à son Pere eternel,
Lequel est Tout et Celluy seul qui Est:
Là il trouva son repoz et arrest,   Fol. 326
Clarté sans nuict et beaulté sans laideur,
Santé sans mal, feu plaisant sans ardeur:
Plaisir sans fin et joye sans tristesse,
Force et vertu sans vice ny fallace,
Vie sans mort, sçavoir sans ignorance,
Possession sans travail d'esperance,
Vraye union sans separation,
Amour parfaict sans nulle fiction,
Le ciel sans terre et Dieu sans nul semblable,
Esprit sans chair et tout innominable,
Et verité sans cuyder claire et pure,
Foy sans doubter, netteté sans ordure,
Contantement satisfaict et contant.
Parquoy ce Rien va courant et saultant,

For, what He wants or He may contemplate   3540
He knows how to cause at His preemption.
Not a living creature has exemption.
His fire and forces aren't combatable;
Thus, with himself He is compatible,   3544
Content to have within what satisfies;
For He is All, who holds the earth and skies

Within his arms, who flings them forth to spin
As it may suit Him and He moves therein.   3548
But His goodness, which is ever zealous,
Which is of His glory ever jealous,
At length by dint of love the heavens rent
And for us caused His only Son's descent,   3552
To free us from the prisons' filth and dirt,
Where notionate invention, to our hurt,
Was keeping us; God brought to pass on earth
That each should think himself a thing of worth. 3556
The wish to be of worth and to prevail
Came fast upon illusion, without fail;
Swiftly, to ensnare the heart, came pleasure;
Pains a thousandfold it would admeasure.   3560
Oh, missing birth were better any day
Than through delusion to be led astray.
Of God, of self, of being and birthright
A false belief deprives one of insight;   3564
But, through the Son sent down among us here,
The divers quarrels tend to disappear.
He donned our flesh; CHARACTER In His transmutation,
All to Nothing, lies our liberation.   3568
It was the Nothing that He would affirm
When on the cross He seemed to be mere worm,
Less than man, in self-annihilation,
Bringing pride to its obliteration,   3572
Carnal Adam into Nothing casting,
Jesus drew him to His everlasting
Father, All, One, the single One Who Is:
There he found rest and his own verities,   3576
All light, no dark, all fair, no ugly thing,
Health without illness, brightness without sting,
True endless pleasure, joy without distress,
Great strength and virtue and no viciousness,   3580
Life without death and wisdom without fail,
Possession without covetous travail,
Truest union without separation,
Perfect love without its simulation,   3584
Sky sans earth and God without an equal,
Spirit without flesh and nameless sequel,
The lack of false belief, truth pure and plain,
And faith without a doubt, clean without stain,   3588
Contentment, satisfaction, and content:
To run and skip is therefore Nothing's bent

Ravy d'amour et transporté de joye,
Dedans son Tout, verité, vie et voye:
Il vit ayant sa vie recouverte,
Il croyt voyant sa voye toute ouverte,
Il est sçavant, trouvant la verité.
O povre Rien, qui n'avoys meritté
D'estre, sinon Rien, le nom que tu porte[s],
Comme en ce Tout tu as puyssance forte,
Lequel t'a fait en toy premier entrer
Et puys en luy par vive foy rentrer,
Te donnant mort, puys resurrection,
Damnation et puys salvation,
Qui du hault ciel jusqu'en enfer t'abbesse
Pour te monstrer ta grande petitesse,
Et puys du fondz d'enfer plain de martire
Jusqu'au plus hault du ciel il te retire; Fol. 326 v°
Il t'a perdu, tourmenté, esprouvé,
Jusques à Riens, et puys t'a retrouvé.
O puyssant Tout, plain d'amour indicible!
O povre Rien, encloz en impossible,
Qui es tyré de tes lyens horribles
Par les effectz du Tout, qui sont terribles,
Aveuglissant les yeulx qu'il illumine,
Faisant boiteux affin que myeulx chemine
L'home impuyssant, le navrant pour guerir,
Et luy couppant les piedz pour myeulx courir!
O povre Rien, très riche devenu,
Dedans ce Tout que t'est il advenu?
O prisonnier dedans la lettre morte,
Par ung cuyder qui te fermoit la porte,
Tant qu'en lisant plus de lettre apprenoys
Et moins au vray sçavoir tu parvenois,
Quelle clarté t'a l'esprit revelé,
Qui dans la lettre es encloz et cellé?
La lettre occit le vivant qui se fie,
Mais l'home mort cest Esprit viviffie,
Très heureux Rien, qui par ce feu celeste
Prison, lyens, cuyder qui tant moleste,
Pilliers, muraille, et tous cruelz ustilz
Sont si brullez qu'on demande: «Où sont ilz?»
Car leur memoire avec le son perit
Et de leur mal le malade guerit.
O joyeulx Rien, qui par clarté sans umbre
Peulx cheminer, ne craignant nulle encombre,
Qui te sçauroit plus tenir ne garder,
Emprisonner, lier ou regarder?   Fol. 327
Nul, car il n'est œil sachant si bien veoir
Qui hors du Tout te puysse appercevoir.
L'humaine main sçaura bien besongner
S'elle te peult hors du Tout empoigner,
Et dans le Tout tu es trop imprenable,
Car il te fait à soy mesmes semblable;

When it is seized by love and overjoyed,
And in His All—truth, life and way—is buoyed: 3592
He lives who has recovered life; he may
Believe on seeing his wide open way;
He's savant when the truth he has observed.
O humble Nothing who had not deserved   3596
To be except you bore that name along,
Since it is in this All that you are strong,
That caused you first inside yourself to turn
And then through active faith to Him return,   3600
After death he grants you restoration:
First damnation, secondly salvation.
He who from heaven lowers you to hell,
Exposing your great smallness to you well,   3604
From hellish depths of martyrdom and pain,
To heaven's pinnacle draws you again.
He has turned you loose, tried, and aggrieved you
Unto Nothing, and then has retrieved you.   3608
Love-filled is All, oh, not to be described!
Poor Null, in helplessness so circumscribed,
Through these effects of All you are rescued
From terrifying bonds of servitude.   3612
It blinds the eye to which it brings a guide;
It lames so that a weakling gathers stride,
And mortifies the man whom it would heal;
It cuts the feet so that they run with zeal!   3616
O now that you have riches without toll,
Poor Null, what's happened to you in this Whole?
O prisoner within dead written lore,
Thanks to an error that once closed your door,   3620
The more you learned of letter as you read,
The less you reached the truth of what was said.
What light is it that Spirit has revealed
To you who're in the letter closed and sealed?   3624
The letter kills the life that gives it trust,
But to the dead this Spirit gives new thrust;
And by celestial fire, O heir of joys,
The prison, bonds, and error that destroys,   3628
The pillars, walls, all tools of cruelty
Are burnt till one inquires, "Where can they be?"
For, with the sound also their mem'ry ceased
And from their plague the sick one was released. 3632
You, joyful Null, who, light-borne, free of taint,
Can go your way, not fearful of restraint,
Pray, who would know how you could be restrained,
Imprisoned, bound, or glimpse of you be gained? 3636
There is no eye that can so well perceive
That, outside All, your image would receive.
The work of human hand will not be small
If it can wrest you from the grasp of All;   3640
And, in the All, you can by none be caught,
For it is in His image you are wrought;

Et puysque Tout l'homme ne peult
   comprendre,
Rien dedans Tout aussy ne sçauroit prandre.
O petit grand! O Rien en Tout fondu!
O Tout gaigné par Rien en toy perdu!
O puyssant Rien, que tu a beau voller
Et en enfer dedans toy devaller,
Qui sur toy n'a povoir ny seigneurie,
Car dedans n'est ung rien sans moquerie!
Et ce grand Tout auquel tu es conjoinct,
Qui du serpent la teste brise et poingt,
Et de l'enfer rompt les portes ferrées,
Et du peché les dentz par trop serrées,
T'a exempté de leur authorité.
Puys, tout ardant d'amour et charité,
Tu prens ung vol dedans le Tout si hault
Que le povoir de tes plumes deffault
A declairer ce qui n'est pas licitte
De prononcer, et lors desir t'incitte
De faire ung vol à la partie dextre,
Et puys tourner après à la senestre;
Et de ton Dieu les bienfaictz contemplant
En l'home et beste, animaulx et en plant,
Où tu peulx veoir si grande difference
Que, faisant d'un à l'autre conference,

Fol. 372 v°

Ne trouveras au dehors rien semblable.
Mais quoy! Voicy ung cas esmerveillable
Qu'ung seul en tous est estre et mouvement,
Vie, penser, raison et sentyment;
Bien monstre icy le Tout son grant povoir,
Quand luy seul est l'estre, vie et mouvoir
De ce qui est si different sur terre
Que l'œil de chair en les regardant erre,
En s'arrestant à la diversité,
Division, douleur, adversité,
Car au dehors n'a que division
Qui donne au cueur mortelle passion;
Et cestuy là, qui le dehors adore,
Il trouvera tenebre exterieure;
Mais en voyant ce dehors divisé,
Si ung en tous par foy est advisé.
Ceste union dedans la multitude,
Ceste douceur dedans l'escorce rude
Rend si contant l'esprit qui voit cela,
Qu'en liberté l'œil deçà et delà
Se peult tourner à veoir les creatures
Qui de Dieu sont masques ou couvertures;
Et ne doit point craindre d'estre pris l'œil,
Ny de dehors sentir joye ny dueil
Quand ung seul voit au dedans seulement,
Qui du dehors a le gouvernement.

And, since man can not comprehend the Whole,
Of Null in All he could not grasp control.   3644
Oh, tiny greatness! In the All engrossed!
All, gained by Nothing, lost in you, its host!
Oh, potent Nothing, it would be in vain
To sink within yourself to hell's domain,   3648
Which over you can have no sovereignty,
Since, inside, it is but a mockery.
And this great All that has you in its grip,
The one that breaks the serpent, head to tip.   3652
He who from hell the ironclad gates has wrenched
And pulled the teeth of sin, though tightly clenched,
Exempted you from their authority.
Then, all aglow with love and charity,   3656
So high into the All you rise and sail,
The power of your pens can only fail
To clarify that which is recondite,
Not said; and then desire comes to incite   3660
You to take wing: at first upon the right,
And later turning to the left in flight,
Contemplating your God's benefactions,
Beasts and plants and men of many factions,   3664
Where you can see such great disparity
When you inspect for similarity,

Outside you'll not find a duplication—
But, a case for wonder and elation!—   3668
One in all is life and motivation,
Being, thinking, reason, and sensation.
How well the All displays here His great force.
When He alone is being, life, and course   3672
Of what, on earth, has such variety
That eye of flesh bent on their scrutiny
Must err in dwelling on diversity,
Division, suff'ring, and adversity   3676
Because outside all is so wide apart
It brings a mortal passion to the heart;
And he who worships at the outer shell
Will find the outer darkness there as well.   3680
But, on seeing this same shell divided,
If by faith to One in All one's guided
To unity within the multitude,
The sweetness inside where the bark is crude   3684
Makes so content the mind that finds this out
The eye can turn itself here and about,
With full liberty to view the creatures,
Which are masks behind which lie God's features; 3688
He need not fear his eye be captured there,
Nor, outside, sense a pleasure or despair
When he beholds inside a single whole
That over the external has control.   3692

Cest ung, ce Tout en tout va requerant,
Et plus en voyt plus en ung est ardant:
Leur difference et multitude et nombre
Ne peult donner obscurité et umbre Fol. 328
A ce seul Tout, mais plus le rend louable,
Plus il se voit en chose innumerable.
O saige Rien, qui tiens la droicte voye
Tousjours au Tout, sans que tu te desvoye
Pour le plaisir de la varieté,
Par laquelle est, l'yver comme l'esté,
Nature belle, qui le dehors admire,
Car au vray Tout et non en toy te myre,
Sans t'arrester à ces choses caduques,
Tenebreuses, empeschantes, offusques,
Combien que l'œil charnel belles les trouve;
Ainsy ne faiz qui en as fait l'espreuve,
Car la beaulté d'un seul si fort te plaist
Que le dehors, tant soit beau, te desplaist,
Sinon d'autant qu'il doit servir d'eschelle,
Pour adresser le voller de ton [aile]
Par la facture au Facteur, et montant
Aller tousjours ses louanges chantant,
Et des bienfaictz luy tout seul recongnoistre
Sans advouer dans le cueur autre maistre.
Mais parler fault çà bas comme les hommes,
Vivant comme eulx tant qu'avec eulx nous
        sommes,
Non pas suyvans leurs œuvres et couraiges,
Mais ouy bien, sans peché, leurs langaiges.
Puys ce Rien volle à la senestre main,
Où tous tourmentz et douleurs voit à plain,
Dont le nombre est à nommer indicible,
Tant que quasi au juste il n'est possible
De traverser ce desert espineux
Sans se piquer ou estre bien poureux; Fol. 328 v°
Mais il est dit que nully n'est blessé
Que de soy mesmes, et cela je le sçay;
Et qui le croit comme moy, si le tienne.
Souvienne vous de ce bon saint Estienne,
Qui au milieu des pierres combattant
Pour son Seigneur, le voyoit en estant
Dedans les cyeulx aux dextres de son pere,
Qui luy faisoit la mort et vitupere
Doulce trouver, jusqu'à ne la sentir.
Et saint Laurens sur le gril voy rostir:
Martirisoit à force moqueries
Tous les tirans, leur donnant fascheries
Plus qu'eulx a luy, car plus le tourmentoient,
Le tourmentant en repoz le mettoient,
Car en tourment ung Dieu tout seul voyoit,
S'esjouissoit voyant ce qu'il croyoit.
Le bon larron, voyant Jesus en croix,

He seeks this One, this All, on every hand
And finds his ardor for the One expand:
Their variety and their profusion
Can not cast a darkness and confusion   3696
Upon this single All; more praise they bring
The All when folk see it a countless thing.
Wise Nothing to pursue the direct way
Always to All, and never go astray   3700
For pleasure in variety, which taunts
Him who admires outsides, as nature flaunts
Her beauty winter, summer, spring, and fall,
Because you truly view yourself in All,   3704
Not in yourself! Not stopping to inspect
Things shady, hampering, perfections wrecked,
Carnal eyes might grant them admiration;
Not so you who've made the exploration.   3708
Beauty of the One so greatly charms you,
The outside, however fair, alarms you
Except as it serves as ladder, mooring
Of design to train your wings for soaring,   3712
Through the product to the maker winging,
Ever, as you climb, His praises singing;
You know Him from the good deeds on His part
And own no other master in your heart.   3716
But we must speak as men while here on earth
And live as they while we yet share their berth,
Not following their daring works and deeds,
But sinless, of their speeches take some heed. 3720
This Nothing next flies on the larboard hand
Where all the pains and torments can be scanned,
The number inexpressible. In fact,
So great, it is impossible intact   3724
To cross this wilderness of thorny waste
Without encountering pricks of distaste
Or tasting fear; yet none is hurt, they say,
But by himself. I know it is this way.   3728
You who think as I, persist! May, even,
This remind you of that good saint, Stephen,
Who, being stoned for taking his Lord's stand,
Beheld Him on the Father's dexter hand   3732
Above, which let him find his own death mete
To be ignored and the abuses sweet.
Also I find it mete to ponder still
Saint Lawrence roasted on the grill: 3736
This saint did martyr and profoundly mock
Then all the tyrants, dealing them more shock
Than they dealt him; for as he met their test,
Their multiplied torments set him at rest;   3740
He saw but God when by his pain aggrieved,
Rejoiced to witness what he had believed.
The good thief, seeing Jesus on the tree

Que l'on eust dit le plus meschant des troys,
Pour ce que plus que tous fut tourmenté,
Combien qu'il fust par le dehors tempté
De l'estimer le roy des malfaicteurs,
Pour estre tel jugé des grans docteurs,
Princes, prelatz et gens de vie austere,
Par foy congneut dedans ce grand mistere
Ce Tout caché, lequel il confessa,
Et ce Tout là sa priere exaulça.
Et qui vouldra les Esciptures lire,
Il trouvera qu'au milieu du martyre
Ce Tout estoit si à clair advisé
Qu'il n'y avoit nul tant martirisé, Fol. 329
Qui ne sentist plus de joye certaine
Dedans l'esprit, que de tourment et peyne
Au corps, sachant ne leur estre donné
Rien qui ne fust par le Tout ordonné.
Et qui dira les saïnctz privilegiez
Et des tourmentz par grace soulagez,
Qui leur faisoit trouver la mort plaisante,
Ce qui n'est plus? O parolle nuysante!
Le braz de Dieu est il donc abregé
Par qui estoit le martir soulagé?
N'est pas sa main et bonté aussy prompte
De les garder qu'onques fut? O la honte
Que doit avoir ce charnel jugement,
Que verité de nostre temps desment!
Car l'on a veu, voire de nostre temps,
Plusieurs chrestiens du martyre contans,
Et qui auroit la foy du bon larron
Les congnoistroit, mais icy nous lerrons
De les nombrer, car il y en a tant
Que d'en dire ung je me tiens pour contant.
C'est en Turquie, où vers le grant Seigneur
La Forest fut du roy ambassadeur:
Et en ce temps ung Turc Dieu inspira
Tant que la Bible à lire il desira,
Que si bien lut, et à son bon prouffit,
Qu'aveques luy treize chrestiens [il] fist.
Lors baptisez, se mirent à prescher
Ouvertement sans espergner leur chair,
Sachans qu'après ceste corruption
Retourneroient par resurrection Fol. 329 v°
En l'union du Tout et de ses membres,
Pour demourer en ses celestes chambres.
Le Turc, sachant ses predications
Causer partout grandes esmotions,
Prendre les fist, et les martiriza
Des plus cruelz tourmentz qu'il advisa,
L'un après l'autre, et par jours differens.
Mais eulx, n'estans tardifz ne differans,
D'un joyeulx cueur les tourmens enduroient,

To be declared the worst of all the three,   3744
Since from torment He was least exempted—
Looking from the outside, one was tempted
To believe Him king of malefactors,
Judged as such by doctors, his detractors,   3748
The princes, prelates, folk of sober mien—
In this great mystery, through faith, had seen
The hidden All, whom he accepted there;
And lo, that self-same All fulfilled his prayer. 3752
Whoever wants to read the Holy Word
Will find amidst what martyrdom occurred:
All, so clearly that the deed seemed chartered,
And there was no mortal yet so martyred   3756
Who then did not more certain joy attain
In spirit than in body he felt pain
Through knowing that to him was nothing sent
That was not by the All's divine intent.   3760
Who is to say that saints likewise ordained—
Who are, through like torments, by grace sustained—
Grace that shows them death a joyous fusing—
Come no more? Oh, hurtful word accusing!   3764
God's own arm is then abbreviated,
By which martyrdom was moderated?
Are not His hand and goodness quick to fly
To their defense as once? What shame must lie   3768
With this base feeling, one that quite denies
The truth that in our day before us lies!
For we have seen, indeed in our own time,
Some Christians martyred who felt joy sublime.   3772
Whoever had the faith of that good thief
Would know them. Here, though, I shall take relief
From their enumeration so profuse,
Content to name but one, with my excuse.   3776
LaForest was the king's ambassador
To that great lord, the Turkish Emperor,
When, lo, an Ottoman who was inspired
To read the Bible, something God desired,   3780
Read with so much profit he converted
Thirteen to our Christ, it is asserted;
In turn, when baptized, these began to preach
In freedom, without sparing flesh, for each   3784
Knew that past the corporal dissection
He'd return by dint of resurrection
To union of his members with the All,
To haunt All's chambers and celestial hall.   3788
Lord Turk, learning that this predication
Was the cause of general elation,
Then ordered seizure that they might receive
The worst torments the ruler could conceive,   3792
One, then another, on successive days.
And they, not having slow nor craven ways,
Found joy through tortures that were on them poured

Voyant ce Tout que tout seul adoroient.	And only saw the All that they adored; 3796
Le maistre fut le dernier amené	The teacher was the last one introduced
Sus ce teatre, où il fut proumené	Upon the scene whereon there were produced
[Eulx] par huict jours de tourmentz tous nouveaulx,	Each day all new torments, eight days and trips,
Luy arrachant les membres par lambeaux,	Returns for taking members off by strips, 3800
Ung jour ung œil; l'autre, pied, doigt ou main;	One day an eye, next finger, hand, or foot:
Mais ce tourment cruel et inhumain,	And while inhuman torture was there put
Plus par douleur le corps afoiblissoit,	Upon him, as his body sank with pain,
Et plus la foy au cueur establissoit,	The faith was strengthened in his heart again 3804
Qui luy dura jusques au dernier poinct	Which lasted through the moment of his fall,
Que par mort fut Rien à son Tout conjoinct.	When Nothing was united with the All.
Et ceste mort fut de telle valeur,	Of so much merit was this man's demise
Que luy voyant porter tant de douleur	That, seeing him bear so much sacrifice, 3808
Sans vaciller, si perseveramment,	Persevering without vascillation,
Oyant aussy son divin preschement,	Marking as divine the predication
Vivant, mourant du Dieu qu'il affermoit	That in both life and death he had affirmed,
Et que par mort son sermon confirmoit,	And that by death his sermon was confirmed, 3812
Plus de six mille estans ses auditeurs	Six thousand plus, being his spectators,
Furent de luy par foy imitateurs,	Thanks to faith became his imitators;
Sachant très bien qu'on les alloit cerchant,	Certain they were sought for more than chiding,
Mais nul d'entre eulx ne s'alloit point cachant;	Still not one of them went into hiding, 3816
Fol. 330	
Plustost venoient dire: «Je suys des siens,»	But came forth saying, "I am one of his!"
Participant de sa mort et lyens,	Associating in his obsequies.
Tant que cinq cens le Turc en fist deffaire;	The prince killed half a thousand of their race;
Mais en voyant d'un deffaict deux reffaire,	But seeing two arise to take each place 3820
Et que leur mort ung leurre au peuple estoit,	And people being drawn by their decease
Dont des chrestiens le grand nombre augmentoit,	So that the Christian numbers showed increase,
Il deffendit de plus ne les cercher,	He ruled them safe from search and harmful reach,
Mais si quelqu'un publiquement prescher	Though one presuming publicly to preach 3824
Ce Jesuchrist l'on trouvoit, qu'il fust pris	Of Jesus Christ was to be seized if found
Et dedans l'eau bien secrettement mys.	And held in water secretly till drowned.
Ainsy cessa sa fureur ce grand prince;	The prince's fury died, but it had served
Mais, maulgré luy, est plaine sa province	To fill his province with what it observed: 3828
Du divin [plan] de ce martir louable:	Divine plan in this death commendable.
C'est de ce temps, l'histoire est veritable.	This modern story is dependable.
Confessons donq que Dieu est mainctenant	God still exists as, let us understand,
Tel qu'il estoit aux siens la main tenant;	When once He led His people by the hand; 3832
Qui voit ce Tout, et qui est bien attainct	Whoever sees the All and feels its touch
De son amour, tourment ne mort ne crainct;	Of love can not fear death and torment much.
Mesmes la mort est agreable à ceulx	And even death's agreeable, they find
Qui ont ce Tout tant imprimé en eulx	Who have the All so printed in the mind 3836
Que tout partout et en tout ilz en voyent,	That everywhere, in all, some part they see,
En quelque mort ou tristesse qu'ilz soyent.	Whatever death or sorrow there may be.
La glorieuse et excellente mere,	The mother excellent and glorious, the one
Qui Dieu avoit pour filz et Dieu pour pere,	Who had God as father and as her son, 3840
Le temple pur de la divinité	The all pure temple of divinity,
Où habitoit toute la Trinité,	The dwelling of the whole of trinity,
Plaine de grace et de perfection,	Lady full of grace and of perfection,

Fit du cousteau tranchant d'affection
D'aspre douleur en l'ame transpercée,
Mais foy la tint dessus ses piedz dressée,
                      Fol. 330 v°
Tant qu'en ung corps saige, constant et stable,
Portoit ung cueur mort à son filz semblable.
Ainsy sa mort dedans son filz passa,
Mais quand du monde à son Dieu trepassa,
En lieu de mort la vie elle goustoit,
Car en son Tout morte et vivante estoit.
Sainct Jehan aussy, Marie Magdelaine,
Qui du rocher en la celeste plaine
Sailloit sans mal, c'estoit que dans la croix
Souffrirent mort, parquoy en ces destroictz
Mort ne povoit les mortz en Christ tenir,
N'ayant en eulx que le seul souvenir
De leur Jesus, leur Tout, que tant aymoient
Que pour le veoir la mort vie estimoient;

Car qui de Christ gouste la mort cruelle
N'a peur ny mal en la mort corporelle.
Si l'un me dit: «Vous parlez des parfaictz,
«Parfaictz en distz, en penser et en faictz,

Des imparfaictz aussi parler n'entendz»;
Mais tout le but, Amye, où je pretendz,
C'est vous monstrer par parolle ou histoire
Que qui ce Tout en tout peult veoir et croyre,
Il est en paix et liberté, sans peur
D'estre empesché de ce monde trompeur,
Car tous ses biens et beaultez il desprise,
Et ses tourmentz et la mort qui tout brise.
Et de mon temps j'en ay veu plus qu'assez,
Qui de ce monde a Dieu sont trespassez
Joyeusement, avec telle asseurance,
Qu'à leur parler et à leur contenance Fol. 331
L'on povoit bien juger ceulx là s'en vont
Veoir leur espoux, où desjà leurs cueurs sont;
Et s'il vous plaist d'en ouyr quelque compte
C'est bien raison que je le vous racompte,
D'Alençon fut duchesse Marguerite
Qui de Lorraine estoit, et si meritte.
D'avoir louange est aux hommes permis,
Voyant en eulx ce que Dieu y a mis,
Ceste cy doit de tous estre louée)
Car à la fin après s'estre vouée
A servir Dieu, sans cesser jour et nuict,
Ce clair soleil qui en tenebres luict,
Estant enclose en sa religion,
Luy declaira qu'en toute region
Et en tout lieu failloit le Tout cercher,
Non en ung seul, soit muraille ou rocher,

From trenchant blade of keen affection,   3844
Did suffer bitter pain when stabbed in soul.
It was but faith that kept her standing whole,
Until, in stable body, she would bear
A dead heart that to Jesus would compare.   3848
The death of this dear son passed for her own.
But, when to God from this world she had flown,
She had tasted life, not death, at curfew;
Dead or live, she found in All her purview;   3852
Saint John likewise and Mary Magdalene,
Who from the rock to heaven's plane was seen
To rise unharmed. For it was in the cross
They suffered death; these instances of loss   3856
Show death a foe unable to restrain
The dead in Christ, to whom no thoughts remain
But of their Jesus, their All, so esteemed
That death, where they would see Him, lifelike
    seemed.   3860
Whoever tastes the cruel death of Christ
Waives fear and harm in death, for His sufficed.
If one tell me, "Those you have selected,
Were in word and deed and thought
    perfected.   3864
Of those less perfect, I don't hear you speak,"
It's still, my Dear, the total end I seek,
Showing you by word or illustration:
One who sees the All in all creation   3868
Lives in peace and freedom, without the fear
To be embroiled by this deceitful sphere.
For all its goods and charms he holds but scorn,
Like death's and torment's making all forlorn;   3872
Enough and more have I seen in my time
Who passed from this world unto God sublime
Full joyously and with such confidence,
To judge by speech and by the countenance,   3876
One is assured that such ones go afar
To see mates where their hearts already are;
And, if you would be pleased to hear a tale,
I'll tell it; such a reason should prevail.   3880
The Duchess Marguerite of Alençon
Was from Lorraine, and a deserving one—
For gentlemen to have praise is allowed,
For it's by God's gift that they are endowed!—   3884
She, too, ought by all folk to be noted;
For, in the end, she, too, was devoted
To the serving of God both day and night,
For, in the dark, her beacon Sun brought the light.   3888
She, while one cloistered, to religion bound,
Declared the All in every region found
And to be sought there, not one place alone,
No matter if it were a wall or stone.   3892

Tant qu'à la fin la superstition
Elle laissa, et la devotion
Que Dieu demande [en une ame amoureuse]
Elle receut, estant religieuse.
Car, sans ung mot delaisser de sa reigle,
Son œil de foy, regardant comme l'aigle
Le vray soleil où estoit sa fiance,
Trouvoit en luy repos de conscience;
Son corps estoit de muraille enfermé,
Et tout son cueur en amour confermé
En liberté avec son Tout vivante,
L'amour duquel la rendoit languissante.
Mais ung beau jour de Toussainctz, sa
    promesse
Luy tint l'espoux; ayant ouy sa messe
Fol. 331 v°
Receut son Dieu, puys le sermon ouy,
Vespres aussy, d'un visaige esjouy,
Dist à ses seurs, en congnoissant sa fin,
Le prononsant purement en la fin:
«Resjouyssez, filles, en Dieu voz cueurs,
«[Encor] ung coup, ayez joye.» Ses seurs
Luy demandant la cause de sa joye,
Dist: «L'heure vient qu'il veult que je le voye,
«Ce doulx espoulx, cest amy perdurable,
«Qui rend la mort sans craincte desirable.»

En ce disant, se coucha sur ung lict
Comme attendant la mort en grant delict
Et demanda le dernier sacrement,
Lequel receut d'un sain entendement.
A ses enfans escrivit ung langaige,
Qui bien sentoit du divin le ramaige,
Les exortant à tout ce que doit faire
Ung vray chrestien, pour tousjours à Dieu
    plaire.
Après avoir à tous les siens pourveu,
A son abbesse elle requist que leu
Fust du Seigneur au long la Passion,
Et en l'oyant, par grande affection
Levoit les yeulx et au ciel regardoit,
En demonstrant que son desir ardoit
D'y parvenir, disant souvent: «Helas!
«Mon Redempteur, romps mes lyens et laqs
«Affin qu'à toy l'hostie de louanges
«Je sacrifie aveques tous les anges.»
Puys, par amour, comme estant hors de soy,
    soy,
Fol. 332
Disant: «Mon Dieu, tyre moy après toy.»
Enfin, oyant parler [la saige abbesse]
Disant que Dieu par charité s'abbesse
Pour embrasser l'ame, et n'est empesché

She forsook at last all superstition;
Being of religious disposition,
She received the call to such devotion
As God asks of amative emotion;   3896
And, as the eagle views the sun with trust,
While carefully obeying rules she must,
She'd eyes transfixed on God, true sun, to find
In Him where lay her trust, her peace of mind; 3900
Her body was behind the wall enclosed,
And all her heart, in love confirmed, reposed
At liberty true life with All to find,
For love of whom she languished and declined. 3904
The promise of the bridegroom came to pass.

One sunny All-Saints Day she heard the mass,

Received her God, the sermon did embrace
And later vespers, and with glowing face   3908
She told the sisters, knowing death was near—
And to the end her words were plain and clear:
"In God, my daughters, let your hearts be glad."
Once more, "Be glad!" To sisters that she had 3912
Inquiring what the cause for joy might be:
"He wishes me to see Him now," said she,
"This sweet bridegroom, this ever loyal Friend
Who makes death, stripped of fear, a welcome
    end."   3916
On saying this, she went to bed, as might
Someone awaiting death with great delight,
And asked that last rites be administered,
While she received with mind for what she heard. 3920
She wrote her children in a language fine,
Reflective of her heritage divine,
Exhorting them to all that one should do
When Christian, always God's will to
    pursue.   3924
When to her people she had made bequest,
The abbess was the one whom she addressed;
To have the Passion read was her request
And, hearing it, the duchess lay, and blessed 3928
With love, she raised her eyes to heaven, showed
That in her heart a great desire now glowed
To go to Him. "O," her lips kept tracing,
"Savoir mine, please break my bonds and lacing. 3932
My sacrifice to you now let me raise
And with the angels offer you my praise."
As if beyond herself then, with her love

She said, "God, draw me after you above."   3936
And last, she heard as her wise abbess told
How God in charity stoops to enfold
The soul and that He would not be deterred

De l'espouser pour ce qu'elle a peché,
Elle, sentant ceste misericorde,
Si joyeuse est quand sa bonté recorde
Qu'elle s'aproche et au second Adam
Dist tenui avec nunc dimittam;
[Disoit] ce mot la dame par amour
Cria: «Helas, quand viendra ce bon jour?»
Et, de ferveur, son abbesse embrassa
Et en disant: «Jesus, Jesus,», passa
Du val de pleur au mont de tout plaisir,
Où de longtemps habittoit par desir.
Mais aussitost qu'elle eut finé de dire:
«Jesus», se print doulcement à soubzrire,
Car ce Tout là, qu'en tout elle avoit creu,
Sans nul obstacle estoit lors d'elle veu.
Encore on peut respondre: ces nonnains,
Qui ont les cueurs si reformez et sainctz,
Pour declarer leur vie vertueuse
Pevent avoir la mort bien gracieuse;
Mais pour monstrer que la foy au mourir
Sçait la mort vaincre et l'homme secourir,
Je vous diray ce qu'ay veu par exprès
De son bon filz, lequel mourut après,
Charles dernier, duc aussi d'Alençon,
Dont je pourroys faire longue leçon,
Si tous les faictz par escript vouloys mettre,
Et son trespas dire sans rien obmettre; Fol. 323 v°
Car tant y a de choses qui m'incitent
A les escrire et qui tant le merittent,
Que j'en lerray le plus, prenant le meins,
Car ennuyer par la longueur je crains.
Venons au jour de sa mort: je vous dy
Que le matin du grand et sainct mardy,
Cinq jours après qu'il print ung pluresis,
Ne pensant point mourir, estant assis
Dedans son lict et sa femme lisant
Propoz de Dieu, et par jeu luy disant:
«Promis m'avez, Monsieur, de recevoir,
«Mais vous n'avez pas fait vostre devoir.
«Or, puysqu'avez au dymanche failly,
«Que ce mardy soit de vous assailly.»
Ce qu'il voulut, et du lict se leva,
Et à genoulz devant l'autel s'en va
Se confesser et recevoir sans craincte,
Par ferme foy et charité non faincte.
Ce faict, au lict derechef retourna,
Puys se leva et à table disna,
Parlant à tous ainsy qu'ung homme sain;
Mais il avoit la mort dedans le sain.
Après se mist en ung lict, et sa femme
Il appella pour consoler son ame,
La priant lire et de son Dieu parler,

From wedding her because she might have erred; 3940
She, feeling this compassion, so glad is
That she draws near, recounting goodness His,
And to the second Adam witnesses,
Then tenui with nunc dimittam says. 3944
Midway, the lady, with love overcome
Cried out, "Alas! When will this greeting come?"
With fervor then, she clasped her abbess near
And calling, "Jesus, Jesus!" left our sphere, 3948
This vale of tears, for that most joyous peak
That her desire long since had gone to seek.
As soon as she'd called "Jesus" in this style,
All wreathed in sweetness, she began to smile. 3952
For All-in-All, in which she had believed
Was then without an obstacle perceived.
Since one may still object and say, "These nuns
Whose hearts are such reformed and saintly ones, 3956
Whose lives present so virtuous a face,
Can have in death thereby a wreath of grace;
But, now to show in dying that faith can
Transcend one's death and help the dying man, 3960
I'll tell you what I saw while there beside
Her good son Charles, who subsequently died,
The final Charles, the Duke of Alençon,
Whose life were ample lesson for someone 3964
If all its facts I might put down in writ,
To tell his death and no detail omit;
But so many things I find exciting,
So deserving to be put in writing, 3968
I'll leave out major portions, telling less
Because I fear to bore through lengthiness.
Let us, I say, come to the day he died.
That morn, Shrove Tuesday, he was mortified 3972
With pleurisy (his fifth day completed);
He'd no thought to die, in bed was seated,
Hearing words of God his wife was reading,
When she said, as if to tease, half-pleading: 3976
"Your Grace, you promised me you would commune,
But in this duty you have left lacune.
Since you've not done on Sunday what you ought,
Let Tuesday be the day of your onslaught," 3980
Which he desired and from the bed arose,
Lo, on his knees, before the altar goes,
Confesses and communes, by no fear pained,
Sustained by solid faith and love unfeigned. 3984
This done, again he went to bed, reclined,
Then rose again and at the table dined;
And, like a healthy man, spoke with the rest
Of us, but he had death within his chest. 3988
When he had gone to bed, he called his wife
To come console his spirit leaving life.
He said to read and of his God to speak

Sans le laisser, ny loing de luy aller:
«Car je sens bien, dist il, ma derniere heure
«Qui ne fera de m'aprocher demeure.»
Ainsy sa mort joyeusement jugea,
Puys demanda quelque chose et mangea,
Fol. 333
Et se voulut lever et proumener,
Puys au grand lict pour la fin retourner.
Et qui l'eust veu marcher si fermement,
Ne l'eust jugé mourir si promptement.
Estant au lict, il fist sa femme lire
La Passion; lors commança à dire
Sus chaque article et chacun poinct notable
Chose qui fut à tous esmerveillable:
Car luy, n'ayant jamais leu ni apris,
Lequel l'on n'eust pour [ung] orateur pris,
Parla si bien, que cinq docteurs presens
Furent longtemps pour l'escouter taisans;
Car il disoit: «O mon Dieu, je sçay bien
«Que j'ai peché et que je ne vaulx rien;
«Et qu'ung seul bien ne sçauroys presenter
«Qui ta justice en rien sceust contanter.»
Puys confessant ses maulx par le menu,
Dist: «Je suys plus que nul à Dieu tenu,
«Qui m'a tant fait de biens en ma jeunesse,
«Et empesché les ennuys de vieillesse.
«Trente six ans, sans grande maladie,
«Vivre m'a fait, et fault que je le dye,
«Et guerre et paix conservant mon honneur,
«Servant, aymant mon souverain Seigneur.»
Lors, regardant madame la Regente,
Luy dist: «Madame, à vous je me lamente,
«Vous suppliant ne [le] celler au Roy:
«C'est que depuys le piteux desarroy
«De sa prison, j'ay eu tel desconfort
«Et tel ennuy, qu'il m'a donné la mort;
Fol. 333 v°
«Laquelle, autant que vivant je l'ay craincte,
«Belle la treuve et la prans sans contraincte;
«Car quand au monde, onques le cueur n'y
euz.
«Ny amusé à ses biens je ne fuz.
«Et n'ayant peu prisonnier ny mort estre,
«Servant, mon roy, pere, frere et bon maistre,
«Plus rien çà bas de partir ne m'engarde
«Pour voller hault, où l'arriver me tarde.»
Baisant sa main, luy dist: «Je ne demande
«Que vostre grace, et je [vous] recommande
«Celle qu'avez conjoincte en mariage,
«Quinze ans y a, avecques moy; tant saige
«Et vertueuse envers moi l'ay trouvée
«Qu'elle peult bien de moy estre approuvée.»

And not to leave, some distant spot to seek; 3992
"I really feel," he said, "my final hour
Will not be long in coming to my bower."
Thus cheerfully his death he'd calculate.
He asked for something to be brought, and
ate. 3996
He wished to rise that he might walk about
Then go to his great bed to see life out.
Whoever might have seen him walk so well
Would hardly have been able to foretell 4000
Prompt death. Abed, he told his wife to read
The Passion; he began next to proceed
Upon each point and item notable,
A thing which all found strange and quotable: 4004
Not a reader nor a knowledge-seeker,
One whom none would take to be a speaker,
Charles spoke at length and so convincingly
Five doctors present heard him quietly; 4008
For he said, "I, O God of mine, well know
That I have sinned and now, unworthy, go,
For I have not a merit to present
To make thy justice in the least content." 4012
He said, confessing sins in full detail:
"To God I'm most beholden; Him I hail
Who in my youth did such good things for me
And kept me from the ills of age: for He 4016
To thirty-six without a grave disease
Has let me live; and I must say this, please:
In war and peace my honor was intact.
I served, and love for my leige never lacked." 4020
Looking then in the *Régente's* direction,
Said, "I lean, ma'am, on your kind affection
And beg you not to hold back from the king
That since the sorrowful surrendering 4024
And his imprisonment I have such wound
And heaviness, it's weighed me to the ground;

This death, which, while I lived I viewed with fear,
Will find fair welcome now as it draws near. 4028
The world, I never had much heart for it,

And from its goods enjoyed no benefit.
Neither killed nor captured for my master
To serve father, brother, king — disaster! 4032
So nothing further here below prevents
My rising, and my yearning is intense.
"I only ask," he said, and kissed her hand,
"Your pardon, and commend, you understand, 4036
The one whom fifteen years ago you gave
With marriage vows to me. So well-behaved
I found her and so virtuous with me
That I approve her to the last degree." 4040

Mais regardant sa femme de ce pas,
Derriere luy dist: «[Ne me] laissez pas.»
Qui, nonobstant maternelle deffense,
Ne voulut pas au mary faire offense,
Mais l'embrassant et s'approchant de luy
Luy monstroit Dieu, son secours et appuy.
Lors regardant entre les chevaliers,
Il appella monsieur de Chandeniers,
Disant: «Je craindz de faire fondre en pleurs
«Mes officiers et povres serviteurs,
«En leur disant l'adieu qui leur desplaist:
«Vouz leur direz, compere, s'il vous plaist,
«Les priant tous de se reconforter.
«Ma femme aussi ne sçauroit supporter
«Après ma mort parler à eux ensemble;
«Dont myeulx que nul le ferez, ce me
    semble.»   Fol. 334
A maistre Jehan Gœvrot, son medecin,
Qui arriva ce jour, il dist: «Ma fin
«Est aujourd'huy: Il fault que je deffine,
«En vous priant de donner medecine
«En conservant celle qui m'a servi
«Et mon vouloir jusqu'à la mort suyvi.»
Et se tournant vers elle luy donna
Son medecin, et puys luy ordonna
Ce qu'il vouloit de son enterrement
Et serviteurs, sans autre testament:
Car il sçavoit que son vouloir feroit
Mort comme vif, et luy obeyroit.
Puys l'unction l'evesque de Lisieux
Luy apporta, luy disant tout le myeulx
Que faire peut, à quoi il respondit:
«O mon evesque, où est ce grand credit
«Qu'avoit l'Eglise, en donnant garison
«Par unction et devotte oraison?
«Plus ne voyons l'Eglise primitive
«Prier par foy et charité naïfve.«
—«Monsieur, dist il, ce sacrement vous vaille
«Pour vous donner victoire en la bataille
«Que l'ennemy mainctenant vous appreste.»
Il respondit: «Jesus luy a la teste
«Si bien rompue et deffaicte et brisée,
«Que sa force est de moy trop desprisée.»
Et regardant dedans ung grant tableau
D'un crucifix, il dist: «L'homme nouveau
«En ceste croix pendu me renouvelle,
«En m'asseurant de la bonne nouvelle:
                                    Fol. 334 v°
«C'est que le Filz a Dieu mys en ce monde
«Pour effacer nostre peché immunde.»
Et tout remply d'une ferveur benigne,
Joignant les mains, crya: «Bonté divine,

And, looking at his wife close thereupon
Behind him, said, "Don't leave me!" She was one
Who, in spite of orders from her mother,
Would not cross her husband for another;   4044
Approaching and embracing him, she stayed
And showed him God was his relief and aid.
He glanced among his knights who might remain
And called on Chandeniers the chamberlain: 4048
"I fear the flow of tears that sorrow stirs;
Amongst my household and my officers   -
It might displease if I bade them adieu.
So, comrade, please, I leave such word to you. 4052
You'll bid them all be of good mind and cheer.
My wife can't bear the duty to appear
To speak to them assembled when I go,
And you will do it best of all, I
    know."   4056
To Master John Gœvrot, his physician
Come that day, he said of his condition:
"Today's my last, and I must specify
That you give medicine to certify   4060
The health of her who's served me and intends
To carry out my wishes till life ends."
Turning, he put his doctor in her hands
And gave his wife his last detailed commands, 4064
Orders that he had for his interment
And, for household members, last conferment,
Full-knowing she would carry out his will;
When he was dead, she would obey him still. 4068
The bishop of Lisieux brought unction then
And spoke to him the best words of his ken,
To which Duke Charles replied not without grief,
"Lord Bishop, where is that once great belief 4072
The Church had because she would bring healing
Through her unction and her prayers appealing?
The church is not the one we used to see
At pray'r with faith and trustful amity."   4076
The bishop said, "This sacrament avails
To give you victory when strife assails
Such as the enemy prepares for you
This hour." To which the duke said that he knew, 4080
And, "Jesus crushed and ground the devil's head
Till it's strength is the one that I least dread";
And gazing at a painted Christ coloss,
"The New Man," said he, "hung upon the cross, 4084
Brings sweet renewal to this person, too,
Assuring me that His good news is true:

God did convey His Son on earth through grace
That he might our own unclean sin erase!"   4088
Quite filled with fervor utterly benign,
His hands entwined, he cried, "O, Good divine,

83

«Dedans ce corps en la croix attaché
«Je voy vaincu et couvert mon peché.
«O! Moy pecheur, meschant, infame et lasche,
«Dans ce costé par vive foy me cache!
«J'ay meritté, Seigneur, d'estre battu;
«Mais en ce corps dont je suis revestu,
«Il n'y a lieu où vous n'ayez frappé,
«Et en luy mort suys par vous eschappé.
«Vous me devez mettre à damnation:
«Je le sçay bien, c'est ma confusion;
«Mais vostre filz est pour moy condamné
«Jouant pour moy le roolle du damné.
«Vous m'arguez de n'avoir obeys
«Voz mandemens mais les avoir haÿs:

«Je le confesse et en ay congnoissance.
«Mais regardez la grande obeyssance
«De vostre enfant qui a tout accomply
«Vostre vouloir, et lequel m'a remply
«D'un [seur] espoir que ses œuvres sont
        miennes,
«Et qui plus est, il fait les myennes siennes;
«Et mes pechez par luy sont satisfaictz,
«En me donnant part à tous ses bienfaictz.
«O mon bon Dieu, je le croy fermement:
«Parquoy vous prie et requiers humblement
«N'attendre pas que le soleil se couche,
«Pour me tyrer de ma mortelle cousche,
«Mais aujourd'huy, par ce soleil luysant,
                    Fol. 335
«Comme au larron, ce paradise plaisant
«Me faictes veoir. Seigneur: c'est vostre face,
«Affin que là ma louange parface.
«Puysque le Filz, d'un amoureux couraige,
«N'a crainct pour moy passer ce dur passaige,
«Passer m'y veulx sans craindre nul alarme;
«Car ce n'est pas raison que le gendarme,
«Passant canon, lance, espée ou meschef,
«D'un cueur joyeulx ne suyve son bon chef.
«Je m'y en voys; mon Dieu, avansez-vous,
«Car ce mourir plus que vivre m'est doulx.»
Puys dist: «Je sens mes membres et mon corps,
«[Mais sans douloir] l'un après l'autre mortz.
«Chacun disoit la mort de douleur plaine
«[Et] je me meurs, et n'ay ni mal ny peyne.
«O mon Seigneur, je voy la raison forte,
«Car ma douleur vostre filz en croix porte;
«Il a pour moy beu cest amer bruvage,
«Ne me laissant en corps ny en couraige
«Mal ny ennuy, sinon l'ardant desir
«D'estre avec luy en l'eternel plaisir.»
Après l'oyant lire ung peu se taisa;

In you nailed on the cross, there to succumb,
I see my sin included, overcome.   4092
I, a sinner loose and foul, find hiding
Within this cleft side, through faith abiding!
O Lord, at best, I merit to be scourged;
But in this body where I am immerged,   4096
There is no spot you have not touched for me;
And through His death, by you, I am set free.
Oh, you ought to send me to damnation!
Knowing this is my humiliation.   4100
And yet, for me, your Son was one condemned
And played for me the role of the contemned.
You may reply that I have not obeyed
Commandments and with disregard have
        strayed;   4104
I so confess and take full cognizance;
But, look upon the great obedience
Of your own Son who carried out your will
In full. My heart is one that He did fill   4108
With certainty: His works suffice for
        mine;
And further, He takes mine by this design.
He, for my own sins, gave satisfaction
Giving me a part in His good action.   4112
O God, I firmly hold what He did teach,
Therefore, I humbly pray you and beseech
You not to wait until the sun grows dark
To extricate me from my mortal bark;   4116
But, on this day, while sunborne rays still shine,

As did the thief see Paradise divine,
Let me too, see, O Lord, your face and raise
To you at last my hymn of perfect praise.   4120
And, since your Son with loving fortitude
For me feared not His passage on the rood,
I hope to pass there scorning all alarms.
There is no reason that the man-at-arms   4124
Who braves mishaps of cannon, lance, and sword
Should fail to follow with glad heart his Lord.
That I may make my way there, Lord, lead on!
To die grows sweeter than to live anon,   4128
I feel my body and my limbs," he said.
"But without paining; one by one they're dead.
Though people used to say death full of pain,
I die, and by discomfort am not slain.   4132
My Lord, I see good reason not to mourn,
Because, upon the Cross my pain was borne.
Your Son for me has drained this bitter drink,
Not letting me in heart and body sink   4136
With illness and distress, but fired with this:
A wish to share with Him eternal bliss."
When he had heard her read, he briefly hushed,

Puys embrassant sa femme il la baisa,
Disant: «Adieu pour ung bien peu de temps,
«Lequel passé nous nous verrons contans.»
En se tournant, les yeulx au ciel leva
Et à son Dieu sa voix foible esleva,
Disant: «A vous sans douleur je m'en voys.»
Son *In manus* dist, puys en doulce voix,
Comme amoureux de son Dieu, dist: «Jesus!»
Fol. 335 v°
Lequel finy, l'ame volla là sus;
Mais en faisant du corps au ciel passaige,
Le clair soleil sur ce pasle visaige
Ung beau rayon fist si très fort reluyre,
Qui sembloit estre un cheriot pour conduyre
L'espouse au ciel, l'ame à son createur.
Et ce soleil, qu'avec ung ardant cueur
Avoit à Dieu prié ne l'oster pas,
Mais qu'avec luy peust faire son trespas,
Luy fut donné comme il le demandoit,
Pour le mener au lieu qu'il pretendoit.
Assez de mots dist, monstrant qu'il voyoit

Dieu tout en tous, ce que si bien croyoit
[Que] luy, qui fut de la mort tant craintif,
Estoit d'aller à la mort bien hastif.
Et si l'on dit tel prince en sa jeunesse
N'ayant en soy malice ne finesse
Ne devoit pas de la mort faire compte,
Las! qui auroit veu ce que je racompte,
Diroit que Foy est ung maistre d'escole,
Qui a la fin fait jouer ung tel roolle
A l'inocent qui ne fault d'un seul mot,
Et le sçavant sans Foy se monstre un sot.
Mais, s'il vous plaist, Amye, d'une femme
Qui de son temps par sus toutes eut fame,
Je vous diroy commant elle mourut,
Et comme Foy mourant la secourut.
Ung vilaige est que l'on [appelle] Grès,
Près de Paris, lieu remply de regrets,
Car là mourut Loyse de Savoye, Fol. 336.
Qui de vertu avoit suyvi la voye,
Mere du Roy Françoys, qui avoit [d'age]
Cinquante cinq ans, l'an de son voyaige.
Voyant la fin peu à peu aprocher
Loing de son filz qu'elle tenoit tant cher,
Lequel fuyant la peste fut constrainct
De s'esloigner, dont il eut regret mainct;
Pas ne pensoit si tost perdre sa mere,
Dont il porta douleur trop plus qu'amaire:
Elle ayant fait de sa vie le cours
En longs ennuys et en plaisirs bien cours,
Ce que chacun peult clairement sçavoir;

Embracing her; his lips against hers brushed,   4140
Then said, "Farewell, there is but little time
Before we meet again in joy sublime,"
And turning, heavenward he raised his eyes.
Allowed his feeble voice to God to rise.   4144
"Unpained to come to You, I now leave here,"
And his *In Manus* said, then "Jesus, hear!"
Like one who loves his God, his voice was
   soft;
When it was done, the soul had soared aloft.   4148
But, passing from the body to on high,
On this pale visage, the bright sun supply
So strongly caused to shine a goodly beam
A chariot was fetching, it would seem,   4152
The bride, the soul, to heaven, to its Source.
Not to remove the sun from this day's course
Had been his ardent plea to God, unless
He crossed as well; and God saw fit to bless   4156
Him, honor his request as He retired
Him to the place to which Duke Charles aspired.
Charles showed through his discourse that he
   perceived
God all in everyone, and so believed   4160
That he whom death had once brought such distress
Would go, embracing it with eagerness.
And if one say such prince in his young days
Who had not malice nor deceitful ways   4164
Should hardly have found death so great a state,
Oh my! Had he but seen what I relate,
He would call faith the master of a school
Who guides the simple from the dunce's stool   4168
Till he at last lacks neither word nor rule;
The wise man without faith appears the fool.
But, if it please you, Dear, I now shall rhyme
About the one most noted in her time,   4172
And I shall tell you how she came to die
And how her faith, to help her, did apply.
There is in France a village known as Gretz,
Near Paris, seat of manifold regrets   4176
Because there died one Louise of Savoy,
Who'd followed virtue's path and scorned to toy.
This mother of King Francis, then alive,
(The year of passing she was fifty-five)   4180
Was seeing bit by bit the end encroach
While still the son she loved did not approach;
He'd been obliged to flee the pestilence
And with regret had made withdrawal thence;   4184
He'd not thought so soon to lose his mother,
So his grief was bitter like no other.
Life for her had run its course with measure
Long in difficulty, short in pleasure.   4188
As everyone must clearly be aware:

En tous estatz ayant fait son devoir
Avec honneur et conscience pure,
Autant ou plus que fist onq creature.
Unze ans avoit quand mary elle prist,
Saige et prudent, duquel beaucoup aprist;
[Avec] luy huict ans elle demoura,
Mais ce bon temps gueres ne luy dura.
Fille et filz eut, à elle obeyssans,
Rempliz d'esprit, de vertuz et bon sens.
Veufve elle fut en l'age [de] dix neuf,
Et sans vouloir reprendre mary neuf,
Bien qu'elle fust de grans roys demandée,
Viduité eut tant recommandée
[Qu'en] la gardant vesquit si chastement
[Qu'en] son parler, regard et vestement,
De chasteté à tous l'exemple estoit;
Et dans son œil très beau elle portoit
Avec doulceur si grande magesté

Fol. 336 v°

Qu'elle incittoit chacun à chasteté.
De sa bonté, las! assez esprouverent
Ses serviteurs meschans, qui controuverent
Mille moyens pour nuyre à leur maistresse,
Et luy oster en si grande jeunesse
De ses enfans l'administration.
Mais nonobstant la demonstration
De leurs cueurs plains de mensonge et malice,
Par sa doulceur elle couvrit leur vice.
Aux faulx tesmoings leur faultes pardonna,
Sans rien oster leurs gaiges leur donna,
Disant: «Dieu seul par ces hommes me tante,
«Ses verges sont, par quoy je m'en contante.»
Ce Tout voyoit qui tout seul l'affligeoit,
Les homes rien que verges ne jugeoit;
Car de la main de Dieu le coup venoit,
Lequel voyant, aux verges pardonnoit.
Sa grand prudence et son bon jugement
Fut bien congneu quand le gouvernement
De son royaulme elle seulle soustint,
Dont très grand bien au roy son filz advint:

Car, quand il fut de prison retourné,
Trouva le tout si très bien ordonné,
[Par tout le pays,] soit privé ou estrange,
Qu'il en donna à sa mere louange,
Et elle à Dieu, sachant qu'en foible main
Il avoit fait ung acte souverain.
Voyant son filz et ses filz revenuz
De la prison où tant furent tenuz,

Ce qu'elle avoit porté passiemment Fol. 337
En son esprit, mais la peyne et tourment

In all conditions she took faithful care;
With honor and pure conscience she performed
To best or equal any creature formed.   4192
Eleven were her years when she was wed:
He wise and prudent, she by him was led.
Eight years with him she was allowed to spend,
But this good life came to untimely end.   4196
Her son and lass gave her obedience;
She gave them spirit, virtue, and good sense.
She was a widow in her nineteenth year
With no wish a new husband to endear;   4200
Although she was petitioned by great kings,
Her widowhood she'd praised in barterings
Until she kept it, and remaining very chaste
In all, her dress and speech and her good taste,   4204
She stood as an example for the whole,
And in her eyes (of beauty to extol)
She bore with sweetness such great majesty
That she incited each to chastity.   4208
Her goodness underwent sufficient trial
From servitors contriving methods vile,
A thousand ways to do their mistress harm
And to remove quite early from her arm,   4212
Right to guide her children's education.
But, notwithstanding the demonstration
Of falseness, malice trying to entice,
With gentleness she overcame their vice,   4216
Pardoned fault in those who bore false witness,
Did not trim their wages, but in fitness
Stated, "God, through these men, is tempting me;
They are His scourges I'll bear patiently."   4220
She saw that All alone did chasten her;
These were but scourges; this she could infer
Because the hand of God had dealt the blow.
In turn, she would on them her grace bestow.   4224
Her prudence and good judgment were well known
When on Louise the government was thrown,
And single-handedly she held the helm,
Whence good came to her son the king, and
    realm: 4228
When from imprisonment he was exchanged,
He found affairs of state so well arranged
In all, both foreign and domestic ways,
That to his mother for it he gave praise,   4232
And she to God, that through her feeble hand
The Master had been governing the land.
She saw King Francis and his sons returned
From prison where they were quite long
    interned;   4236
A weight she bore, and she did not complain,
But she then found that pain and mental strain

Qu'elle endura rendit son corps deffaict,
Alors qu'elle eut son desir satisfaict,
Et ne fist plus que se diminuer
Et au salut de l'ame estudier;
Tant que souvent seulle en son lict estant,
Ce [qu'a] ouy qui l'aloit escoutant,
Parloit à Dieu comme espouse à espoux,
Disant: «Seigneur, las! pourquoi tardez vous?
«J'ai fait çà bas tout ce que j'ay peu faire,
«Je ne suys plus au monde necessaire:
«Plaise vous donc pour vostre m'advouer
«En me tirant à vous pour vous louer.»
Puys ses bienfaictz alloit ramentevant,
L'en merciant, mais c'estoit si souvent
Que son rideau n'estoit plus tost tyré
Que son esprit ne fust hault retyré.
Dedans son lict quatre heures s'enfermoit
Pour deviser [à Celluy] qu'elle aymoit;
Et povoit on, en oyant ses souspirs,
Juger qu'à Dieu avoit mys ses desirs.
Le dernier jour venu, ceste princesse
Fist préparer devant elle la messe,
Et fist sa fille à la fin recevoir,
Ce qu'elle eust fait [s'elle] eust eu le povoir.
Elle appella son pere confesseur
En lui disant: «Mon pere, il est tout seur
«Que Dieu m'a fait l'honneur de m'appeller,
«Et de bon cueur je veulx à luy aller;
«Car s'il m'avoit donné la carte blanche

Fol. 337 v°

«Pour me passer ceste mortelle planche,
«Je n'eusse osé demander tant de biens
«Qu'il m'a donnez, que tous de luy je tiens,
«Et de ses dons et biens j'ay mal usé;
«Mais mon peché [me] peult estre excusé,
«Car de sa grace et loy il m'a fait part,
«Et longuement, avant ce mien depart:
«Son Filz m'a fait recevoir pour saulveur,
«Par qui j'ay eu de luy [toute] faveur;
«Tant qu'en luy seul de mon salut m'asseure,
«Et que peché faisant en moy demeure,
«Et qui m'avoit damnation aquise,
«Est tout estainct par sa bonté exquise;
«Il est mon Dieu et ma salvation.»
Puys elle fist tout bas confession
Devotement, ayant aux yeulx les larmes.
Après luy dist telz ou semblables termes:
«Mon mal est tel que ne puys nullement
«Recevoir Dieu sacramentellement;
«Mais allez moy une hostie querir
«En la parroisse, affin qu'avant mourir,
«En la voyant, puysse ramentevoir

Had undone the body thus mistreated.
Since her dearest purpose was completed,   4240
She need do no more. Strength would diminish
As she sought salvation in life's finish,
And so, alone, she often stayed in bed;
Some people listened and heard what she said, 4244
She spoke now in a wife-to-husband way
To God: "Alas, Milord, why this delay?
I've done all is this world I could," she hurled.
"I am no longer needed in this world: 4248
So, may it please you to make me your own.
Take me, that I may make your greatness known."
Her blessings then she endlessly would name
And give Him thanks. But it so often came   4252
About, no sooner was her curtain drawn
Than up to heaven was her spirit gone!
There in her bed four hours she would stay
To tell her loved one what she had to say,   4256
And one could judge from hearing how she sighed
She'd placed her wants with God to be supplied.
When came the day this princess was to pass,
She ordered that they bring her Holy Mass   4260
And had her daughter at the last assume
What she now lacked the power to consume.
She called her father-contessor to her,
Saying, "Father, it must be very sure   4264
God honors me to call me to Him; so,
Whole-heartedly to Him I want to go;
For had he permitted me to order

Things to help me cross the mortal border,   4268
Not ever had I dared to ask such good
As He's bestowed, the only one who could;
Some of His gifts and goods I have ill-used.
My sin, however, still can be excused   4272
Because Christ's grace and law included me.
Long since before this farewell that you see
God let me receive His Son as Savior —
Grace that came from His, not my behavior: 4276
Upon Him solely my salvation rests.
Whatever sin my record now attests —
Though it's earned for me a just damnation —
Is expunged, thanks to His expiation —   4280
Goodness exquisite, my God's salvation!"
Softly she confessed and poured oblation,
Having eyes brimmed over with devotion.
Then came some such words in her emotion: 4284
"My malady is such I can not hold
The sacrament of God, to be consoled;
Pray go and ask the parish — say it's I —
To send the Host, so that before I die,   4288
Beholding, I'll be able to recall:

«Que Dieu se fait à l'homme recevoir.»
Ce que l'on fist; et quand l'hostie vid,
S'escriant dist: «Jesus, filz de David,
«Qui sur la croix pour moy fuz estendu,
«Et par amour cueur et costé fendu,
«Je vous adore, ô mon Dieu et mon roy;
«Pere et amy tel je vous tiens et croy,
«Vous requerant de mes pechez pardon

Fol. 338

«En la vertu de ce très riche don
«De vostre amour que vous m'avez donnée,
«Laquelle amour ne m'a habandonnée:
«Je l'ay tousjours [en] fiance parfaicte.
«Or mainctenant qu'aproche la deffaicte
«De la prison de ce vieil corps charnel,
«Las! plaise vous, o mon pere eternel,
«Entre voz braz l'ame et l'esprit reprendre
«Que de bon cueur entre voz mains vois
      rendre.
«Je sçay, Seigneur, que celluy qui a creu
«Entierement par foy vous a receu:
«Je vous croy myen, vous le m'avez promis,
«Donc vous recoy, o l'amy des amys,
«En mon esprit qui par foy vous embrasse.
«O le pain vif duquel la douhaceur passe.
«Toute douhaceur, en foy je vous recoy:
«Par ceste foy ainsy recevez moy;
«Je ne suys pas de recevoir deceue
«Le vray amy duquel je suis receue.
«Je vous recoy spirituellement,
«Ne vous povant recevoir autrement,
«Croyant si bien ceste reception
«Que seure suys de ma salvation.»
L'hostie fut lors de là transportée;
Elle du tout en Dieu reconfortée
Print l'unction que très bien entendit,
Et aux endroictz que failloit respondit.
Puys se monstrant de Dieu espouse et fille,
Va commander de lire l'evangile,
Et commançant au sermon fructueux

Fol. 338 v°

Dapres la cene, que d'un cueur vertueux
Elle escoutoit, et tant que l'on lisoit,
Sans sentir mal, ung seul mot ne disoit,
Mais quand ung peu l'on cessoit la lecture,
Se pleignoit fort, car sa povre nature
Eut grand tourment de pierre et de gravelle,
Et qui pis fut, elle eut une nouvelle
Forte à porter, c'est qu'au terme prefix
N'estoit possible avoir le roy son filz.
Lors fist ung cry quand elle ouyt cela,
Et en pleurant amerement parla:

God makes Himself available to all."
"Twas done; and when she saw the Host was fetched,
She cried, "O Jesus, son of David, stretched   4292
Upon the cross for me, who took my part,
And, for His love, was pierced in side and heart,
God, King, I love you, on you I depend;
I hold you both my father and my friend,   4296
Requesting pardon for my sins of you.

By virtue of this precious gift, mine too,
Your love that you have given unto me
That has not left me to catastrophe: 4300
I always cling to it with perfect trust.
And now behold, about to turn to dust,
The prison of this old body's kernel.
Take my soul, please, Father mine, eternal;   4304
Take my spirit in your embrace once more,
Which, with good heart, to you I now
      restore.
I know, O Lord, that this one who believed,
Through faith exclusively, yourself received;   4308
That you are mine, as promised, I believe.
So You, O Friend of friends, I thus receive
In my spirit and through my faith embrace
You, Bread of Life, whose sweetness has a taste 4312
Beyond all sweets; in faith receive I you:
Receive me thus as by this faith is due.
About receiving I am not deceived:
He's one, the True Friend by whom I'm received. 4316
It is in spirit that I must partake
Because no effort can my body make.
Well-believing this accreditation,
I am now assured of my salvation!"   4320
Directly was the Host from there removed.
She knew in full the comfort that God proved
And took the unction, which she understood;
She answered in the places that one should,   4324
Then showed herself God's daughter and His spouse,
Someone to read the Gospel had them rouse,
To open with the sermon of much fruit

That closed the final meal. With mind acute,   4328
As long as they would read to her, she heard.
She felt no pain and uttered not a word.
But when, in reading wearied, they had slacked,
Her plaint was clamorous, her body wracked   4332
With torment; her passages were graveled;
And, much worse, bad news by now had traveled
That prior to the time agreed upon
It was not possible to fetch her son.   4336
She made outcry when first she heard the news.
She spoke through tears too bitter to refuse.

«O mon enfant! ne te verray je point!
«Me fauldras tu, mon filz, au dernier poinct!
«Fault il partir de ce terrestre lieu
«Sans te baiser pour le dernier adieu!»
Puys dist, levant au ciel ses pleurans yeulx,
«Vous l'avez fait, mon Seigneur, pour le
    myeulx;
«Car luy ne moy ne l'eussions sceu porter,
«Encores moins l'un l'autre conforter.
«Trop grande estoit l'amour d'entre nous deux
«Où plus ne fault penser, et je le veulx.
«Mais, Seigneur Dieu, soyez luy favorable,
«Et à ses grans affaires secourable.
«Il portera [tant,] tant et tant d'ennuys.
«De ceste mort, parquoy, tant que je puys,
«Je vous requiers, par vostre passion,
«De luy donner la benediction
«A luy, aux siens et à toute sa race,
«Et le tenir en vostre bonne grace.»
Et puys la croix, de triumphe baniere, Fol. 339
Entre ses mains luy mist La Bourdaisiere,
Qu'elle baisa, en disant doulcement:
«Ainsy fut mys pour moy le vray amant.
Après, prenant sa fille par la main,»
Dist: «Marguerite, encore est mon cueur plain
«De ceste amour portée à vous si forte,
«Et à mon filz, ce qu'encores j'y porte;
«Et dans mon cueur le sens si vehement
«Que pour n'avoir en mon entendement
«Rien que Dieu seul, que seul doy desirer,
«Je vous requiers d'ung peu vous retirer
«D'auprès de moy; car quand je vous regarde
«D'avoir plaisir en mon cueur je n'ay grade.
«Las! forte amour parler à vous m'empesche,
«Mais ung seul mot pour la fin je vous presche,
«C'est qu'en mon cueur je sens la foy si ferme,
«Le don de Dieu par lequel il m'afferme
«De mon salut, dont le plaisir je gouste;
«N'en faictes plus, m'amye, nulle doubte.»
A ces propoz sa fille fort pleura,
Et de ses yeulx soudain se retira
Et non pas loing, car jusques au dernier
Ne la laissa, et le bon cordelier
Mist entre deux, regardant à loisir
Sa bonne mere en lict mortel gesir,
Qui escoutoit la lecture divine,
Les yeulx en hault, sans parolle ne myne,
Comme personne en extase ravie.
Mais ung des siens qui bien l'avoit servie,
Fut bien longtemps à la persuader Fol. 339 v°
De quelque chose en fin leur commander,
En la priant avant que s'en aller

"My child! Has my last time to see you passed?
Will you be lacking to me at the last?   4340
My son, must I vacate this earthly place
And leave no farewell kiss upon your face?"
Raising eyes to heaven all the wetter:
"As you've done it, Lord, it must be
    better.   4344
For neither could have borne it, much less known
What comfort to the other could be shown.
It was too great, the love between us two.
I must dismiss it, which I'll try to do.   4348
Show favor, Lord, if it shall be your whim,
And in affairs of greatness, succor him.
So many difficulties he must bear
Because I die; so, while I can, a prayer   4352
I say, mindful of the crucifixion:
Grant to him, I pray, a benediction
On him and his, all children of his race,
And keep him in the path of your good grace."4356
The cross and victory for which it stands,
La Bourdaisière placed then between her hands,
She kissed it as she murmured tenderly:
"In this way was the true love shown for me."   4360
She took her daughter later by the hand
And said, "My heart's still full of that strong brand
Of love that I have borne you, Marguerite,
And for my son I hold love still complete;   4364
It has in my heart such deep dimension
That, to hold not it in my attention
But our Lord God, the one I should desire,
I ask you just a little to retire;   4368
For, looking at you, I've no mind to find
Rejoicing in my heart. To speech inclined,
I can not give to God the love I owe.
I preach one word to you before I go: 4372
That in my heart I sense the faith so strong
It must be God's gift meaning I belong
Among the saved. My pleasure bears this out.
Of this, my dear, pray have no further doubt."   4376
At these remarks, her daughter's weeping grew.
She quickly from her mother's eyes withdrew,
But not far off, because until the end
She did not leave her, and she placed their friend, 4380
A Gray Friar, 'twixt them, to watch at leisure
Louise, who lay waiting for death's seizure
And was list'ning now the Word to capture,
Mutely, eyes above, like one in rapture,   4384
Without expression, in ecstatic spell.
But someone who had always served her well
Consumed some time persuading her to state
Some final task she would to them dictate,   4388
And begged some word she might at least impart,

89

Vouloir les siens d'un seul mot consoller.
Elle luy dist: «Cessez vos vainz propoz;
«Mainctenant est mon esprit en repoz,
«Plus n'est çà bas, vous me rompez la teste.»
Sa fille alors, qui du secours fut preste,
Dist: «Laissez la: elle attend la promesse
«De la divine et admirable haultesse;
«Tous serviteurs, enfans, honneurs et biens
«N'estime plus sinon ordure et fiens;
«Tous les mortelz pour l'Immortel oublye,
«Voyant son Dieu qui l'a tant anoblie,
«Qui la reçoit pour espouse et pour femme.»
Dont respondit à sa fille la dame:
«C'est très bien dit, m'amye, il est ainsy.»
Et sans bouger ses yeulx d'en hault aussi,
Sans plus parler la croix elle baisoit,
Et d'ouyr clair tousjours signe faisoit.
Et tost après jecta un regard doulx
Devers le ciel, là où son Tout en tous
En soubzriant sembloit veoir clairement.
Et sur ce poinct fist son trespassement,
Si doulcement que sa fille sans plus
S'en apperceut, car trèstout le surplus
Se debattoit s'elle estoit morte ou non.
Ainsy passa, digne d'heureux renom,
Celle qui eut et vivante et mourante
Foy en Dieu seul, amour et vraye attente.
Par ceste mort, Amye, il fault congnoistre

Fol. 340

Que plus Dieu fait la tentation croistre
Et plus il est du [tempté] adjuteur
Qui par luy met à riens le vieulx tempteur.
Si de la foy, par ce dernier exemple,
Vous ne voyez la vertu assez ample,
Souvienne vous, Amye, aussi fait il,
Du roy Françoys, son filz, prince gentil,
Gentil de nom, de race et de vertuz,
Qui à la guerre a souvent combattuz
Ses ennemys, emportant la victoire,
Et, s'il fut prins, il n'en eut moins de gloire;
Qui du seigneur de Langé sa cronique
Verra, sçaura qu'il a eu la pratique
De gouverner, soit en paix soit en guerre,
Tout son royaulme, ou myeulx toute la terre.
De son sçavoir et de l'amour aux lettres
De ses escriptz tant en prose qu'en mettres,
Je m'en tairay: ilz sont assez congneuz.
De son trespas le bon Castellanus,
Qu'il avoit fait evesque de Mascons,
En a escript affin que ne doubtons
Que co roy là, tant beau, saige et bien né,
De biens, d'honneurs grandement fortuné,

To soothe her people ere she should depart.
She said to him, "Do hush you words and noise!
My spirit is now in repose, its poise   4392
No more on earth! You drive me from my mind!"
Her daughter, quick to aid, was close behind.
"Leave her," she said. "For she but waits to see
The promise of divine sublimity.   4396
Goods, children, servants, honors, though profuse,
She deems no more than surplus and refuse.
For heaven she forgets all mortal things;
God raises her among the noblest kings.   4400
For his wife and spouse he will have sought her."
Countess Louise answered then her daughter:
"That is well said, my dear. It's true. You're right!"
Her fading eyes not straying from the height, 4404
She kissed the cross, and no more did she tell
But gave some sign that she could still hear well
And straightway turned to All her tender glance.
She seemed to see with smiling countenance,   4408
In clarity, her God, All-engrossing;
And that moment made her final crossing
Quietly; her daughter, but no other,
Noticed; all the rest asked if her mother   4412
Were yet dead; it involved them in dispute.
Thus passed one worthy of elite repute,
Living and dying, for love she was known,
True expectation, faith in God alone.   4416
And through this death, Dear, you must recognize

As clear: the more God lets temptation rise
The more He shows Himself the tempted's friend
Who helps Him bring Old Tempter to an end.   4420
Find you virtue in this last example
No adducement to a faith more ample?
May I remind you, Dear, the same did He
With her son Francis, prince of royalty,   4424
In virtue, race, and name superior,
Who frequently engaged in waging war
And over foes was oft victorious;
And, captured, was then no less glorious.   4428
Whoever sees De Langé's chronicle
Will know that his regime [canonical]
Prevailed in time of peace and time of war:
Of all his realm, nay earth, the governor.   4432
Of his love of letters and his learning,
Writings prose and verse, his fine phrase-turning,
I'll say nothing; they're adequately known.
Good Castellanus, of his death, has shown   4436
(Macon bishop whom François selected)
Writing lest some question be injected,
That this handsome, wise king, family proud,
With goods and honors splendidly endowed,   4440

N'eut on son cueur la foy vive et ardante,
Qui par dehors n'estoit tant evidente
Qu'on le jugeast ung devot Saint Loÿs;
Mais, par ung mot qu'ung jour de luy j'ouys,
Ce qu'avez fait come je croy, m'Amye,
Ceste foy vive en luy ne doubtay mye,
Disant: «Sachez icy, en ce festin,

Fol. 340 v°

«Si Dieu mandoit que demain au matin
«Il me faillust par mort le veoir au ciel,
«En ce banquet n'y a sucre ne miel
«Qui si doulx soit à la friande langue
«Comme à mon cueur seroit ceste harangue,
«Et ne desire à vivre longuement
«Pour d'un tel bien avoir retardement;
«Digne n'est pas d'avoir ung si bon maistre
«Qui n'a desir par mort avec luy estre.»
Je diray plus que onques je ne viz,
En ces plaisans et gracieux devis,
Que l'on eust dit: «C'est homme icy habunde,
Sans craindre Dieu, en tous plaisirs du monde»;
Qui se quelqu'un soudain propoz tenoit
Parlant de Dieu, la larme luy venoit
A l'œil, monstrant l'esprit n'estre empesché
D'aymer son Dieu, nonobstant qu'à peché
Servist le corps par sa fragilité;
Car de peché venoit humilité.
Si parfaict fut en sa condition,
Que si peché quelque imperfection
N'eust myse en luy, dont estoit exempé,
De trop d'orgueil il eust esté tempté.
Si haultement son bon esprit volloit
Et de son Dieu si vivement parloit,
Que si Satan Dieu ne luy eust donné
Dedans sa chair, eguillon ordonné
Pour abbesser de soy mesmes l'estime,
Orgueil l'eust mys au plus grant de la cime.
Donc en la chair à peché il servoit, Fol. 341
Mais en l'esprit la foy il conservoit,
Qui le faisoit en soy humilier,
Et à Dieu par forte amour lyer;
Et ceste foy, laquelle avoit receue
De bien longtempts, monstra à son yssue
Ce que voz yeulx ont veu et non les miens,
Dont vous heureuse et moy malheureux tiens.
Souvienne vous que sa mort il congneut;
Souvienne vous qu'humblement il receut
Ses sacremens, que tous il demanda;
Souvienne vous de ce qu'il commanda
Au roy son filz, par grande affection,
Auquel donna sa benediction;
Souvienne vous comme il se confessa

Had in his heart faith and endeavorment,
That outside was not quite so evident
That one would take him for a devotee
Like good Saint Louis; I think you, like me,   4444
My dear, could doubt his faith no more the day
That you and I heard he had this to say:
"Know ye here, around this good feasting drawn:

If God commanded that, tomorrow's dawn   4448
Through death, in heaven I must our Lord greet,
This banquet has no honey and no sweet
To tempt my palate, which would love such meal,
As to my heart such news would have appeal;   4452
And I don't want to live a lengthy while
Delaying all the good things of this style.
Unworthy of a Lord whose heart's so fond,
Is one who'd spurn to be with Him, beyond,"   4456
And I shall add that there has never been
Among the pleasantries one that could mean:
"This man without the fear of God doth take
His fill of worldly pleasures, like a rake."   4460
And if someone should offer a remark
On God, the tears, as if one struck a spark,
Filled his eyes: his soul was not impeded,
Loving God, although he had conceded   4464
His flesh to sin through instability;
For, from this sin had come humility.
And so splendid was this king's condition,
Had not sin been in his composition —   4468
Imperfection otherwise exempted —
To excessive pride he'd have been tempted.
So high did Francis' spirit used to soar,
And of our Lord so sanguinely he'd roar —   4472
Had God omitted from him the devil
(Shaft inside his flesh designed to level
A bloated estimation of himself),
Why, pride had sent him to its highest shelf!   4476
If it was sin that in the flesh he served,
It still was faith the spirit had preserved
That caused him to be humble in his pride
And to his God by strong love always tied.   4480
This faith, the one he had received long since,
Appeared to grace the farewell of this prince,
To which your eyes were able to attest,
Not mine. I was deprived while you were blessed. 4484
Remember that his death he had perceived.
Recall that it was humbly he received
The sacraments, all by him requested.
Think of orders that he then suggested   4488
To the crown's heir, Henri, how he caressed
With great affection this king, son he blessed.
Remember, he confessed himself to be

Pecheur damné, et jamais ne cessa
De tous ses maulx humblement s'accuser
Sans se vouloir d'un tout seul excuser;
Souvienne vous que biens ny royaulté,
Sçavoir, povoir, force, santé, beaulté,

D'habandonner ne monstroit nul regret,
Ce qu'il disoit tout hault, non en secret;
Souvienne vous comme son cueur ardoit
Parlant de Dieu, duquel il attendoit
De son salut vraye finition,
Se confiant en ceste passion
De Jesuchrist, dont le meritte est tel
Qu'il n'y a nul peché ne si mortel
Que par ce sang ne soit estainct sans faincte,
Demandant grace en s'asseurant sans craincte
Que Dieu est bon, et sa promesse il tient,
Fol. 341 v°
Quand humblement vers luy le pecheur vient.
Souvienne vous qu'en eslevant ses yeulx,
Comme voyant par foy son Tout aux cyeulx,
Luy demandoit de cueur humble et humain
Qu'il luy donnast sa très puyssante main,
Se confessant remply de pesanteur
Par son peché, parquoy du Redempteur,
De ceste main clouée en croix l'aïde
Il demandoit, sachant que c'est la guyde
Qui peult mener le povre viateur
Entre les braz du puyssant Createur.
Souvienne vous que ses braz estandoit
Et sa main grande ouverte à Dieu tendoit,
Duquel par foy congnoissoit le secours
Estre très seur à son dernier discours;
Souvienne vous de l'ardeur de sa foy
Qui le poussoit à Dieu dessus soy,
En s'asseurant que sa misericorde
Luy pardonnoit sa vie salle et orde,
Et que sa grace en sa main il tenoit
Ou ses pechez sa bonté pardonnoit.
Souvienne vous de ses propoz et dictz,
Et comme en foy demandoit paradis
Que justement disoit avoir perdu
Par son peché, mais que du tout rendu
Il luy estoit par le sang et meritte
De Jesuchrist, par lequel l'homme heritte,
Non pas par soy, le celeste heritaige;
Souvienne vous comme en ferme courage
Il s'asseuroit en Dieu, par la bonté Fol. 342
Duquel peché et l'enfer est dumpté.
Las! je sçay bien que vous n'oublierez pas
Qu'ung peu avant qu'il deust passer le pas,
A dire adieu aux siens il s'efforça,

A lost soul and recited stubbornly   4492
The sins of which he wished himself accused,
Unwilling for a one to be excused.
Think of it! Not wealth nor royal duty,
Knowledge, power, strength, not health nor
  beauty   4496
To be jettisoned cost him one regret,
A thought he spoke aloud, no secret fret.
Remember also how his heart would light
At talk of God, on whom he kept his sight: 4500
Source and aim of ultimate salvation;
He put trust in Jesus's oblation,
Wherein he knew Christ's merit to be such
That there could be no mortal sin too much   4504
But by this blood were cleansed—it could not fail—
And, asking mercy, trusting without wail
That God is good and to His promise true

When sinners humbly come His peace to sue.   4508
Recall, it was in faith he raised his eyes
Like one who saw his All amid the skies;
With humble, human heart he shed command
And asked that God lend him His stalwart hand,   4512
Confessed himself one filled with heaviness
Of sin, asked aid of Him who made redress,
That hand that on the cross was nailed, to lead
Him, knowing that it can so intercede,   4516
Shepherding the erring supplicator
To the mighty arms of the Creator.
Pray recall the monarch's arms beseeching,
That his open hand for God was reaching,   4520
The one he'd known through faith to be help's source,
As in his last speech he affirmed with force.
Pray recall his faith and its resplendence
Lighting him to God and to transcendence,   4524
Assuring him God's mercy would include
A pardon for his life though soiled and lewd,
And that His grace our Lord then to him gave,
In that God's goodness all his sins forgave.   4528
And now recall remarks, his words precise,
And how in faith he asked for paradise,
Which, in all justice, said he, he had lost
Through sin; but everything sin should have cost   4532
Was returned through Jesus' blood and merit,
Through whom man's permitted to inherit —
Not through himself — celestial heritage.
Recall with what firm courage he'd allege   4536
His trust: God's goodness was the medium
By which one's sin and hell were overcome.
Yes, I well know that you will not forget
That, just before the step, not passing yet,   4540
To all his own he tried to bid adieu.

Et par amour ung chacun embrassa,
Les consolant de son soudain depart,
Dont vostre cueur sentit de dueil sa part.
Souvienne vous que son esprit ce jour
Dedans son corps ne peut faire sejour,
Car, ayant pris son dernier sacrement,
En declairant au long par testament
Ce qu'il vouloit, ayant dit le surplus
A son cher filz, voyant qu'il n'avoit plus
Chose çà bas qu'il faillust ordonner,
Devers son Dieu se print à retourner,
Remply d'amour ardante et de foy forte,
Laissa son corps et passa par la porte
De ceste mort, que si doulce esprouva
Que dedans elle et vie et Tout trouva;
Ce que l'on vit, car son corps sain et fort
Ne fist semblant de ce dernier effort:
Pas n'est raison que le corps douleur sente
A ce jour là, puysque l'ame est contante.
Ainsy ce roy en son Tout fut receu,
Car il avoit ce Tout par foy conceu
Tant que prison, maladie ou douleur,
Tristesse, ennuy, perte d'amys, malheur,
Ne l'ont point fait tant soit peu murmurer,
Mais doulcement tous ses maulx endurer;
Prosperité ne l'a mys en orgueil   Fol. 342 v°
Pour mescongnoistre ou destourner son oeil
De son Seigneur, où par foy revenoit;
Et si peché çà bas le proumenoit
En le menant en region loingtaine,
Il retournoit souvent à la fontaine
De penitence, parquoy Jesus, venu
Pour les pecheurs qui l'ont creu et congneu,
Rompant du sens charnel le jugement,
L'a prins à soy, où eternellement
Avec luy regne, et çà bas a regné,
Car il estoit pour estre vray roy né.
A ce Rien donq, que long temps j'ay laissé,
Retourner fault, lequel s'est abessé
A regarder par la senestre bende
Son tout en tous qui tous les maulx amende,
Car, soit en mort, tristesse ou passion,
Ce Tout, qui est remply d'affection,
Ne sçauroit tant nostre corps lapider
Que nostre esprit il ne vienne aÿder;
Et qui le voit au milieu du tourment
Le tourmenteur tourmentant doulcement,
Non pas ainsy que l'avons desservi
Pour ne l'avoir ny aymé ny servi,
Mais ung petit, comme enfans, nous chastie,
Nous departant ung peu de sa rostie
Affin qu'ayons memoire que rostir

With love he clasped each one—they were not few—
Consoling each that he must soon depart.
Your share of grief is still felt in your heart.   4544
That day, recall, his spirit, though confined
In body, could no longer stay behind.
He, having taken final sacrament,
Explained his wish at length by testament,   4548
And told the rest to his son dear [since birth];
And seeing he'd no further task on earth
That of necessity was his concern,
To God he undertook then to return;   4552
And, filled with ardent love, strong faith innate,
He left his body and passed through the gate
Of death. It proved sweetness. He discovered
In it both the All and life recovered!   4556
One saw, because his body strong and whole
Lacked signs of any final effort's toll.
No reason had his body to feel pain
That day, for joy holds sway in soul's domain.   4560
Thus was this king into the All received
Because he had, through faith, this All perceived
Till prison, suffering, or sickliness,
Grief, worry, loss of friends, until distress   4564
Could force from him no tiniest complaint,
But he could bear his ills with self-restraint.
Prosperity did not inflate his pride,
Make him deny, or turn his eye aside   4568
From God, where, heeding faith, he would adhere;
And if, on earth, sin causing him to veer,
He was led off to region far astray,
He oft returned with penitent dismay   4572
To Jesus, fount of penitence, who came
To sinners that believed and called His name;
Who, separating truth from carnal sense,
Took Francis to Himself; from which day hence   4576
He reigns with him; as here below he reigned,
Because he was a true king foreordained.
To Nothing, whom I have some while ignored,
I must return, to that one who was lowered   4580
To look left-hand to see His all in All
Which compensates for evils that befall.
For, in death or pain or sad dejection,
All is filled with such sincere affection   4584
It could not, in such way, our bodies stone
And fail to help our spirits, to atone.
One sees Him in the midst of one's distress:
Tormentor punishing with tenderness,   4588
Not in proportion as we have deserved
Who've loved Him little and but little served.
He chastens as for children one makes shift:
He deals to us small portion of His shrift,   4592
Giving us remembrance through the token

S'est fait pour nous, et que devons sentir
En nostre cueur ung grand contantement,
Quand ung morceau nous donne seulement
De son dur pain, qu'il a pour nous masché,
Fol. 343
Voire avallé en la croix attaché;
Nous l'avallons, mais point ne le goustons
Quand de sa mort la vertu nous doubtons;
Et onques nul, qui à luy s'attendit,
Son ame à Dieu en douleur ne rendit.
Mais ceulx qui n'ont ny amour ny foy vive
En ce Tout là, quand ce vient à la rive
Et qu'on leur dit: «Amy, mourir vous fault»,
Oyant cryer Jesus, le cueur leur fault,
Et tant plus sont affoibliz et malades,
Les fault tenir, tant ilz font de gambades.

J'en ay congneu en extresme vieillesse,
Plains de tous maulx et de grande foiblesse,
Qui à la mort en fais[oie]nt des grimaces
De piedz, de mains, comme bouffons en farces:
C'estoit l'esprit voyant son jugement,
Qui craignoit tant ce dur departement
D'ame et de corps, que la chair tourmentoit,
Qui quant à soy peu de douleur sentoit.
J'en ay congneu, ainsy que j'ay compté,
Desquelz la foy avoit le cueur dumpté,
Qui en mourant d'un gracieux couraige
Sans faire myne, ainsy qu'ung bel ymaige,
Ont ce dur pas saulté, que leurs corps
Fussent puyssans, jeunes et sains et fortz.
J'en ay congneu de vie bien mondayne
Par le dehors, où foy n'a esté vaine,
Car à la mort les a tant secouruz
Qu'à leur Saulveur sans doubter sont couruz;
Et confessant leur juste damnement Fol. 343 v°
Ilz ont trouvé en luy leur saulvement,
Ne se fians qu'en ses œuvres parfaictes,
Et de celles que vivant [avoient] faictes,
Ne trouvoient rien qu'ordure et puanteur;
En s'arrestant du tout au Redempteur,
Qui leur estoit misericordieux
Comme peché leur estoit odieux,
Et puys que Rien devant luy [s'estimoient,]
Trouvoient en luy le Tout que tant aymoient.
L'ayant trouvé après l'avoir perdu,
Ont leur esprit si doulcement rendu
Entre ses mains, que Dieu estoit louable
Rendant la mort [et] doulce et amyable.
J'en ay congneu de vie pure et munde

Autant qu'on peult veoir et juger le monde

That for us His body was thus broken;
We, in our hearts, a great content should sense
When but a piece He does to us dispense   4596
Of His hard bread that for us He has chewed,
Yea, swallowed while attached upon the rood.
We partake without appreciation
When we doubt the consubstantiation.   4600
No one who ever counted on the Lord,
In suffering his soul to God restored.
But those who have not love nor faith that burns
In All, come where the shore to current turns   4604
And being told, "You are about to die,"
Lose heart when they hear someone's "Jesus cry";
So much the more enfeebled and made ill,
They must be held, limbs dancing with death's
chill;   4608
And I have seen some folk extremely old
Who, having every illness flesh can hold,
Made their deathbed gestures and grimaces
Like the clowns of farce, both limbs and faces.   4612
This was the spirit facing its last test,
Which feared hard separation from the rest:
The split of soul from bodily torments,
Which, on its part, meant little it could sense.   4616
As I have said above, I have known some
Whose heart by faith had been so overcome
That, dying, having courage through God's grace,
Their features formed a perfect picture face;   4620
Without grimace the cruel step was leapt.
Though they'd strong bodies, healthy, young, adept.
I have known some whose lives appeared mundane
Outside, in whose case faith was nowise vain;   4624
At death by faith these folk were succoréd
For they'd no doubt and to their Savior sped.
By confessing they deserved damnation,
They had found in Him, Lord Christ, salvation.   4628
These, trusting only in His words complete —
While in their own life's work, accomplished feat,
They'd nothing not malodor nor foul waste —
Found, when with the Redeemer all was placed,   4632
The One who was to them compassionate,
As sin became the object of their hate
And they, beside Him, Nothing in their thought,
In Him, the whole that they so loved they caught.   4636
And, having found All after all was lost,
So meekly gave the spirit as they crossed
Into His hands that God won from them praise
For giving death a mild and kindly phase.   4640
I have known some whose lives would show no
smudge
As far as persons of the world could judge,

94

Jeusneurs, prieurs, faisans grandes merveilles,
Mais quand failloit crier à leurs aureilles
Ce mot: «Jesus», en lieu d'un grant mercys,
L'on les voyoit estonnez et transiz
En crainte et peur, cherchans pardons [et]
    bulles,
Pour s'asseurer dix mille scrupules;
Car leurs bienfaictz où ilz s'estoient fundez,
Quant à la mort et pesez et sundez,
Les leur monstroit la divine justice,
Devant laquelle est nostre vertu vice;
Ilz se trouvoient appuyez d'un roseau
Qui leur perçoit jusques à l'os la peau,
Car, sans la foy, n'y a œuvre plaisante
Au Createur et qui ne soyt nuysante
A celluy-là qui du tout s'y confie. Fol. 344
Et j'en ay veu, je le vous certiffie,
De tourmentez pour n'avoir pas apris
De se fier au meritte et grant pris
De Jesuchrist, lequel par grace est nostre,
Dont leur povre ame en craincte passant oultre
Leurs corps faisans tant effroyables mynes
Que l'on povoit congnoistre leurs ruynes.
Las! le corps fort ny la vie joyeuse
Ne rend la mort dure et laborieuse;
Le faible aussy ny la vie apparente
Ne fait la mort amye ny parente;
Mais la foy vive rend au cueur la mort belle,
Comme elle est laide au pecheur infidelle.
O leger Rien, volant du fondz d'enfer
Jusqu'au plus hault dont partit Lucifer,
Puys d'Orient jusques en Occident,
Le bien et mal t'est monstré évident.
Que trouves tu, çà et là te tournant?
Tu trouves Tout en tous tout contenant;
Tout en enfer tu voys justicier
Ceulx qui n'ont sceu ce Tout remercier
De ses bienfaictz, ne de luy les tenir,
Sans congnoissance, amour ny souvenir
De sa bonté; mais ce Tout incongneu
Et refusé du grand bien, qu'obtenu
Avoit pour eulx de grace entierement,
Est en enfer le plus amer tourment:
Car voyant Dieu, duquel ils sont bannis,
Tant plus est bon, et tant plus sont punys,
Et n'est douleur qui soit tant importable
                                Fol. 344v°
Qu'estre privé du seul bien desirable.
Que trouve[s] tu en la prosperité,
En l'orient, en la diversité,
A cette dextre où est toute habundance?
Tout y est seul en sa belle ordonnance,

Great fasters, marvel-workers, and pray-ers,
But when one cried "Jesus!" in their ears,   4644
One saw great fright instead of gratitude;
In sudden shock and chill they could be viewed,
In their conduct showing apprehension,
They sought pardons, bulls, and such attention. 4648
For, when good deeds, on which they had founded
Hope regarding death, were weighed and sounded,
God's merit showed their own would not suffice.
In contrast, all our virtue is but vice.   4652
They found themselves supported by a reed
That pierced their skins and to the bone would lead;
Because, without the faith, no work can charm
The great Creator; it but brings to harm   4656
The one who'd wholly on himself rely.
And some of them—this I can certify—
I saw in torment since they had not learned
To trust themselves to merit Jesus earned,   4660
That through God's grace is ours in our despond,
And these poor souls who feared to pass beyond
Had twisted body and such fearful face
That one could read their ruin and disgrace.   4664
It is not health nor custom to exult
In life that renders dying difficult;
Yet, plodding like a sickly peregrine
Does not make death one's lover nor his kin.   4668
Warm faith gives death a beauty with largess;
But, to the faithless sinner, ugliness.
Light Nothing, winging from the depths of hell
To that most high whence Lucifero fell,   4672
Then sweeping from the east to occident,
The good and bad to you is evident.
What do you find here and there as you twirl?
Do you find All contained in all, awhirl?   4676
In hell's depths do you see true justice fall
On those who did not learn to thank the All
And not to take from Him His benefits
Without requital, love, or thought that fits   4680
His goodness; but this All that they disdained
Ungrateful for the great good He'd obtained
For them, through God's grace, for their enjoyment
Is in Hades its most bitter torment: 4684
For, seeing God, from whom they are exiled,
So excellent, the damned feel more reviled;
No punishment exists that is so dire:
To be denied the one good they desire.   4688
What do you find amid prosperity
And in the East, in the diversity
Upon the right where all abundance is?
There's only All in its fine ordnancies;   4692

95

Et rien que Tout n'y peulx considerer,
Qu'en chascun lieu veulx et doibz reverer,
Le congnoissant le bien des biens, l'honneur
De tous honneurs, la vray plaisir du cueur,
Vertu par qui porte fleur, fueille et fruict,
Ignoramment l'arbre; et ung cueur instruict
De ce seul Tout ne fait, ne dit, ne pense
Que ce que veult le Tout, lequel l'avance
Ou le retarde ainsy qu'il détermine.
Quand tous ces biens au vray tu examine,
Tu dis heureux ceulz qui ce Tout congnoissent
Dans les beaultez qui dehors apparoissent,
Et malheureux qui s'arreste à l'externe.
Sans passer oultre au Tout qui tout governe.
Que trouves tu en l'occident senestre,
En mort, trouvant ennuy depuis la teste
Jusqu'à la fin en guerre et en procès,
En maladie, en injure, en excès,
Portans gibetz, lances, canons, espée
Dont la vie est avant son but coupée?
Le Tout en tous qui glorieusement
Les uns punit voire à leur damnement,
Et ses esleuz chastie en amytié,
Ayant tousjours à la fin d'eulx pitié;
Et [qui] ce Tout dans les maulx peult
    comprendre,   Fol. 345
Il luy sera facile de les prendre
Bien doulcement, et qui ne l'y peult voir
S'en va tumber au fondz du desespoir;
Qui meurt sans Tout en desespoir habunde;
Qui meurt en Tout n'a point de mort seconde.
O Rien, qui es plain de felicité
En renonçant aux yeulx de cecité,
Voyant des yeulx du Tout et non des tiens,
Au fondz d'enfer, en tous maulx, en tous biens,
[Ton seul Tout] voys. Mais dy moy plus avant;
Quand tu t'en vas sus les ælles du vent,
Que trouves tu au ciel entre les sainctz?
Tu trouves Tout, duquel ilz sont tous plains,
Tout, qui de tous est la beatitude,
Tout, seul vivant en ceste multitude,
Tout, qui en tous s'ayme par son amour,
Tout, qui se loue en tous et nuict et jour;
Tout, ung seul feu, qui par ses estincelles
Purge, nettoye et fait apparoir belles,
Sans vice aucun, les lampes attachées
A ce hault ciel, qui ont esté tachées,
Estant çà bas, par peché qui ne tasche
Que de noircir nostre blanc par sa tache.
Mais ce feu chault ayant purgé le verre,
Le separant de sa boue et sa terre,
Le rend si clair, et net de toute ordure,

No other thing but All can you see here
That in each place you must and would revere,
Knowing Him of all things good the measure,
Honor of all honors, heart's true pleasure,   4696
The force by which the tree is made to bear
Its flower, leaf and fruit — though unaware.
Hearts taught by unique All do but opine
And speak and act as wills the All divine,   4700
Advanced, retarded, as All must decide.
When all these goods in true light you have eyed,
You call those blest who see that All is here
Inside the beauties which outside appear,   4704
And curst the ones who stop at the outside,
Not penetrating to see All preside.
What do you find upon the left-hand, west,
In death, as you consider the distressed,   4708
From start to end in war and court process,
In illness, insult, in outrageousness,
In prisons, gibbets, lances, cannon, blade
By which life is before its goal waylaid?   4712
All, who by His glory's revelation
Punishes some people with damnation,
And chastens His elect as would a friend
Does always show them mercy in the end;   4716
And if the concept of the Whole is kept

In trials, pains are easy to accept;
If one can not perceive the great All there,
One tumbles to the bottom of despair.   4720
Who dies without All, in despair abounds;
Who dies in All gives death no second rounds;
Your joys, O Nothing, mount up to the skies
As you now strip the blindfold from your eyes   4724
To see through eyes of All, and not your own;
In every good and ill, hell's nether zone,
Your single All you see. But tell me more
While rising on the wings of wind to soar;   4728
In heaven's saints what do you find instilled?
You find the All, with which they all are filled,
That is of each the full beatitude,
Sole animation of this multitude.   4732
All, that's by all men loved through His own love,
Is praised in all, both night and day above:
A single flame which with its many sparks
Cleans, purifies, and with new beauty marks   4736
The lamps now without stain that have been swung
In this high heaven, which were stained and hung
In bonds below by sin that merely strains
To polish our clear crystal by its stains.   4740
But this hot fire, once having purged the glass
In separating it from earth and mass,
Makes it so clear and clean of every dross

Qu'il est luysant encontre sa nature;
Ce Tout, ce feu, ceste vraye lumiere,
En toute lampe et en toute maniere,
Reluit si fort en tous les sainctz et sainctes,

Fol. 345 v°

Qui lampes sont sans jamais estre estainctes,
Par ce feu là qui en soy les rassemble
Que feu chacune et non verre ressemble;
Et plus ce feu à bas les a polies,
Et plus là hault sont claires et jolies.
Qui plus çà bas de poliment reçoit,
Là hault plus clair le feu s'y apperçoit,
Et tant plus est le verre extenué,
Poly, fourby, en soy diminué,
Plus la beaulté du feu [s'y] monstre claire,
Et plus ce feu par elles nous esclaire,
Et les vertuz et graces naturelles
De ce feu là voyt on reluyre en elles;
Et qui ce feu en elles ne verroit,
Ceste lueur venir d'elles croyroit,
Mais qui congnoist le Tout en tous n'a garde
De se tromper en chose qu'il regarde.
O contant Riens, qui plus Riens t'apperçoys
Et plus le Tout tu congnoys et conçoys.
Las! que ce Tout plus ardant que nul cierge
Tu as congneu en la benoiste Vierge,
Mere du filz qui à rien nous a mys
Pour à la fin au Tout estre remis!
O que ce Rien pleut à ceste pucelle
Quand elle dist: «Voicy de Dieu l'ancelle»,
Quand elle dist que sa nichilité,
Son povre Rien, bassesse, humilité,
Son Dieu avoit par pitié regardée,
Et qu'elle estoit par ce regard gardée
De l'ord venin du veneneux serpent,

Fol. 346

Qui sur tout homme au monde le respand;
Plus qu'autre femme en son cueur elle avoit
Ce Rien, lequel gardoit et conservoit
En s'unissant à luy de son bon gré,
Et s'abessant jusqu'au plus bas degré
Du povre Rien; le vray Tout, desireux
De ce Rien là dont il est amoureux,
Pour ce qu'à Rien soubzmyse la trouva,
Dedans son Tout si très hault l'esleva
Qu'on ne sçauroit dire au celeste lieu
Si elle est lampe ou si elle est pur feu,
Car si fort est son verre cristalin
Puriffié que le beau feu divin
S'y voit si clair, l'ayant puriffiée,
Que sa lampe est toute déiffiée.
Purgée fut par preservation
De tous pechez, par tribulation,

That, counter to its nature, it has gloss; 4744
This All, this fire, true illumination
In each lamp and every situation,
Glows in saints and lends such strong distinction
They are lamps not destined for extinction 4748
By the fire that in itself assembles
Them; but fire, not glass, each one resembles;
And, as the fire below has polished them,
The more above they shine like some bright gem. 4752
The more one gets of polishing below,
The brighter in the sky he's seen to glow.
As the glass is furbished, levigated,
In itself reduced, extenuated, 4756
The beauties of the fire more clearly flare;
And, through them, thus, the more it lights us there.
In them, also, one sees that light to glow,
Its virtues and its natural grace to show. 4760
And he who would not see in them this fire
Would take each lamp to be its own supplier.
Whoever, though, the All in all can meet,
In things he looks on, does not fear deceit. 4764
The more you see yourself, O Nothing, small,
Content, the more you meet and know the All.
More brilliant than a taper ever shone,
All, in the Blesséd Virgin, you have known, 4768
The mother of Him who set us at naught
So that to All at last once more we're brought!
Oh, how this Nothing pleased the maiden sweet
Who said: "Behold in me the Lord's helpmeet." 4772
She said that God saw her nihility,
Poor-Nothing lowliness, humility,
And through pity looked in her direction;
And that this regard gave her protection 4776
From the loathesome serpent's venal poison
That it gives each male on earth in foison.
More than the other women, she possessed
This Nothing, which she guarded in her breast, 4780
Uniting with it and of her own grace,
Demoting herself to the lowest place
Of merest Naught. The true All, one eager
For that Nothing, lover of the meager, 4784
Finding her to Nothingness submitted,
Raised her to His All, so high admitted
That none could say in His divine empire
If she were lamp or if she were pure fire 4788
Because, so greatly is her crystaline
Glass purified, fair fire divine within
Is seen, so clear that since He purified
This lamp, it is quite wholly deified. 4792
She was made pure due to preservation
From all sins and to her tribulation,

Et par la foy en Celluy qu'elle creut,
Dont charité si fort en elle acreut,
Que par son feu monstra la lampe pure
Sans le povoir d'humaine creature,
Dont par sus tous plaine de Dieu reluict
Au lieu où est jour eternel sans nuict.
Diligent Rien regardant ceste lampe,
Où Tout en Rien se voit myeulx qu'en
l'estampe,
Je m'esbahy qu'en ce lieu ne t'arrestes,
Mais je voy bien que ton vol tu aprestes
D'aller plus hault, et que ton vol et course
N'aura repoz [jusqu'à] ce qu'à la source
Soys arrivé; or sus, Rien, que dis tu Fol. 346 v°
En aprochant la divine vertu?
Ne voys tu pas en ung Dieu troys personnes?
Racomptes m'en, mais quoy? mot tu ne
sonnes?
Ne voys tu pas une seulle unité,
Ung tout seul Dieu en une trinité,
Puyssant et saige et bon: ce sont bien troys,
Mais en ces troys seule deité croys.
Ne voys tu pas le grant povoir du Pere,
Qui tout a fait et qui partout impere?
Ne vois tu pas du Filz la sapience
Par qui avons du Pere la science,
Qui triumpher fait nostre humanité?
Ne voys tu pas l'amour, la charité
Du Saint Esprit qui chacun illumine,
Luy declarant comme il fault qu'il chemine?
Et ces troys là ne sont qu'ung toutesfoys;
O Rien, ravy où es tu ceste foys?
Amoureux Rien, forte amour te fait fondre,
Tant que ne sens ou ne me veulx respondre!
Ceste clarté te fait en toy tenir
Et en ce Tout pour jamais mainctenir;
Ce grant esprit et ce feu consummant
Met Rien en Tout, comme au commancement
En Rien avoit mys l'homme et sa puyssance,
Et mainctenant donne à Rien jouyssance
De ce Tout là qui pour luy s'est courbé
Affin que Rien en luy fust absorbé.
O puyssant Tout, Elisée prophete,
Qui sur l'enfant, le mort, la chose infecte,
Te fait petit, courbé et à luy joinct, Fol. 347
Parquoy le mort, où vie n'estoit point,
Receut de toy ce qu'en toy seul estoit;
Ainsy ce Rien qui nul bien ne congnoist,

Par ce grand Tout, qui pour luy fut petit,

Ravit d'en hault, la force et appetit.

Also by faith in this One whom she knew.
His love in her so greatly did accrue   4796
That, through her lamp, Pure Light's epiphany
Shone without dint of man's ability;
Whence over all it shines, filled with God's light
Where there is but eternal day, no night.   4800
Choice Nothing, watching where is seen more bright
Than in the print the All-in-Nothing's light,

I'm shocked that at this point you do not rest.
I see that you prepare your flight addressed   4804
To go much higher, that your flight and course
Will know no rest until the very source
You've reached. Aloft now, Null, what do you say
As you draw near God's virtue on your way?   4808
Do you not see one God in three there found?
Tell me of this. But what? No word you sound?

Do you not see a whole in trinity,
A singleness in God's divinity?   4812
The powerful, the wise, the good? Yea, three;
But in these three, I think, one deity.
You see the father magisterial
Who made the whole and reigns imperial?   4816
Do you not see the wisdom of the Son
Through whom our knowledge of the Father's won,
That leads humanity to victory?
Do you not see love's benedictory,   4820
The Holy Ghost that brings to each the light
Instructing him how he must go aright?
And those three, are they, notwithstanding, one?
This time, O Nothing, whither are you spun?   4824
Love's made you insensate, caused you to melt?
Or don't you wish to tell me what you felt?
The light now makes you in yourself inhere
And in the All forevermore appear.   4828
The Spirit and its fire's consuming burst
Puts Nothing inside All, as, at the first,
In Naught, man and his force it located
And now sees that Nothing is elated   4832
By this great All that for his sake was bent
So that the Nothing into it was blent.
Your prophet called Elisha, O great All,
Above the child, the dead, the thing of pall,   4836
Inclined and joined with it, is You in small;
The dead thereby, where life was not at all,
Received from you what you alone enclose;
And, thus, this Naught, which no such beauty
knows,   4840
Through this great All, which for the Naught was
slight,
Took, from on high, a strength, and appetite.

98

O Rien, en Tout tu es en liberté,
En doulx repoz, en ferme seureté;
Tu ne craindz plus d'estre mys en prison
Ny des beaultez la fine trahyson;
Biens et honneurs et plaisirs tu regardes,
Mais avec toy tu as si bonnes gardes
Que leur povoir ne te pourroit toucher,
Pour ce qu'en toy n'y a morceau de chair;
Car cest Esprit, dont ta liberté tiens,
T'a delivré de tous charnelz lyens.
Parquoy voyant, parlant, beuvant, mangeant,
Ainsy que ceulx que les sotz vont jugeant
Hommes communs, qui de vie commune
Vivent partout sans en choisir pas une,
Pour au dehors se monstrer plus parfaictz,
Ce nonobstant tu ne portes nul faix
De ce peché qui entre par les sens,
Car tu ne voys, ny goustes, ny ne sens
Que ce Tout seul couvert de sa facture:
Cestuy seul est ton regard, ta pasture,
Luy seul tu voys, tu entans et tu manges,
Tu viz de luy et tout en luy te renges;
En luy tu as le sçavoir, les sciences,
Et voys à clair le fondz des consciences;
En luy tu as puyssance et majesté   Fol. 347 v°
Parquoy le mal est de toy rejecté;
Là Bien [es tu] sans contradiction,
Sans sentir plus la malediction
Qui rend la chair à la vertu rebelle.
Tu as trouvé justice originelle
Que le cuyder de l'homme avoit chassée.
Assez l'avoys suyvie et pourchassée,
Mais nul povoir n'avoys de la tenir
[Jusqu'à ce jour qu'à Tout as] peu venir;
Et en ce Tout, o Rien, tu es parfaict,
Bon, juste et sainct, car Cestuy qui t'a fait
Rien, povre et nud, meins qu'ung petit festu,
T'a si très bien de son Tout revestu
Que de malice, ignorance, impuyssance,
En toy se pert toute la congnoissance.
Et puysque Tout t'environne et te cœuvre
Et très à clair l'arche de paix descœuvre,
Povoir, sçavoir et bonté infinie
Pour tout jamais te feront compaignye.
O divin Rien, divinement mys bas,
Divinement monté au vray soulas,
Au vray plaisir, à la joye indicible,
Qui de tous maulx t'a rendu impassible,
De tout peché, de tourment et danger,
Pour en tel lieu si heureux te ranger,
Je te requiers ung petit qu'il te plaise
Nous declarer quelle est ceste grande aise

You, Nothing, in All are at liberty,
In sweet repose, in firm security,   4844
Fear no more to spend a prison season,
Nor by beauties to be dealt fine treason;
Pleasures, wealth, and honors you may review,
But you have such good guardians with you   4848
Their spell could not again contaminate
You, for there is no flesh in your to sate.
The Spirit from whom comes your liberty,
From all the carnal bonds has set you free,   4852
So, though seeing, speaking, eating, drinking
Like the ones whom idiots go thinking
Common men, those whose lives are common run
Live without choosing any special one   4856
That they may look more perfect on display,
You have no load to bear in any way
Of sin that would through senses have entered;
You see, taste, and feel but what is centered   4860
In one All, *His* work covering the sum:
He is your whole concern and pabulum,
The One alone you see, hear, and devour;
You live by placing yourself in His bow'r   4864
In Him you have the lore and sciences
And clearly see heart-deep alliances.
Majesty from Him you have affected
So that evil is by you rejected.   4868
There you are, quite free of contradiction,
No more subject to the malediction
That sets the flesh at odds with purity.
You've found primordial law's security   4872
That man's false faith had heedlessly dismissed.
In search you did sufficiently persist,
But still lacked the power to retain it
Till this day, come unto All, you'd gain it;   4876
And in this All, you, Nothing, are complete,
Good, just and saintly. He by whose receipt
You were made poor and nude, less than a straw,
Has clothed you in His All once more—His law!— 4880
So well that ignorance you do not know,
Nor weakness, and all malice you forego.
And, since the All surrounds and covers you
And brings the ark of peace within your view,   4884
Strength, knowledge, goodness to infinity
Forevermore will you keep company.
O Nothingness divine, divinely sent
To earth, divinely raised to true content,   4888
True pleasure, and to joy one can not tell,
Which made you free of every evil's spell,
Of sin, of pain and danger one might face
To put you in so fortunate a place,   4892
I make a small request, that you will please
Make plain for us what is this boundless ease

Qu'en ce Tout là toy, Rien, experimente,
Qui sans finer tousjours croist et augmente.
Las! tu ne veulx ou ne nous peulx
respondre!   Fol. 348.
Si grant plaisir as de te sentir fondre
Et de te perdre en ce Tout amoureux,
Sans lequel Rien est tousjours langoureux,
Auquel tu as plaisir si amplement
Qu'en toy n'y a penser ne sentement,
Voir ny parler, estre et vie, car Tout,
Qui par sa grace et bonté t'ayme moult,
T'a transformé en Tout, dont je concluz
Qu'en ce Rien là, qui par ce Tout n'est plus,
Parfaictement liberté se recœuvre
Car ce grand Tout fait de Rien son chef
d'œuvre,
Et ce doulx feu de l'esprit consummant
Toute raison de l'humain jugement,
Qui tout cuyder d'estre et sçavoir assomme,
Qui le pur Rien faict concevoir en l'homme;
C'est luy par qui en liberté entiere,
En sa justice et nature premiere,
L'homme est remis, car joinct par cest esprit
A Rien, à mort, à croix en Jesuchrist,
Est fait en luy Rien, mort, crucifié;
Aussy en luy il est déifié,
Uny au Tout et au souverain Bien
Pour estre fait aveques Jesus Rien.
O feu ardant, doulx esprit d'amour plain,
Qui ayant mys Rien à rien, dans le sein
Du puyssant Tout, du grand Tout l'a remis!
O forte amour, à qui Tout est soubzmys
De recevoir ce Rien par ton mistere!
Ceste voix là ne puys ny ne doy taire:
Où l'Esprit est divin et vehement, Fol. 348 v°
La liberté y est parfaictement.

You know as Naught in All, which it foments,
That endlessly increases and augments!   4896
To us you won't or can not answer send?

So great's your pleasure as you come to blend
And lose yourself inside this loving All,
Without which Nothing always comes to pall,   4900
In whom you've pleasure of such amplitude,
No thoughts nor feelings to yourself allude,
No sight, nor speech, no being, nor life touch;
For, All, with grace and goodness does so much 4904
Love you, it's made you All? Then I conclude:
In Nothingness, no longer so construed,
Does liberty, through All, find full release:
For All, of Nothing, makes His masterpiece;   4908

As the Spirit's gentle conflagration
Kindles human reason's arbitration
To subsume being and knowing and plan
And plant pure Nothing in the mind of man;   4912
Man is restored to liberty entire,
To his perfection, to his nature prior,
In All, joined by this Spirit, to accord
With Nothing, death, and cross in Jesus Lord, 4916
In Him made nothing, dead, one crucified,
As in Him also man is deified,
United with the All and sovereign Good
To be with Jesus lifted from selfhood.   4920
O ardent fire, sweet spirit that redressed
Within the All's, the great Almighty's breast,
The Nothing that to nothing it debased!
O great love under whom the whole is placed   4924
Absorbing Nothing through your mystery!
That voice can not, must not be stilled by me:
Where spirit is divine and vigorous,
There liberty in full exists for us.   4928

FIN DU TROISIÈME ET DERNIER LIVRE
DES PRISONS.

END OF THE THIRD AND LAST BOOK OF
LES PRISONS

TEXTUAL NOTES AND VARIANTS

KEY TO MSS AND PRINTINGS IN TEXTUAL NOTES

a = MS. 24.298

b = MS. 1522

c = Excerpt from Leroux de Lincy and Anatole de Montaiglon

d = Abel Lefranc edition, When **d** is listed as sharing a variant and where there appears in the note an accent or apostrophe, it is to be recalled that Lefranc alone used these.

Canto I

Verse 9. a. estimois rires.

19. d. Oh!   a. Ou que voyant souvent.

24. a. Prez bois voiez jardins.

38. a. sa sa.

42. a. Bien qu il a.

51. a. fust.

53. a. fust.

62. d. N'avons. Gaston Paris, "Les Dernières Poésies de Marguerite de Navarre," in *Journal des Savants,* June, 1896, p. 367: N'av'ous. MSS unclear.

66. a, b, d. Si on. Charles Comte, "Le Texte de Marguerite de Navarre" in *Revue de Métrique et de Versification,* vol. I, N° 3, p. 112: S'on.

73. d. harmonie.

80. a, b, d. qu'autre parolle ne voix. Comte, *loc. cit.:* que parolle ne voix.

82. a. En mon oreille.

89-90. a. Ma liberte/ Ma passion.

98. a. Line missing.

107. a. la fenestre.

109. a. Ne d ung baston de ne de deux toises toucher.

115. a. avec.

116. a. The verse is treated as two lines, broken after the sixth syllable.

118. a. les esbatz.

124. a, b, d. seulle. Pierre Courteault, *Revue Critique d'Histoire de la Littérature,* XXX, N° 26, p. 110: seul. *It is the male prisoner who speaks.* b. d estre si icy seulle.

136. a. *Line missing.*

145. a. Il vous plaist de.

151. a. que plus me fortz me tenez.   b. et plus fortz me tenez.   d. que plus fort me tenez.

157. a. Donques.

161. a, d. beau.   b. bien.

165. a. aide. *Diaeresis in b and* d *is deliberate archaism to complete meter.*

167. d. Amye.   a, b, amye.

168. a. a la prison.

169. a. Puis ca puis la puis aimant sa beaulte.

177. a. et aimois.

179. a. par esprouvee.

184. a. *Line missing.*

186. a. Mise a neant.

189. a. que me donnoit.

195. a. Lasse.

200. a. que *omitted.*

204. a. Fors pour luy voyant le temps venue.

205-06. b. *Lines missing.*

207. b. par mon bien.   a, d. pour mon bien.

211. b. pour ouverture plaine.   a, d. par ouverture plaine.

220. *Line must end on fem. syl. for rhyme. Note changed spelling as in MS a, a corrector writes:*   chascuné et chascung̣. ne

231. a. mais plus ne la veoir.

239. a. Pensant le bien gagner.

257. a, b. repare.   d. reparay, *a change to indicate past def., for clarity.*

264. a. la premiere muraille.

265. a. mon doux passee.

271. a. Jouvray.   b. Jouvre.   d. J'ouvray.

272. a. Mais je ne ny voy.

273. a. Et nest.

277. a. Je relieray vous pierres.

290. a. Confirmant mieulx aymant n estre ne.

291. a. Que ne n estre point.

292. a. du dieu mes amoureux.

295. a. ma *omitted.*

298. a. *et* omitted.

299. a. *et* omitted.
304. a, d. envie.   b. amie. Gaston Paris,
    loc. cit.: amie. *The logic of this latter*
    reading is borne out by v. 313, "Si fut
    ce vous," *where the narrator is*
    addressing his lady.
305. a. cest la sa.
309. a. Donner foi si estrange a chose si
    estrange.
311. a. Sil v. [?] fust venu dun tel cas
    madvertir.
313. a. Sil fut ce ne fut autre main.
316. a. Soubz ung regard pour me faire
    advouer.
324. a. Et mon labeur.
328. a. *Line missing, probably caused by*
    rhyme of homonyms.
330-331. a. *Two lines missing.*
331. b, d. je suis ne la place. *Logic suggests*
    de la place.
338. a, b. Je me trouve.   d. Je me trouvay.
339. a. Non celluy. *de* omitted.
341. a, b. Qui.   d. Qu'il.
344. a. aboys.   b. auxboys.   d. aux
    boys. Comte, *op cit.,* p. 114: aux
    aboys, *taking* sanglier *as two syllables.*
    Gustave Lanson, compte rendu de
    Dernières Poésies, in *Revue de*
    l'Histoire littéraire de la France, 1896,
    p. 294: aux bois.
373. a. pour scavoir ce que cestoit.
378. a. Elle te vouldroit tenir.
388. a. donc.   b. car.   d. or.
392. a. ma vye.   b. m amye.
    c. ma mye.
393. d *brackets* s *although it occurs in*
    b: ailleurs.
397. a, b, d. desplyez. *Ryme suggests*
    desployez.
404. a. Que premiere et que nul oeil n en
    pleure. la *omitted.*
406. a, b. navoit.   d. m'avoit.
422. a. dons.   b. dons *stricken and* maulx
    written above.
423. b. Que je ne pense.   a. peusse.
    Unclear between me *and* ne.
    d. Que je me pensay. Paris, *J. des S.,*

1896, p. 367: Que je ne me peusse.
429-30. a. desmollit/ desmollit.
441. b. grosseaux monsseaux.   a. gros
    monceaux.
445. a. sermens.   b, d. sermons. Paris,
    loc. cit.: sermons.
449. a, b, d. justement. Paris, *J. des S.,*
    p. 367: vistement.
451. a. sa vue ou parler. ou *stricken and* le
    written above.
459. a. su bout.
462. b. proposans.   a. transpesans.
    d. transpersans.
465-66. a. plaisoit/complaisoit.
    d. plaisoyt/complaisoyt.
    b. playra/complaira.
476. a. gracieuses.
480. a. d'istoires et mensonges.
484. a, b. feignois.   d. forgeoys.
    a, b. propoz.   d. repoz.
485. a. Line missing.
486. a. Line missing.
500. a, b. enfer.   d. l'enfer.
502. a. ou je ne tenoys.
510. a, b. ay.   d. aye.
525. a. j ay intelligence.
526. a. ma vengeance.
540. d. sceur.   a. b. sceu.   Courteault,
    op. cit., p. 510, *and* Compte, *op. cit.,*
    p. 102: sceu.
549. a, b. Refaictes la.   d. Refaictes
    là.   a, b, d. si elle. Comte, *op. cit.,*
    p. 112: Refaictes la, s'elle.
553. Lefranc. *D. P.,* p. 141, *inserts* là. *This*
    change in line 7 of his page probably
    caused the accent in v. 549, *his third*
    line by confusion with it.
561. d. tont.
570. a. Je n'esjouy voir huys de bien celler.
    b, d. l'huys.
575. b, d. Que lhuys naura mal ne perte.
    Comte, *op. cit.,* p. 114, *points to the*
    correct rhythm of MS. a, *adding his*
    own apostrophes: Que l'huys n'aura
    par elle mal ne perte.

Canto II

622. d. Ne.   a, b. Me.
624. a. veult.
625. a. portans. verdz.

626. a. envie.
636. d. leur grandeur.
640. a. et ce quil veult Il peult.

662. a. nettes et claires.
668. a. allumine.
671. a. par voz aspres effortz.
674. a. defaites.
679. a, b. exercite. d. exercice. Paris, *op. cit.*, p. 367: exercite. a. *verses 680 and 681 are reversed in order from our basic text* b. *In* b, *v. 685 occurs in right margin of 684. Although text is clearly* messagers, *logic suggests* messages.

690. a. se regard.
692. a. me.
693. a.. je voidz. b. La Ou je viz, *the* La *added in left margin.* a, d. Là où.
695. a. Je voidz.
697. a. J advisay. b. Advisay. d. J'advisay.
698. a. cest grandz estangz.
699. a, b. cerf, sanglier (*periods between species in* a). d. cerfz, sangliers.

704. b. pleignent. a, d. prennent.
709. a. Quelque puissance cruaute ou fureur.
711. a. son *written above* empire.
715-16. a. passant/ chassant.
716. a. et autres de cordages.
771-72. a. entreprinse/ prinse.
732. a. toutefoys.
734. a. *Line missing.*
763. a, b. lesse. d. lessay.
764. a. *et omitted before* villes.
768. a. a dorure.
774. a. brusle.
783. a. Las.
795. a. debvoir.
806. b. ou prouffitable. a. et proufitable. d. et prouffitable.

811-812. b. autanticques/ autanticques. a, d. anticques/ autanticques.
812. b. cloches. a, d. clochers.
813. a. ouvrages.
822. b. ouy de diverses manieres. a, d. oys en diverses manieres. Lefranc adds trema, insuring meter: oÿs.

826. a. De veoir ardantz cierges et flambeaux. d. De veoir ardans cierges et flambeaux.
828. a. oreilles. *estonnantes shows gender*

and number agreement with *cloches* although *estonnantes* has a direct object, usage acceptable at that time.
829. d. lors.
834. b. meinctes. a, d. mainctes.
854. a. champs.
857. a. champs.
867-68. a, b. entre/ rencontre. d. entray/ rencontray.
869. a, b. povres et chtifs. d. *omits* et, *rectifying meter.*
892. a. d'acquerre *stricken and* acquere *written above.*
895-96. a. Car par vertu par les armes a ce [?] accreue.
896. b, d. a creue. *Both MSS* a *and* b *show* a *connected to* creue. *It seems to us that Lefranc does well to make the separation since the past indefinite is consistent with the line above.*
905. a. Masques mommons et commedies.
906. a. Entrerent lors furent donc estourdies.
907. a. au bois.
908. a. *Line missing.*
910. a. *Line missing.* b. d. mon ymaige. Gaston Paris, *J. des S.,* juin, 1896, p. 367: non ymaige.
911. d. Et. Paris, *loc cit., restores* Mais *of* a *and* b.
917. a. Et ainsy.
922. b. este *stricken and illegible change written above.*
925. d, *note* (2): Qui me fist = Ce que me fist.
941. a. Et mon honneur sur l'amour pure. 947. qui = que.
952. a. Mais toutefoys jamais ne me marieray.
956. a. *Line missing.*
966. a. *Line missing.*
968. que c'est = ce que c'est que.
970. a. scauray.
975. a. Comment ilz serviz et obeys. sont *omitted.*
976. a. Comment de ceux.
983. a. la fureur.
984. a. brusler.
989. a. Ne m'estonnay de veoir hoster la vie.
991. *Quotation marks added by* Lefranc.
992. a. se me semble.
994. b. *Written in right margin of 993 on two levels.* S'ilz *is missing before* y veulent

994. b. *Written in right margin of 993 on two levels. S'ilz is missing before y veulent* pretendre.
1013-1014. b, d. bien/bien.   a. *Two lines missing.*
1019. a, b. commance.   d. commançay.
1020. b. m avance.   d. m'advançay.
      a. m avncer.
1023. a. Et peu a peu en degre a degre.
1024. a. tant que eusse.
1032. d. Pour avoirs biens.
1043. a. ne me persuadois.   b. je me persuadoys, je *stricken,* ne *substituted above.*   d. je me persuadoys. *Verse is short by one syllable.*
1044. a. Et d acquerir.
1045. a, d. Et vray honneur.
      b. Ce vray honneur.
1048. a. en vouloir.
1049. a. meriter tous biens.
1053. b. leurs histoires.
      a, d. les histoires.
1059. a. Car a tous eulx.
1071. a. Donc.
1089. a. jay trouve
1108. a. sentez grand douleur.
1111. a, b, d. avarice lorde. Comte, *loc cit.:* avarice horde [horridum], Cf. v. 1484.
1119. a. Je connois que prisonnier vous estes.
1143. a. Me fait avoir au monde estime.
1149. a. Et si vous dit.
1165. d. avoir.
1171. a, b. Ne travailler.
      d. Et travailler.
1175. b. *Last two words stricken and correction of uncertain legibility written above.*
1183. par qui = par lequel.
1189. a, b. tenez.   d. teniez.
1191. a. Mieulx vous voulluste.
1197. a. Ou je vous lye prins et captif.
1200. a. *Line missing.*
1205. a. Le bien il vous monstre.
1210. b. doit.   a, d. doibt.
1212. a. engrave et hente.   b. engra [*last two letters uncertain*] et plante.   d. engrané et planté. Paris, *loc. cit.:* engravé et enté. Comte, *op. cit.,* p. 118: engrané et enté.
1220. a. Et l impossible.
1223. a. son feu si peu senty.
1226. a. or et noircy.

1232. a. fust ce le jour de Pasques.
      b, d. fusse le.
1236. a, d. par estime receue.
      b. en estime receue.
1243. a, b, d. si elle. Comte, *op. cit.:* s'elle.
1247. a, b. Et me diriez.   d. Et ne diriez.
1268. a, d. Quant.
1275. a. ny de plus ay envie.
1296. a, b, d. jusques à. Comte, *loc. cit.:* jusqu'à.
1311. a. les ris.
1318. a. Vouldroit jamais avoir si riche este.
1326. a. faict.
1327. a. donnoit.
1328. a. et le plus doux traictement.
1345. a. fortunes.
1357. a. pensant a la fin attaindre.
1376. a. Quaux trois tirans ont eu foi en amour.   b. foy en amour.
      d. foy et amour.
1387. a. Car le desir nouveau desir qui la deceu.
1427. a. Que son ame avoit en la perdant.
1438. a, d. Quant.
1444. b. publique.
1460. a. C est ung bien.
1462. qui = lesquelles.
1489. a. avec.
1515-16. a, b, d. estoffes/ philozophes. *We reverse line order for logic.*
1518. a. et *omitted before* cassé.
1520. a. Tel qu'autour.
1527. a, b, d. Que l'on a prins pour vertu acquerir. Comte, *loc. cit.:* prinses, *the mute syllable not to count at the cesura.*
1529. b. chaste.   a, d. chasteté.
1531. a. la patience.
1524. *is added in right margin of 1533 in seemingly different hand.*
1545-46. b, d. Par qui seront rempliz vos vicieux/ Lyens. Paris, *op. cit.,* p. 367: rompuz. Pierre Courteault, *Revue Critique,* t. XXX, N° 26, p. 509: rompuz.   a. rompuz.
1564. a, b. espargne.   d. espargnay.
1582. dont = de ce que.   b. *Caret follows* Et *and* mercier dont *is written above.*
1588. a. chef *omitted.*
1607. Qui = Ce qui. Cf. Abel Lefranc, *Dernières Poésies* (Paris: Champion, 1896), p. 180, n. (1).

1641 *is written in right hand margin of* 1640.

1642. a. Car ilz sont trois meurtriers inhumains.   b, d. Car ilz sont trop meurtriers inhumains. Comte, *op. cit.*, p. 115: meurtriers (*two syllables*) et inhumains.

1660. a, b, d. de Beatrix et de Dente. Comte, *op. cit.*, p. 112: "L'ancienne forme française est à rétablir ici: de Bietrix et de Dante." Cf. a, b, d, *verse* 1673: Dante.

1661. a. Je n oubliay vous dire.   b, d. Je n'oubliay de vous dire. Comte, *loc. cit.*, supports MS. a.

1662. a. Mectoit en lieu.

1663. d. l'ourse.   a, b. *unclear*. Paris, *loc. cit.*, lonze. Cf. Dante, *Inferno I*, 32: lonza.

1664. a, d. l'on trouve.

1686. a, b. la fuyant hors du monde. d. là fuyant hors du monde. Paris, *loc. cit.*: la suyant.

1692. a. Quant.

1700. b. en *written in small hand above* accented à *before* moy.   a, d. en moy.

1703. d. Qui n'est plus tel.   a, b. Quy = Qu'il *since si of* 1701 *requires it.*

1712. a. onques.

Canto III

1734. a. pauvres.

1735. a. recepvoir.

1737. a. fie.   b. fye.   d. fyay.

1738. a. defie.   b. jedifie.   d. edifiay.

1742. a. ceincture.

1745. a, b. commence.   d. commençay.

1746. a, b. haulse.   d. haulsay.

1751. a. philosophie.

1755. a, b, d. clers. Paris, *J. des S.*, juin, 1896, p. 367: clos.

1760. a. du scavant.   b, d. des scavantz, *imperfect rhyme for* avant.

1763. a. de *omitted before* la poesie.

1766. a. debvoir.

1775. a. J ambrasse donques ces livres en ung temple.   b. J assemble donc ces livres en ung tas.   d. J'assemblay donc ces livres en ung tas.

1778. a. ou la main passetemps trouvay.

1784. a. les scay.

1786. a, b. grave.   d. gravés.

1789. a. pouvoir.

1802. a. volupte.

1808. a. Celuy quy Peult courir dedans la plaine.

1811. a, b, d. d'honneur. Comte, *op cit.*, p. 102: d'honneurs.

1813. a, b, d. fin. *Cf note* 1212 *which shows the possibility of confusing* n *with* v. *A reversal of consonant order would then yield a rhyme for* naïf, *a word frequently found in the company of* argent *as well as in the company of* plaisir: vif.

1818. a. tant en y a.

1821. a. cache dedans.

1830. a. ne moiens ou petis.

1832. a. Dieu veult en ceulx ou il fit esclarer.

1833. a. Par ces raisons.

1841. a. Et *omitted.*

1846. a. jusque a.

1862.   a. poison.   b. poisson.   d. poissons.

1868. a. ypocrites.

1871. a. Et quant il ont.

1874. a. Que tout appart.

1876. a. Mais. mathematique.

1877. a. philosophie.

1880. a. Quant.

1891. a. fond entendre.

1895. a. ne peult a la prosperite.

1915. a. En recueilliz.   b, d. J'en.

1920. a. polly.

1921. a. est trouvee.

1922. a. *Line missing.*

1923. d. aÿde. *Trema rectifies meter but destroys rhyme.* Cf. Comte, *op. cit.*, p. 118. *We take the liberty of supplying* ung. quy = lequel, *of which the antecedant is* langaige, v. 1920.

1926. a. a tort.

1928. a, d. Quant.

1930. b, d. droit.   a. droict, *consistent with* 1917 *and* 1926.

1934. a. poinct ny touche. en saillant *omitted.*

1961. a. ou bien aditioner.

1963. a. En la voulant rendre.

1968-69. a. En aprenant au st esprit que cest de nul contrainct, *distracted copying which omitted six words and combined two verses into one.* b. Mais cesprit qui nest nul de nul contrainct. d. Mais cet esprit qui n'est de nul contrainct.

1985. a. pillier *omitted.*

1988. a. Dont les plus pres sont mis mieulx l'entendent.

1900. a, b, d. estoient coustumiers. Comte, *op. cit.,* p. 115: plus coustumiers *(three syllables), rectifying meter.*

1992. a. Mais.

1993. d. les espritz.

1994. a. escriz estoit.

1998. a. une si bonne sentence.

2004. b, d. nuees fort nuysantes.   a. nues fors et nuysantes; Comte *concurs, op. cit.,* p. 113.

2005. a. fonds eslevees.

2008. a. voyr soubmys.

2013. a. ferme et lequel.

2015-16. a, d. vigueur/ rigueur. b. vigueur/ vigueur.

2029. a. prier et pleurer, *weak rhyme.*

2035. a. acquerroys, *rhyme word omitted.*

2049. a, d. d'a b et c e petis.   a. Le fundement fut a b a c et petis. Comte, *op. cit.,* p. 112, *suggests using* MS 24.298 *as guide and to suppress* et.

2051. b. tous plains.   a, d. tout plains.

2060. a. *Line missing.*   b. Que.   d. Car.

2061. a. Mesclaroit.   b. Mesclareroient. d. Ne m'esclairoient.

2063. a, b, d. car. *Logic suggests change to* que *to complete* Qu'il me sembloit *of* v. 2058.

2076. a. *Line missing.*

2085. a. Dressoit mon coeur.

2086. a. *Line missing.*

2087. a. *Line repeated.*

2092. a. L autre sur moy et jusques aux cieulx voller.   b. L autre sur moy et jusques aux cyeulx volloit. d. L'autre sur moy et jusqu'aux cieulx volloit. Paris, *J. des S.,* p. 367: L'autre sur mer et jusqu'aux cieulx voller.

2096. a, b. ou estre mis desja au ranc. d. ou d'estre.

2099. a. Je ne desirois le plaisant fruict manger.

2100. a. Et tout savoir.

2110. b. *First hemistich added in left margin.*

2112. b. bien *omitted before* disputé. *It is found in* a *and* d *and required for meter.*

2118. a. *First hemistich omitted.*

2122. b. l'on.   a, d. on.

2141. b. Ainsy quy fut.   a, d. qu'il.

2161. a. par une amour.

2162. d. Il ne transmist aussy son soleil fort.

2177. a. aigu.

2178. a. *Line missing.*

2180. a. Et.

2195. a, d. droict.   b. droit. Cotgrave: droict.

2196. a, d. Frappe le myen.   b. Fraper le myen.   a. a plus profond. b, d. au.

2201. a. revelle.

2211. a. qui de lui fut espris.   d. qui luy estoit espris.   b. quy luy fut espris.

2234. a, b. que œil.   d. qu'œil.

2235. a. la la *after* voix.

2241. *Capitalization originates in Lefranc edition for deification.*

2247. a. avec.

2247-48. a. debattre/ debattre.

2248. a. cest *for* sçait. 2248. qui = ce qui, celui qui. *Capitalization originates in Lefranc edition, suggesting personification.*

2260. a. avec.

2261. a. je ne faisois.

2262. a. ma foy.

2284. a. pas nest.

2285. Psource que = Parce que. a, b, d. veult. Paris, *loc. cit.*: vient.

2296. a. dé *omitted before* l'enfer.

2309. a, d. Peché en Dieu n'est pas. b. Peche en dieu ne nest pas.

2332. a. Et *omitted.*

2334. a. tous *omitted.*

2337. a, b. Fors que Benjamin qui ce mot consola.   d. Fors Benjamin que ce mot consola.

2345. a. est.   b, d. c'est.

2348. a. ne peult de.

2356. a, b. force.   d. forces.

2357. a. Que me.

2358. a. qui.

2360. a, d. pour les renouveler.   b. par les renouveler.

2363-64. docteurs/ doubteux, *the r being mute, rhyme.*

2387. a. tous rien. *The MSS are erratic in their capitalization of the proper names that follow.*

2392. a, b, d. Plus clairement qu'en nul si ne mais. Comte, *op. cit.,* p. 114: qu'en nul si ne nul mais, *rectifying meter.*

2418. a. En noubliant.

2421. a. Mais que estre celeste.

2435. a. respandre.

2435. a. respandre.

2444. a. luy *omitted.*

2468. a, b, d. et hommes et chevaulx. Comte, *op. cit.,* p. 112: garder veult homes et chevaulx.

2471. a, d. trouve.   b. trouvé.

2472. a. jusques au bout.

2480. a, b. quil.   d. qui.

2492. a. en lhomme jointe la science.   b. ennente la science.   d. inventé la science. Paris, *loc. cit., concurs with* MS. b.

2510. a. esgal.

2528. a, d. L'eternel Dieu où n'y a si ne mais.   b. L eternal dieu qui seray a jamais, *distracted copying in the second hemistich from the line above.*

2541. a. esjouy.

2542. a. d. Quant.   entendiz.   b. entendz, *short meter.*

2543. a. Et le secret d un scavoir si subtil.   b. Et le secret d un scavoir subtil.   d. Et que le secret d'un scavoir si subtil. Paul Courteault, *in Revue critique d'Histoire de littérature,* Paris, juin, 1896, p. 508:"[que] *renders the verse false … ."* [our translation].

2553. a. est.

2560. a, b. trouve.   d. trouvay.

2568. a, b. Qui les avez par fureur poetique.   d. Qui les a fait, *completing a causal idiom converting an apostrophe into an exclamation.* Faisiez *(two syllables) would retain the person of the verb.*

2584. b, d. faulte.   a. fausse. *Paris, loc. cit.:* la fable.

2601. a, d. mers.   b. miles.

2618 *is written in right margin of* 2617.

2625. a, b. Qui.   d. Que.

2626. a. lequel il nest rien.

2629. a. dabondance.

2635. a. se feu.

2636. a. avec.

2642. a. prenne *omitted.*   a, b. souffrira.   d. souffrera.

2652. a. plus *omitted.*

2654. a. a descouvert.

2656. b. la mer *for* l'amer *but it is to contrast with* doulceur.

2658. a, b. voy poesie belle.   d. voy la poesie belle. Comte, *op. cit.,* p. 114, *concurs with* MSS a *and* b.

2671 *and* 2683, MS. b *uses* l'horateur, *in* 2673, l'orateur.   a, d. l'orateur *in both places.*

2675. a. *The second* est *is omitted.*

2680. a, b. Ny commencer, moyenner ny parfaire.   d. Ny communier, moyenner ny parfaire. *Paris, loc. cit.:* commencer. Comte, *op. cit.,* p. 113. *removes the first Ny to adjust the meter.*

2684. a. moy.

2686. a. sens *omitted.*

2695. a. trouve.

2697. a. dans ces beaulx livres.

2702. a. viz *omitted.*

2707. a, b, d. Renouveler leur vie par ce feu cler. *To remove excess syllable,* Comte, *loc. cit., makes two suggestions:* (1) a ce feu *and* (2) en ce feu.

2720. a. jusques au.

2737. a. l espee et la lance offenser.

2738. a. Quelque orgueilleux qui se cuide au cuider.

2749. a. tel chef.

2750. *Line written in the right margin of* 2749.

2772. a, d. seul roy.   b. roy *omitted.*

2784. a. a *omitted before* tiré.

2789. a. avec.

2811. Ouy bien *is a set phrase and does not constitute a shift to the second person singular.*

2816. a, b. trouve.   d. trouvay.

2824. a. de *omitted.*

2826. a, b, d. Des loix d'en haut sont seurs et parentes. *Comte, op. cit.,* p. 114, *rectifies meter:* sont et seurs et parentes.

2845. a. telle.

2848. a. patience.
2857. a, b. un dieu est.   d. c'est, *improving syntax.*
2879. a. sens.
2889. a. n'ont *omitted before* langue.
2896. a. y *added after* qui.
2900. a, b. ancre.   d. encre.
2912. a. les ungs.
2939. a. qui = qu'il.
2944. a. Ce qui en est faulx ce que nous regardons.
2947. a. a valeur.
2695. a. Ung seul vray.
2988. a, b. Et.   d. Est.
3000-01. a. faict/ faict.   b. fait/ fait.
    d. fait/ faict. Livres, v. 2997 *is the logical subject, so we presume to correct:* font/ font.
3003. soient *is two syllables here.*
3005. b, d. doctrines.   a. doctrine. Comte, *op. cit.,* p. 112: doctrine, *correct meter.*
3012. a, b. que a fer ou cloux.   d. qu'à fer ou à cloux *correct meter.*
    a, d. Quant.
3019. *Line is written in the right margin of* 3018.
3023. *Lefranc, D. P.,* p. 230: excercité; *but in his* Glossiare, *D, P.,* p. 448: exerciter *with ref. to* p. 229, *where such does not occur.*
3030. a. d une flamme.
3036. d. Par.   b. Pour.   a. Par cest amour qui brusle tout si soudain. tout *is written above the line.*
3041. a subtil *omitted.*
3043. a, d. nommé.   b. nommer. *A towering flourish is read as a combination of tilde and* er.
3062. a, b. Qui.   d. Que, *which, with* de, *is equivalent of* combien de.
3071. a. qui.
3073. a, d. a la terre.   b. a a terre.
3092. a, b. mesmerveille.
    d. mesmerveillay.
3094. a. fust.
3100. a. de lettres.
3111. a. Et se voyant.
3128. a, b, d. a son ymage. d. à.   *We respectfully substitute a synonym which completes the rhyme and maintains the contour of the word in*

the MSS: à soy semblable *or* à son semblable, *substantivating the adjective.*
3129. b. Ces ons docteurs.   a, d. bons docteurs.
3139. a. de tout leur possible.
3157. b. andemens.   a, d. mandemens.
3180. a. Manne tres doulce et tres necessaire pain.
3185. a. avecq.
3206. a, d. exciter.   b. excitter.
3227. a. aigneau.   b. annieau.
    d. agneay.
3229-30. a, d. Par l'union .../ Pour lequel ... *is more logical line order than MS.*
    b. Pour lequel .../ Par l'union ... .
3252. a, b, d. murailles. Comte, *op. cit.,* p. 112: muraille, *rectifying meter.*
3258. a. car a dextre et senestre.
    b. car *omitted, leaving meter short.*   d. à dextre et à senestre.
3269. a. tropt.
3261. a, b. mesliant.   d. me liant.
3263. a, b, d. Car. *Logic suggests* Par.
3283. a, d. vient à estre.   b. vient estre.
3287. a. Vainquit et moy et mon cueur abatit.
3299. fuz *of verse* 3297 *is understood with* muée.
3334. b. entendement.   a, d. entierement.
3337. a. *unclear.*   b. declairé.
    d. declairer.
3341. a, b. resiouyt.   b. resjouyt.
3346. a. impossible est que d une mortelle aureille.
3352. a, b, d. nos sens. *A prisoner's highly personal experience is being related; logic suggests* mes Cf. 3774 *plural verb, perhaps royal.*
3361. a. laisse.
3385. a. ceste promesse.
3440. a, b. exaulcé.   d. exaulcée.
3484. a. *First hemistich missing.*
3485. a. *Second hemistich missing.*
3506. a, b, d. Rend cuyder et l'homme tout deffaict. Lanson, *Revue d'Histoire littéraire de la France,* p. 294: Rend le cuyder de l'homme.
3510. a. desavancè.   b, d. de science. Lanson, *loc. cit.,* desavance.
3515. a. Et si tres rien qu estre en luy ne seiorne.

3519. b. *Line 3520 is written in the right hand margin of 3519.*

3538. a, b. Qui recongnoist.   d. Qu'il recongnoist.

3597. b. le le nom.   a,b, porte.
d. portes.

3624. a. est encloz et scelle.

3527. a. qui par feu celeste. Rien *is spoken to; qui refers to spirit.*

3629. a. hustilz.

3632. a. le monde malade guerit.

3635. a. hasarder.

3665. a. si grand difference.

3665. b. [fol. 327], *below text and catch words a line is drawn and a footnotes follows: "Monsieur de Lyon a regle ceste page. i553." A small, curving arrow points to the word* page. *If the last four characters represent a date, this edition* b *was under way four years after the death of Marguerite.*

3669. a. Que ung seul en tous ait estre et mouvement.

3684. a. Ceste doulceur dedans l escorce. Rude *is transferred to the next line.*
b, d. douleur.

3689. a. Et il ne doubt poinct craindre d estre pris de l oeil.

3691. a. clairement, *better rhyme.*

3693. a. va regardant.

3696. a. ny monbre.

3709. a. te desplaist [*copied in error from missing line 3710*].

3712. a. esle.   b. elle.   d. aile.

3745. a. fust.

3746. a. fut. *Cause with subjunctive mode and concession with the indicative are archaic constructions.*

3747. a. de l estimer roy.

3760. a. Rien qu il ne fut.

3765. a. donques.

3789. a. leurs predications.

3793. a. par *omitted.*

3799. a, b, d. Par huict jours de tourments tous nouveaulx. Comte, *R. de M., I. N°3, p. 115, suggests:* Eulx par huict jours de tourmentz tous nouveaulx, *rectifying meter and contrasting with* il *of the preceding line.* Paris, *loc. cit.,* suggests Par huict jours tous pleins de tourmentz tous nouveaulx.

3774. a, b. lerron.   d. lerrons. *Deliberate archaism.*

3777. a. en en.

3781. a. bon *omitted before* proffit.

3782. a. qu avec.

3782. a, b. treize chrestiens fist.
d. treize chrestiens il fist, *which we adopt, although* chrestiens *was sometimes three syllables at this time.*

3822. d. le nombre augmentoit. Comte, *op. cit.,* p. 114, *also* a *and* b: le grand nombre augmentoit.

3823-24. a. chercher/ prescher (r *stricken*).
b. chercher/ preschoit.
d. chercher, prescher.

3829. a. du divin plan.   b, d. plant.

3860. a. la vie.

3863. a. cy lon.

3877. juger *is not followed by the usual* que, *meter not permitting.*

3880. a, b. que je le vous racompte.
d. je vous le racompte.

3895. a. en une ame amoureuse.
b, d. à une ane amoureuse.

3912. a, b, d. Encores ung coup. Comte, *op. cit.,* p. 112, *rectifies meter:* Encor.

3913. a. Luy demandant *written twice.*

3933. b, d. Affin qu'a toy hostie de louanges.
a. lhostie, *avoiding hiatus and adding alliteration.*

3934. a. avec t tous *or* avoit tous.

3934. a, b, d. Te sacrifie. Te *duplicates* à toy *of 3933. Must not the original have been* Je, *which needs expression here for clarity?*

3937. a. En fin oiant parler sa sage abbesse.   b. la belle abbesse, belle *stricken,* saige *written above.*
d. Enfin oyant parler la saige abbesse.

3946. a, b, d. Disant. Paris, *J. des S.,* juin, 1896, p. 367: Disoit.

3955. a, b. ont peu.   d. on peut.
a, b. ces.   d. ses.

3958. a. peuvent.

3963. a. aussi *repeated.*

3961. C *begins verses excerpted by* Leroux de Lincy *and* Anatole de Montaiglon *from MS. 1522, printed in their 1880 edition of the Heptaméron, pp. 154-164, in the first of the four volumes.*

3966. a. Si icy tous ses faictz.

3969. MS. c *interrupts for 19 lines.*

3992. a. loing *omitted.*
3996. a. manger.
4014. a. nul *omitted.*
4015. a. bien.
4016. a. Et *omitted.*
4023. a. ne le sceller.   b. ne celler.
   c. ne pas celler.   d. ne le sceller.
4024. a. piteux *omitted.*
4029. a. mon coeur.
4033. a. ne me garde.
4034. a. ou *omitted.*
4036. a, d. et je vous recommande.
   b. c. me recommande.
4038. a. avec.
4042. a, c. Derriere luy dist ne me laissez pas.
   b. Derriere luy dist me ne me laissez
   pas.   d. Derriere luy dist: "Ne me
   laissez pas."
4091. a. dedans.
4093. a. je meschant
4096. a. ce *omitted* before corps.
4098. a. de vous eschappe.
4099. a. mettre *omitted.*
4104. a. Vous mandemens de n avoir obeis.
4109. a. seul.   b. seul; l *stricken, r written
   above in different hand.*   d. seur.
4113. a. O mon Dieu.
4114. a. requiers et prie.
4126. *Line missing.*
4130. a, b. Mes sans douloir. Paris. *loc. cit.,*
   Mais sans douloir.   d. Mes sens,
   douloir l'un après l'autre mortz.
4134. b. Et je me me meurs.
   a, c, d. Et je me meurs.
4136. a. en *missing before* couraige.
4138. a. a l eternel plaisir.
4153. c. *Here begins omission of 17 lines.*
4157. a. comme il demandoit.
4161. a, b. De luy.   d. Que luy, *which more
   logically introduces the result clause.*
4172. a. par dessus tous eut fame.
4172. C *injects title* Mort de Louise de Savoie
   before resuming with v. 4175.
4175. a, b, d. nomme Gretz. Paris, *loc. cit.,*
   appelle, *rectifying meter.*
   c. surnomme.
4179. a, b. deage.   d. d'age.   c. d'eage.
4180. a. l ans.
4186. a, d. qu'amaire.   b, c. que amaire.
4192. a. onques creatures *corrected to* onc
   creatures.
4193. a. ans *omitted.*

4195. a, b, c. Avecques.   d. Avec.
4199. a, b. dix et neuf.   d. l'age de
   dix-neuf.   c. en l'eage dix neuf.
4203-4204. b, c. Que en.   a. Quen.
   d. Qu'en.
4207. a. grand majeste.
4228. a. Du tres grand bien au roy son fils
   advint.   b, d. Dont tres grand
   bien.   c. Dont au roy son fils tres
   grand bien advint.
4230. a, c. si *omitted.*
4231. a, b, d. Le pays partout.   c. La pays
partout. Comte, *op. cit.,* p. 112: Par tout le
   pays, *rectifying meter and syntax.*
4233. b, c. que en.   a. qu en.   d. qu'en.
4244. b,c. que a.   a. qu'a.   d. qu'à
4254. a. en hault.
4256. a. deviser a celle.   b, c. diviser a
   celluy.   d. deviser à Celluy.
4257. a. l on.
4258. *c puts strophic break after this line.*
4262. b, c. se elle.   a. si elle.   d. s'elle.
4269. a. ose *omitted.*
4272. a, b, d. ne.   c. me.
4276. b. tute faveur. a, c, d. toute faveur.
4277. b. qu'en. *Apostrophe added by another
   hand.*
4300. b. ma habandonne, *Ligature above,
   linking the two words.*
4301. a. b. c. La jay toujousjours eu.
   d. Je l'ay tousjours eu.
4306. a. en vos mains.
4323. d. Par l'unction.
4324. c. de dire l'Evangile. *Strophic spacing
   follows.*
4328. a, b. Dapres.   d. D'apres. *The
   opposite of davant.*
4337. a, b, c, d. Lors. *Redundant with
   ensuing "when clause." Original may
   have been* Las!
4349. c. Où plus. a, b, c. Ou plus. *Lefranc
   habitually, but not here, distinguishes
   between 'where' and 'or.'*
4351. b, d. portera tant et tant d'ennuys. MS.
   a, *also* Comte, *op. cit.,* p 114: Il
   portera tant, tant, et tant d'ennuys,
   correct meter.

4368. a. d ung.   d. d'ung.   b, c. de ung.
4376. a, c. nul doubte.
4386. a biens. l'avoit *missing before* servie.
4390. a. con- *of* consoller *duplicated.*

110

4398. a, b, c. fiens. d. siens. Paris, *loc. cit.,*
   fiens.
4401. c. Qu'i.
4413. a, b, c, d. si elle estoit. Comte, *op. cit.,*
   p. 112: s'elle estoit.
4416. *C ends here.*
4419. a, b, d. temple. Paris, *loc. cit.:* tempté
   before adjuteur.
4431. a. *second* soit *omitted.*
4466. a. Car de peche quelques imperfections,
   *comprising first hemistich of 4466 and
   second hemistitch of 4468. second
   hemistich of 4466 is missing, as are
   verse 4467 and first hemistich of 4468.*
4476. a. au plus hault de la cime.
4507. a. que promesse.
4512. a. Qui. b, d. Qu'il.
4559. a. nest nest.
4574. a. les *omitted before* pecheurs.
4601. a. en luy.
4611. a, b. faisant. d. faisoient.
4625. a. tous *before* secouruz.
4626. In MS. 24-298, in order to follow the
   Lefranc MC. 1522 sequence, one must
   proceed at verse 4626 to folio 195 and,
   after 196 verse, return to folio 193. At
   the foot of 196 verso, we read in a
   hand different from the main body,
   *"fin du tiers et dernier livre des
   prisons."* This is an error since the
   poem is resumed on a verso of
   illegible number (presumed 199v°) and
   ends on presumed recto 200, where
   the number is entirely frayed away.
4629. a. parfaictz.
4630. *Subject is* ilz *of v.* 4628. a. qu avoit
   faites. b. avoit faictes. d. avoient
   faictes.
4635. b. sestimoit. a, d. s'estimoient.
4640. a, b, d. *short meter.* a. Rendant la
   mort doulce et amiable.
   b, d. Rendant leur mort doulce et
   amyable. Courteault, *Revue Critique
   d'H. et de L.* t xxx, N°26, p. 509: et
   doulce et amyable.
4644. a. crier *omitted.*
4648. b, d. cherchans pardons bulles.
   a. cherchans pardons et bulles.
   Courteault, *loc. cit., and* Comte, *loc.
   cit., suggest* et *before* bulles.
4669. a. au cœur rend.
4684. a. leur tourment. a, d. le tourment.

4689. a, b. trouve. d. trouves.
4704. a. s aparoissent.
4706. a. atout.
4709. b. geurre.
4714. a. A vous *replaces* Les uns.
4717. a, b. Et que. a, d. Et qui.
4719. a, b. luy. d. l'y.
4723. a. *Confusion in first hemistich before*
   qui est.
4727. a. Tout ton seul void. b. Tout ton
   seul voys. d. Ton seul tout voys.
4728. a. sur les esles.
4730. a. Tout *omitted.* Il sont.
4732. a. Line missing.
4743. a. *Premature notice of the end of the
   work: "fin des vers et dernier livre des
   prisons." The handwriting has a more
   forward slant than the bulk of the
   MS.*
4744. a. Qui = Qu'il.
4751-52. a. pollies/ pollies. jolies *omitted.*
4757. a, b. si monstre. d. s'y monstre.
4806. a. Naura repoz jusqua la source, *short
   meter.* b. jusqus a ce q'a la course,
   long. q has arc above it. d. N'aura
   repoz jusqu'à ce qu'à la source.
4823. a. en ces trois.
4831. a. en la puyssance.
4834. a. en *omitted before* luy.
4842. d. La vie d'en hault *with footnote
   which says to understand* received, *a
   word not expressed in text.* a, b, *and*
   Comte, *op. cit.,* p. 113: Ravit d'en
   hault, *eliminate necessity of such note
   and correct the meter.*
4848. a. aveques.
4869. a. estoit. b, d. estois. *Logic suggests
   present tense here and the preceding
   adverb suggests inversion,* es tu.
4876. a. *A later hand has added accent and
   apostrophe and changed* Jusques a ce
   jour que a tout appris venir *to* qu'a
   tout as peu venir. d. *agrees with
   these changes.* b. Jusques a ce jour que
   a tout es peu venir.
4877. a. *The later hand has written* ores
   above o ryens.
4879. a. *The later hand has changed* Bien *to*
   Rien *and* festu *to* vestu.
4897. a. Las tu peulx ou ne nous peulx
   respondre. *Side note in later hand
   reads:* Las tu le veuls mais ne nous

111

peuls respondre.
4898. b. si grand plaisir as te sentir fondre.
a, d. si grand plaisir as de te sentir
fondre.
4920. a. avec.

4927. a. Qué ou.   b. Que ou.   d. Où
l'esprit est divin et vehement. Paris,
loc. cit., "Que *ou* était à garder, sauf à
imprimer *Qu'où.*"

CULTURAL NOTES
Canto I

Verse 1. Amye tant aymée. The identity of this beloved is a matter of speculation. Since the sole narrator is expressing the views of the queen herself, we may assume that the Amye is a gentleman once loved by her or perhaps a composite of such persons. The candidates are six: de Foix, Francis, Bonnivet, Bourbon, d'Albret, and de Montmorency. Her childhood idol, Gaston de Foix, vanished early from her life when he came to prefer another, but he died a hero's death at the battle of Ravenna, some 37 years before the composition of the poem which purports to influence the person addressed. Her only brother, Francis, was one for whom she felt extraordinary affection; however, he died in 1547, his death is a feature of the poem, and we are told that the addressee is someone who was an observer at that event. The admiral Bonnivet invaded her bedroom one night and retreated with scratches that he had to hide by feigning illness. Of this incident, Marguerite's companion, Mme de Châtillon, was soon apprised; whereas, the queen insists that the incident of Canto I was never learned of by father, brother, nor *friend*; Bonnivet died in 1525. The Connêtable de Bourbon, her youthful mother's marital target, announced a long kept secret passion for Marguerite but defected to the side of France's enemies, an affront to Marguerite's interests; Benvenuto Cellini claims to have killed him during the sacking of Rome in 1527. Her none too faithful husband, Henri d'Albret, caused her the type of disillusionment recognizable in the narrative, for theirs was in origin a love match; furthermore, Henri survived her. It seems an essential point, however, that the relationship in the poem was both secret and platonic, which the Albret relationship certainly was not. Verse 472, "Curses then on you and all your scions" would be contradictory to her durable affection for the daughter of this marriage, Jeanne d'Albret, which love survived Jeanne's occasionally vexacious conduct. Finally, there remains the Connêtable de Montmorency with whom Marguerite maintained a long constant correspondence and whose career she furthered at every opportunity. As to disappointing faithlessness, he denounced her as a heretic and seems not to have returned her devotion to him except as duty required. He did indeed survive the poem's composition and was likely present at the death of her brother.

It is no doubt better to view the entire work as something larger than a personal confession and to find with Gaston Paris (*Journal des Savants*, June, 1896, p. 365) that "the author tried to represent human life as a whole . . . and placed herself understandably in the point of view as a man [as did Christine de Pisan] and not of a woman, [which] did not prevent her mingling into this work of fiction more than one personal recollection. Thus in her portrait of an exalted love betrayed, she put more than a trace furnished by her altogether too real experience." Cf. verse and note 1672; Also see note 124 to French text, a reference to the narrator in the feminine gender, *seulle*. It is known that Marguerite read Dante to Francis and that he scorned it.

14. Here begins a series of conceits of the Platonic type made popular by the poets Aretino, Sannazar, Bembo, and chiefly Petrarch. Heroët and Scève were the principal exponents of the figure in France. Their predecessors were Saint-Gelais, Salel and Marot. Since Joachim du Bellay, like

112

Marguerite, satirarizes Petrarchism, it is fitting to compare the lines taken from his "Contre les Pétrarchistes" (Floyd Gray, *Anthologie de la poésie française du XVI siècle* (New York: Meredith, 1967), p. 202:

> "Ce n'est qu'horreur de leurs douleurs,
> Ce n'est encor' de leurs soupirs et pleurs
> Que vents, pluie, et orages:
> Et bref, ce n'est qu'à ouir leurs chansons
> De leurs amours que flammes et glaçons,
> Flesches, liens, et mille autres façons
> De semblables outrages."

To these we add that the lover is unable to express himself in the lady's presence, and that, by being in servitude to her, he arrives at a sense of freedom. Cf. Vianey, *Le Pétrarquisme en France au XVI siècle.*

54. *Gehenna: ge-Hinnon,* valley of torment. Joshua 15; 2 Kings.

70-71. Cf. Dante, *Purgatorio,* XXIV, 57, "dolce stil nuovo," indicating the illustrious school of Guido Guinizzelli.

213. The subject is *her heart,* which wanted the prison undone to her advantage.

220. Literally, *compels me to tell each* [masculine] *and each* [feminine].

228. *dueil,* besides indicating 'mournful lamentation,' could signify 'a duel.'

330-34. *Qui/ Qui/ Qui/ Qui,* anaphora. Cf. 611-615, 959-963, 980-982 *et passim.*

362. French verb is in the third person plural although *vous,* the second person plural is part of the subject.

365. Cf. 4351, Marguerite is drumming on the word *tant.*

429. Cf. Matthew 7:26-27.

498-500. *Satan:* tempter, adversary, old serpent. Cf. Rev. 12-9; Matt. 4:10. *Lucifer:* light-bearer. Cf. Isaiah 14:12.

536. *la* refers to the roof or the covering.

602. Any loosing of bonds in the course of an upward journey, would be, according to Hans Jonas in *The Gnostic Religion,* 2nd ed'n. (Boston: Beacon, 1936), p. 166, an echo of the gnostic document attributed to Hermes Trismegistus, who is praised by Marguerite.

CANTO II

686. Man's head was erect only to praise his Maker. Cf. Ovid, Metamorphoses I, 85.

688. *Solomon's throne:* the planet Saturn.

751. Cf. Job 38:8. "Who shuts up the sea with doors . . . ?"

932. *On courtly principle:* In the Platonist doctrine of Ficino advanced by Cusa and Marguerite's two mentors, Lefèvre and Briçonnet, a gentleman might take a first step toward God, whose essence was ideal beauty, by devoting himself to beauty and goodness in the lady to whom he vowed fidelity of "true-love."

1037. *the plum* replaces *some plume;* both are symbols of victory but are not intended here as literal translation.

1063-55. "From ambassadors they have made cardinals . . . saintly and perfect ones." Thomas àBecket is a case in point.

1073. *"Sounding wiser for this skill* [speech]." G. Lanson comments: "It is speaking well that is taken for total knowledge. The orator is supposed to be ignorant of nothing according to Ciceronian theory, of which one can see the development in the *De Oratore." Revue d'Histoire litté*raire de la France, 1896, p. 294. Quintilian also held the idea of the orator as a good man of excellent mind. Cf. Hans Jonas, *Gnostic Religion,* p. 238.

1092. *"Pale."* Virgil, the voice of reason, speaks indistinctly to Dante in the first canto of the *Inferno.* However, this figure may represent one of Marguerite's mentors.

1128. Robert Marichal has emphasized that Marguerite was unwilling to confound beauty with virtue as did the Hellenes in considering the manifest essence of God upon earth. See *Navire*, p. 28.

1264. *"La belle Hélène,"* Helen of Troy, the fairest maiden, whose beauty inspired the Trojan war.

1266. Marguerite again drums on *tant*. Cf. verses 365 and 4351. Further incantatory *tant's*.

1460. Literally, *This is a link that is made of quicksilver*, possible alchemical associations.

1484. A more comfortable order, *l'avaricé immunde*, would have forfeited a needed syllable.

1545. See 602.

1555. *de science amateur.* Equivalent of the word *philosopher*, derived from the Greek. Possible alchemical reference.

1614. In the French there begins here a series of *plain de*, 'full of' complemented by seven *soubz*, 'beneath.' This incantation, falling near the end of Canto II, recalls the series of *Adieu's* at the close of Canto I. Although some such repetition is present elsewhere, the penultimate position reminds one of a drumroll preparing an important announcement.

1618. *Sans échec . . . joueur matte.* In the game of chess, the cry of "Check" is a warning that the opponent's king is so endangered that he must move it or defend it. If both are impossible, "checkmate" is declared, and the opponent loses the game. *Without check* here could indicate 'without warning.'

1644. *concupiscences.* Cf. 1 John 2:15-16. In Canto II, the traditional "pride of life" will be a focus on intellectual pride.

1667-68. Cf. Dante, Inferno I, 14-17, in Grandgent, p. 13; also footnote 17. *"pianeta*, the sun . . . ."

1672. Francis Hackett, in *Francis the First* (Garden City: Doubleday-Doran, 1935), p. 358, says that the king pronounced Dante "ridiculous."

1695. *Ouy bien* is a set phrase and not a sudden shift to second person singular imperative, "Mark you well!"

CANTO III

1898. Rhetorical figure known as litotes, favored by Greco-Roman orientation.

2013. *seven clasps.* Cf. Revelation 5.

2081. Literally *Asia.*

2126. *prosne.* Randall Cotgrave, *Dictionarie of the French and English Tongues*, London, 1611, facsimile, North Carolina Press, 1968: "the publication made or notice given by a priest unto his parishioners when the service is almost ended."

2134. *toward the fair fruit.* Cf. Genesis 3.

2157. *Dathan and Abiram.* Cf. Numbers 16:27-33.

2159. Cf. Numbers 35:6-15.

2162. *Samson*, in Hebrew, means 'sunlight.' Cf. Judges 16.

2171-72. *hypocrite.* Cf. I Samuel 13:13 and 15:19-35.

2173. *Jupiter*, same as *Jove*, king of the gods, whose weapon was the thunderbolt.

2175-76. *But through kindness, which is His true blade,/ Trenchant sword gleaming, bright and beautiful.* Cf Ephesians 6:17, "the sword of the Spirit which is the word of God."

2231. Cf. John 1:23. *his sextant* added.

2232-33. *who was waiting to learn.* Cf. Exodus 3:14. *"Je suis"* of verse 2234 follows the Latin Vulgate of Jerome.

2245. *"Celluy qui Est"* is closer to the Septuagint. M. A. Screech cites Wilfrid Strabon's Glossa Ordinaria in *Rabelaisian Marriage* (London: Arnold, 1958), p. 79.

2292. *I am He who pardons sins.* Cf. Matthew 9:6; Mark 2:5; Ephesians 1:17.

2301-02. *lumières lumineuses / tenebres tenebreuses.* For appreciation of coherence in this long composition, contrast the nouns here with their cognate adjectives in Canto I, verses 8 and 9.

2322-25. *by this Word are released from peril.* Cf. Matthew 8:23-27.

2336. With the exception of Benjamin, the brothers had sold Joseph into slavery. Cf. Genesis 32.

2350. *Cuyder*, to Marguerite, usually means the belief disputed by her that one could by his independent efforts attain heaven.

2372. *Nothing* as both contrary and component of *all* was an ancient idea revived in Marguerite's time. It occurs frequently in the 1520 correspondence of Briçonnet, as well as in the Cabbala, where the awareness of one's nothingness figures as the lowest springboard from which to rise to the heights of assimilation into the *one* or *all*. The Florentine Neo-Platonists, with their translations, had given these ideas wide circulation; and Briçonnet, with his translations, was their continuator. (See Introduction, Subject Matter and Some Sources, p. xiv.)

2394. *Hermes* Trismegistus, gnostic pagan writer and syncritist, to whom a remnant of Egyptian Hellenistic literature of revelation is attributed, especially a portion called the *Poimandres*. Cf. Hans Jonas, *The Gnostic Religion* (Boston: Beacon, 1963), p. 41.

2403. Cf. Job 19:25, "For I know that my Redeemer liveth and that he shall stand at the latter day upon the earth."

2413. *This light Socrates received.* Cf. Erasmus, "Holy Socrates, pray for us!" Plato's essays, the *Apology, Crito,* and *Phaedo* form a trilogy about the imprisonment and death of Socrates (347 B.C.).

2425. *Plato followed his doctrine very well.* W. H. D. Rouse, in prefacing his translation, *The Great Dialogues of Plato* (E. H. Warmington and P. G. Rouse, eds., New York, New American Library of World Lit., 1956) says: "Socrates wrote nothing himself; but, after his death, his favorite and most billiant pupil, Plato (427-347 B.C.) set up a school of philosophy in 386 in a place called Academy, in an olive grove on the outskirts of Athens, and wrote memories of what he had heard; he made this into a more or less complete system, adding much of his own, no doubt, but grouping all under the name of his beloved teacher."

2463. Literally, 'I am who am.'

2484. The liberal arts comprised grammar, rhetoric, dialectic, arithmetic, music, geometry, and astronomy.

2507-08. In French, the order of these verses is the reverse.

2509. *Of the circle.* Cf. Georges Poulet, *The Metamorphoses of the Circle*, translated from the French by Carley Dawson and Elliott Coleman in collaboration with G. Poulet (Baltimore: Johns Hopkins Press, 1966), intro., p. xl. There the sentence "Deus est sphaera cujus centrum ubique" is said to have made its first appearance in a pseudohermetic manuscript of the twelfth century, *The Book of the Twenty-Four Philosophers,* anonymous.

2579. Literally, "I am who am."

2581. *Metamorphoses,* work of Latin Poet Publius Ovidius Naso.

2586. In Greek tradition Deucalion and Pyrrha survived the flood sent by Jove and repeopled the earth.

2589. *This is the very strong Atlas.* The Titan upon whose shoulders Jove placed the burden of the heavens.

2590. *wise Pallas.* Same as Athena, goddess of war, wisdom and weaving.

2593-94. *By rain of gold impregnated the virgin.* Danaë was daughter of King Acrisius of Argos, who shut her up in a tower because he feared to be killed by a son she would bear. She wanted to see Jove. The king of the gods, in love with her, appeared to her in a shower of golden rain. She thus became the mother of Perseus.

2595. Bacchus was the son of Semele and Jove.

2602. Lefranc, *Dernières Poésies*, p. 215, note (2): "It is a question of the Dioscures."

2606. Actean, a huntsman, came upon the goddess Diana taking a bath; in her anger she changed him into a stag; he was set upon and killed by his own dogs.

2607. 'Literally, *This* [The I Am] *is Leander who for Hero crossed/ This great sea where he died,/ And by his death drew to him his friend,/ Who, by death, like the lover, was put to sleep.'* The sea is the Hellespont; Hero is the girl's name.

2621. Procus, 'suitor,' is confused with Poros, the god of plenty. Cf. Plato's *Symposium*.

2637-38. *Androgyne.* Cf. Plato, *Symposium*, 189-194.

2705-2706. Reversed in English from French order.

2715-22. *Of that great king.* Moses. Cf. Exodus 19 and 20.

2740. *Carthage.* Perhaps Marguerite has in mind Porphory, a third century writer of Phoenician extraction who was known for his quotation from an earlier writer: "We ought then, having been united and made like God, to offer our own conduct as a holy sacrifice to Him." (Eusebius, Dem. ev. 3) cited in Edwin Hatch, "Sacrifice," in *Enc. Brit.* 11th ed'n., XXIII, 985; or she might have meant St. Augustine's teachings in Carthage.

2762. Cf. Genesis 4:2-8; Matthew 23:35.

2884. Assavoir mon. Cf. Glossaire, Lefranc, *D. P.,* p. 446: "certainement affirmation."

2888. *anesse,* fem. Balaam is identified in Numbers 23:22-35.

2901. Literally, *"abuses,"* but the sense here seems 'to be 'usurps,' hence *"out of place."*

2918-20. Literally, *all downhill/ Proceed to lead into a deep pit those/ Who have believed them.* Cf. Matthew 5:14.

2943-45. Literally, *'But to judge of the evil and of the good/ The one that touches the Scripture most closely.'* Lefèvre, commenting on St. Paul, calls Scripture the *"vraye touche pour sçavoir les paroles vraies ou mensongères."* H. P. Clive, *Œuvres choisies,* I, 3.

2977. Saint Bonaventure (1221-1274) names the three attributes of divinity to be goodness, power, and wisdom, as does Maurice Scève's *Microcosme* and as do certain other 16th century philosophic works. See note 4811, also Introduction, Subject Matter and Some Sources, p. xiv.

2991. *Not to depend on mortal man.* Cf. Romans 6:23.

2992. Marguerite seconds Luther, Briçonnet, and others, as she affirms that faith outranks works to the exclusion of reliance upon works. See Introduction, footnote 34 *re* "works" signifying feats of magic.

3038. *ceste femme intentive.* Most probably refers to Saint Catherine of Siena.

3054. supplicious, 'attaching to martyrdom.'

3052. *L'ame charnelle.* Mary of Magdala, among others. Cf. Matthew 28:1-10; Mark 16:1-10; John 20:1-18.

3155-56. Literally, *all the magicians/ Of Pharoah and their ancient arts.* Cf. Exodus 4-12.

3267. *by thousands and by hundreds.* Cf. v. 2879. One may observe that Marguerite uses anticlimax more than once and that it is consistent with her theory of the individual's diminution toward God.

3230. *Adopted son.* Cf. Romans 8:15-17.

3192-98. *Old* appears five times in six lines and again in v. 3203.

3312. Literally, *covering.* Cf. Hebrews 9:4-5, which describes "cherubim overshadowing the mercy seat" and manna inside.

3363-67. *It is of such heaviness that we prefer to speak with the servant.* Cf. Exodus 20:18-19. The people say to Moses, "You speak to us and we will hear; but let not God speak to us lest we die."

3368. Cf. Genesis 4, which narrates the slaying of Abel by Cain.

3370. Literally, *he hid himself from it.* Cf. Genesis 3:8.

3371-74. Cf. Genesis 21:22-30. Abimilech, Philistine king of Gerar, received Abraham as a sojourner because the former was frightened by the destruction of Sodom and Gomorrah and impressed by Abraham's rescue from it. Abimilech requested an alliance with him so that he too might have the protective guidance of God (the Voice). Abraham protested that Abimilech's servants had seized the well and denied water to their sojourner. Abimilech disclaimed responsibility and conceded access to the well to be Abraham's right.

3380. *and wise* added. Cf. Genesis 9:11-13.

3382. Genesis 15:4-5 tells of the promise of heirs to Abraham and Sarah. This is the reference touched by Marguerite's line, *"When of children 'he had lost hope."*

3385. Blessing extracted from the angel by Jacob. Cf. Genesis 32:26-29.

3386. Literally *His Jacob.* Cf. 3391 and 3397, where *His* Joseph and *His* David appear.

3389. News of Joseph reaches his father. Cf. Genesis 32:24-28.

3391-92. Cf. Genesis 43-45.

3396. *Those whom Pharoah wanted to martyr.* Cf. Exodus 19 and 20 on the guidance of Moses.

3399. Marguerite confuses David with Jesus here, perhaps deliberately. Cf. Matthew 3:7. The stories of David are found in 1 Samuel 16 and 1 Kings 2.

3402. *It is this voice that is sent by the Spirit. It is this voice* appears in lines 3397, 3402, 3405, 3409, 3443, and 3449, with four instances of *this voice.*

3422. Cf. Song of Solomon 6:13, "Return, return, O Shulamite; return, return that we may look upon thee."

3443-48. Literally, *who usurps/ the good of the big brother; for he plants himself/ Before the father, where he received blessing/ Being covered with passion/ That the sin he was bearing merited/ Through this skin, one who represented us.* Cf. Genesis 27:16.

3452. Cf. Exodus 17:5,2, where Moses strikes rock and draws water, also Zechariah 8:12, "Yea, they made their hearts as an adamant stone lest they should hear the law and the words which the Lord of Hosts hath sent in His spirit by the former prophets."

3459. Cf. 2 Corinthians 2:17, "Now the Lord is that Spirit; and where the Spirit is, there is liberty." This line is repeated at the conclusion of Canto III and is therefore considered of prime importance by Marguerite.

3592. Alliterative motto: *vérité, vie, et voye.*

3612. Lines 3613-16 present a gnostic path toward God, harmony of antitheses.

3626. Literally, *'vivifies the dead man.'* Cf. 2 Corinthians 3:6.

3658. *plumes* = feathers for flying or quills for writing.

3720. *Jeremiad,* 'warning or lament for disaster brought on by sin, as in the Book of Jeremiah.'

3730. *Saint Stephen,* first Christian martyr. Cf. Acts 7:55-60.

3737. Literally, *'with many mockeries.'* According to St. Ambrose (*De Off.* 1:41; 2:28), Lawrence was martyred around 258 A.D., having resisted seizure of the church treasury by hostile parties.

3743. *the good thief.* Cf. Luke 23:40-43. Barabas. See also verse 3773.

3774. Marguerite here uses a first person plural, for the sake of homonymic rhyme, perhaps, and in verse 3776 reverts to the first person singular.

3777. Lefranc footnote in *Dernières Poésies,* p. 255, cites de Hammer, *Histoire de l'Empire Ottoman,* transl. Helbert, vol. V, pp. 98-99. He sets the date of the event at 1528, La Forest having served until his death in 1529, and identifies the martyr as Kabiz, member of the Oulemas group and teacher of the doctrine that Jesus Christ was superior to Mahomet. The death sentence was imposed by Soliman.

3791. *les* refers to the thirteen converted Christians *treize chrestiens,* of v. 3782.

3825-26. Literally, *'let him be seized/ and put into water' very secretly.* This method of killing was possibly a travesty of baptism.

3858. Cf. 2 Thessalonians 4:16, "The dead in Christ shall rise first."

3881-84. Marguerite de Lorraine (1463-1516), ward and granddaughter of King René d'Anjou, mother-in-law of our poet, was entitled by the Catholic Church to be called "Marguerite the Blesséd." Our poet witnessed her passing as well as those of her own husband and mother, subsequently described, but not that of her brother. We note in the poem her lamenting her absence in the last instance.

3889. *Being cloistered in her religion.* She had retired to the cloister of Sainte-Claire d'Argentan, founded by her. Cf. Lefranc, *D. P.,* p. 259, note (3). *Wall or stone,* a possible Judaism and Islam allusion to the Wailing Wall or Kaaba stone.

3944. *tenui* and *nunc dimittam,* Latin phrases from the last words of Christ, used in prayers of preparation for death, meaning 'I hold' and 'now I surrender.'

3945-46. The subject is Marguerite the Blesséd.

3947-52. Literally, *But as soon as she had finished saying "Jesus," began sweetly to smile.* The poet uses "Jesus" three times in the recital of her mother-in-law's death, twice in verse 3948 and once in verse 3952. At her own death she is reported to have cried out "Jesus" three times. Cf Lefranc, *D. P.,* Intro., p. xxiv.

3963. Charles, fourth duke of Alençon, born in the castle of Alençon, Sept. 2, 1489, married Marguerite d'Angoulême in 1509, and died April 11, 1526.

4020. Literally, *'serving, loving my sovereign lord.'* Francis I is meant.

4022. Louise de Savoie, duchess of Angoulême, Marguerite's and Francis's mother, and mother-in-law to the dying man. Charles, by virtue of an untimely retreat, was blamed for the capture of Francis at Pavia. Louise, at this time, was acting as regent. She was generally spoken of as "Madame."

4043-70. Of historic interest here is the firsthand intimation that Marguerite had acquired some strong affection and respect for her first husband, even to the degree that she champions him against her shrewd and domineering mother, to whose intellect and ambition she owed much of her formation.

4057. Lefrance, *D. P.*, p. 267, n. (1) identifies this Jean Gœvrot as one born at Bellême (Orne), author of *Sommaire de toute medecine* (Alençon: Simon Dubois) and physician to Marguerite de Lorraine, to Charles her son, and to Marguerite d'Alençon (later de Navarre). He served both the households of Francis I and of Henri II.

4072. In Leroux de Lincy and Anatole de Montaiglon, *L'Heptaméron des Nouvelles* de la Reine de Navarre (Paris: 1880, Geneva: Slatkine, 1969, I, 157, n. (1) this priest is identified as Jean IV le Veneur, Cardinal de Tillières, bishop of Lisieux from 1505-1539.

4146. Cf. Luke 23:46 and our footnote to verse 3944.

4151-53. *Which seemed to be a chariot to conduct/ The bride of heaven, the soul, to its Creator.* Cf. the chariot in Ezekiel 5:1-28. The lengthening of the day by divine intervention is a biblical motif in Joshua 10:30. Cf. also *La Chanson de Roland*, vv. 2458-75.

4177. Louise de Savoie, daughter of Philippe, Count of Bresse, later duke of Savoy, and of Marguerite de Bourbon. She was born at le Pont d'Ain (1477), married Charles d'Orleans, Count of Angoulême (not the poet), prince of the royal blood of France in 1488, was widowed in 1496, and died at Gretz (Seine et Marne), Sept. 22, 1533. Cf. Lefranc, *D. P.*, p. 271, n. (3), and Putnam, *Marguerite of Navarre* (New York, 1936), p. 2.

4220. Cf. Hebrews 12:6, "For whom the Lord loveth he . . . scourgeth . . . ."

4306. Literally, *'That with good heart I now restore to your hands.'* Cf. *In Manus. Nunc dimittam*. Of *Nunc dimittis*, found in the Canticle of Solomon, Luke 2:29, T. H. White notes that it came to mean "I've seen it all now; I can die happy." (*The Book of Merlyn*, footnote, p. 29.)

4311. The subject of *embrasse* is *qui*, which refers to esprit.

4351. See 365.

4358. Philippe de Babou, seigneur de la Bourdaisière [bur dez jer *i.p.a.*], superintendant of finances, (d. 2557). Cf. Lefranc, *D. P.*, p. 277, n. (1).

4380. Literally, *the good monk*, i.e., Franciscan friar, also called *cordelier* in the French, because of the rope worn customarily about the waist.

4423. *Souvienne*, impersonal, 'may it occur to you.'

4429. *Memoires du Guillaume du Bellay, seigneur de Langey.* Cf. Lefranc, *D. P.*, p. 280, n. (1).

4430. Literally, *that he had the practice/ Of governing either in peace or in war/ All his kingdom, or rather, all the earth. canonical* added, implying 'well-regulated.'

4436-38. *Le bon Castellanus.* Pierre Duchâtel (d. 1552), a royal reader, bishop of Tulle, Macon, and Orleans, respectively, who pronounced two funeral orations (1547) honoring Francis I, which were published by Balluze (1647) in the *Vita Castellani*. Mention also occurs in de Ruble, *Mariage de Jeanne d'Albret*, p. 223. Both books are cited by Lefranc, *D. P.*, p. 223 and p. 280, n. (2).

4580. *I must.* The French verb is impersonal, *fault*, 'one must.'

4585-86. Literally, *Could not so stone our bodies/ That it does not come to aid our spirit.* Antique reasoning by antithesis.

4645. like 4606, carries a reference to the "Jesus cry."

4658. Final use of the formal *vous*. Intimate form occurs in verse 4675 and thereafter in the poem.

4731-35. All five lines begin with *Tout*. Anaphora. Drumming to lend importance.

4737. Here seems to be an echo of Hasidism: "Not to despise or to leave the body, but so to refine it that an inner light could show through," in Herbert Weiner, *Nine and a Half Mystics: The Kabbala Today* (New York, 1969), p. 146.

4811-16. These three attributes of divinity are traditional, found either in triad or individually. The triad appears here as in St. Bonaventure, *Opera omnia* (Quaracci, 1882-1890), I, 804, and in Denys the Areopagite, *De divinis nominibus, VII. Œuvres complètes du Pseudo-Denys,* trad. Maurice de Gandillac (Paris: Aubier, 1943), p. 143. Marguerite cites Denys.

4835-37. Cf. 1 Kings 4:32-37. The act of healing performed by Elisha.

4855-56. Literally, *who live in common everywhere, without choosing one from them.* Marguerite is deriving an ethic from the general unity, to favor general harmony.

4927-28. Lefranc (*D. P.,* p. 297), notes that, according to La grise, *Le Château de Peau,* p. 144, the motto of the last two lines is found on a dais of black velvet and crimson satin once belonging to Marguerite and very probably executed by her. This piece, called in inventories of the 16th century, "The Dais of Broken Prisons," bears in several places the inscription: *Ubi spiritus ibi libertas.* The same motto figures also on a certain number of pieces of tapestry known to have been made by the Queen of Navarre. Cf. 2 Corinthians 3:17.

APPENDIX

PROPER NOUNS INDEX
The numbers represent verses and their notes.

TABLE OF RHYMES

This index proceeds by the last vowel of the tonic syllable in the first word of the rhyming pair, then by each succeeding letter, then by each preceding letter. The scribes used i and y interchangeably; this ambivalence has been preserved in the texts since it presents no ambiguity there and is characteristic of the period; however, for alphabetical consistency, in this index, wherever y is the last vowel of the tonic syllable the word will be found in the list of y.

A

124

vollé:collé, 325
estimé:blasmé, 285v°
estimé:amyé, 274v°
nommé:aymé, 317
consummé:alumé, 303
fermé:armé, 312
enfermé:confermé, 331
aymé:nommé, 320
né:proumené, 325v°
né:determiné, 297
né:fortuné, 340
amené:proumené, 329v°
regné:né, 342v°
gaigné:n'espargnay, 291v°
obstiné:né, 269v°
condamné:damné, 334v°
donné:né, 296
donné:habandonné, 267
donné:ordonné, 313v°, 329, 340v°
borné:ordonné, 278
retourné:ordonné, 336v°
enchayné:aliené, 266v°
frappé:eschappé, 334v°
huppé:occupé, 287v°
gré:degré, 346
degré:gré, 282v°
inspiré:tiré, 312v°
tiré:desiré, 285
adoré:ignoré, 312v°
honoré:labouré, 318
procuré:asseuré, 275
asseuré:desmesuré, 304v°
delivré:livré, 301v°
enyvré:délivré, 284v°
tyré:retyré, 337
desprisé:brisé, 290v°
advisé:martirisé, 328v°-329
divisé:advisé, 327v°
blessé:sçay, 328v°
adressé:blessé, 280v°-281
laissé:abbessé, 292
laissé:abessé: 301v°, 342v°
usé:excusé, 337v°
excusé:abusé, 289v°
rusé:abusé, 285
varieté:l'esté, 328
fermeté:seureté, 269v°
seureté:dureté, 272
povreté:esté, 287v°
felicité:cecité, 345
felicité:necessité, 266
felicité:incitté, 288
excercité:excité, 316v°
fragilité:humilité, 340v°
nichilité:humilité, 345v°
limité:calamité, 268v°
magnanimité:longanimité, 291
humanité:charité, 346v°
divinité:humanité, 310, 317v°
divinité:Trinité, 330
unité:trinité, 346v°
verité:charité, 297v°
verité:irrité, 302

verité:meritté, 271v°, 284, 315v°, 326
prosperité:l'adversité, 298
prosperité:diversité, 334v°
authorité:charité, 327
l'obscurité:pureté, 312v°
diversité:adversité, 327v°
diversité:necessité, 279
beaulté:cruaulté, 268v°, 281
beaulté:royaulté, 267v°
noveaulté:beaulté, 276v°
cruaulté:royaulté, 277v°
royaulté:beaulté, 341
chanté:contanté, 323v°
planté:santé, 266v°
planté:enté, 285v°
santé:planté, 282v°
santé:contanté, 292v°
tourmenté:tempté, 328v°
bonté:dumpté, 316, 342
volunté:exempté, 325
exempté:tempté, 340v°
compté:dumpté, 343
clarté:eshonté, 271v°
liberté:legereté, 268v°
liberté:seureté, 324, 347
liberté:esté, 265
esté:d'honnesteté, 281
esté:arresté, 284v°
esté:affetté, 283
magesté:chasteté, 336v°
majesté:rejecté, 347v°
osté:costé, 291v°
meritté:verité, 298v°
reputé:disputé, 301v°
extenué:diminué, 345v°
Josué:tué, 302v°
relevé:trouvay, 309
conservé:preservé, 298
esprouvé:retrouvé, 326v°
trouvé:conservé, 297
lyé:alié, 274v°
envoyé:desvoyé, 315v°
refuzé:abusé, 271
aspect:respect, 308v°
respect:aspect, 321v°
subjecte:rejecte, 299
transpercée:pensée, 305v°
transpercée:dressée, 330-330v°
demandée:recommandée, 336
recommandée:demandée, 295
regardée:gardée, 345v°
forgée:alongée, 273
puriffiée:deifiée, 346
aveuglée:desreglée, 271v°-272
aymée:desestimée, 265
aymée:transformée, 318
finée:enluminée, 271v°
illuminée:née, 306v°
donnée:habandonnée, 338
environnée:couronnée, 295
tournée:retournée, 298
espée:couppée, 344v°

desemparée:reparée, 316v°
sacrée:ancrée, 316v°
ferrée:serrée, 266v°
brisée:desprisée, 334
chassée:pourchassée, 347v°
transportée:reconfortée, 338
muée:commuée, 321
nuée:muée, 304v°
louée:vouée, 331
aprouvée:esprouvée, 268
trouvée:approuvée, 333v°
effacées:passées, 311v°
attachées:tachées, 345
ferrées:serrées, 327
amasées:passées, 300v°
nuées:muées, 276v°
eslevées:trouvées, 299v°
chef:derechef, 312
meschef:chef, 335
souef:soif, 280v°
Abel:mortel, 312v°
ciel:miel, 340v°
charnel:eternel, 319, 325v°, 338
paternel:tel, 316v°
tel:mortel, 341
belle:infidelle, 344
belle:telle, 303
rebelle:belle, 266v°
rebelle:originelle, 347v°
pucelle:l'ancelle, 345v°
d'eschelle:aile, 328
Semelle:estincelle, 309v°
eternelle:charnelle, 302v°
grelle:melle, 276v°
mortelle:eternelle, 315v°
immortelle:eternelle, 306v°
immortelle:nouvelle, 319v°
cautelle:eschelle, 282v°
mouëlle:belle, 310v°
cruelle:belle, 265v°
cruelle:eternelle, 269
cruelle:corporelle, 330v°
gravelle:nouvelle, 338v°
revelle:nouvelle, 305v°
nouvelle:renouvelle, 319v°
renouvelle:nouvelle, 334-334v°
rebelles:belles, 313
estincelles:belles, 345
chandelles:estoilles, 300v°
naturelles:elles, 345v°
tremble:ensemble, 315
semble:ensemble, 273
ensemble:semble, 333v°-334
rassemble:ressemble, 345v°
remembre:membre, 312-312v°
membres:chambres, 329v°
femme:ame, 332v°
femme:dame, 281v°, 339v°
femme:fame, 335v°
femme:flamme, 316v°
temple:ample, 279v°
temple:d'exemple, 323v°
exemple:ample, 340

127

poing:soing, 277v°
soing:loing, 313v°
soing:besoing, 276
besoing:soing, 280-280v°
plains:sainctz, 300v°
plains:plains, 322
mains:inhumains, 293
nonnains:sainctz, 332
meins:crains, 332v°
reprins:aprins, 293v°
matins:festins, 265
point:poinct, 338v°
soustint:advint, 336v°
advint:vint, 302
revint:devint, 305
prescript:escript, 319
escripte:descripte, 320
escriptes:hypocrites, 297v°
evangelique:autantique, 315
catholique:etnique, 313v°
s'aplique:musique, 266
cronique:pratique, 340
unique:mathematique, 308
communique:pratique, 320
musique:rethorique, 296v°
poetique:rethorique, 310v°
antique:relique, 273v°
antique:pique, 278v°
antique:brique, 268
antique:rethorique, 298v°
autantique:canonique, 293v°
authentique:mathematique, 297v°
authentique:poetique, 309
anticques:autanticques, 279
fantastiques:mathematiques, 296
chair:cacher, 286v°
chair:aprocher, 304v°
fleschir:enrichir, 282
faillir:saillir, 288v°
saillir:faillir, 269v°
tressaillir:saillir, 281
cueillir:accueillir, 299-299v°
tenir:mainctenir, 346v°
tenir:venir, 347v°
entretenir:souvenir, 274-274v°
venir:tenir, 283v°
venir:entretenir, 301v°
venir:parvenir, 287
revenir:tenir, 272v°
souvenir:tenir, 280v°
souvenir:retenir, 322
souvenir:advenir, 272
veoir:desespoir, 345
veoir:appercevoir, 307, 327
veoir:devoir, 268v°, 295v°
veoir:povoir, 265v°, 290v°, 317v°
espoir:avoir, 292v°
l'espoir:povoir, 322v°
avoir:sçavoir, 282
sçavoir:l'avoir, 296v°
sçavoir:veoir, 295, 303v°

sçavoir:devoir, 336
sçavoir:povoir, 315v°
decevoir:recevoir, 302
recevoir:veoir, 310v°
recevoir:sçavoir, 295, 319
recevoir:decevoir, 286
recevoir:devoir, 332v°
recevoir:povoir, 337
appercevoir:veoir, 300v°
appercevoir:debvoir, 290v°
devoir:avoir, 278v°
devoir:sçavoir, 318
ramentevoir:recevoir, 337v°
povoir:vouloir, 314
povoir:avoir, 285
povoir:devoir, 293
povoir:mouvoir, 327v°
perir:mourir, 306v°
guerir:courir, 326v°
querir:mourir, 337v°
aquerir:querir, 278v°
d'aquerir:querir, 288v°
aquerir:requerir, 323v°
acquerir:perir, 291
mourir:guerir, 305
mourir:courir, 270v°
mourir:secourir, 332
nourrir:mourir, 297
ouvrir:couvrir, 302
desir:plaisir, 335
plaisir:desir, 274v°, 277, 332
plaisir:saisir, 303
plaisir:loysir, 266
loisir:gesir, 339
loysir:plaisir, 281v°
patir:sentir, 324
aneantir:consentir, 270
mentir:repentir, 287v°
sentir:repentire, 304
sentir:martir, 266v°
sentir:rostir, 328v°
departir:martir, 290
m'advertir:desmentir, 270
sortir:assortir, 314v°
bastir:assortir, 278v°
rostir:sentir, 342v°
servir:asservir, 274
servir:suyvir, 297
asservir:servir, 281
suyvir:servir, 311
faire:parfaire, 311
faire:satisfaire, 280
faire:plaire, 310v°, 331v°
faire:complaire, 314v°
faire:necessaire, 337
affaire:necessaire, 317v°
deffaire:reffaire, 330
parfaire:faire, 276
parfaire:salutaire, 304-304v°
claire:esclaire, 345v°
grammaire:sommaire, 300v°
contraire:reffaire, 270
contraire:retraire, 304v°

contraire:attraire, 310
contraire:propiciatoire, 321v°
adversaire:necessaire, 286v°
militaire:retraire, 280v°
militaire:sagitaire, 312
voluntaire:taire, 272
salutaire:retraire, 318
reliquaire:Quaire, 280
l'ire:martire, 312
dire:lire, 309
dire:rire, 268v°
dire:escrire, 293
dire:soubzrire, 332
dire:tire, 285v°
dire:martyre, 266
lire:dire, 292, 333
lire:eslire, 316v°
lire:martyre, 328v°
admire:myre, 328
boire:memoyre, 287v°
gloire:memoire, 321v°
gloire:purgatoire, 314v°-315
gloire:victoire, 291
memoire:gloire, 291v°
croire:gloire, 315v°
purgatoire:memoyre, 289v°
victoire:gloire, 270, 340
histoire:memoyre, 293v°
l'histoire:memoyre, 311v°
histoire:croyre, 330v°
empire:l'empire, 277v°
l'empire:aspire, 282
aspire:pire, 285v°
desire:empire, 267v°
martire:retire, 326-326v°
attire:martyre, 298v°
vesquirent:virent, 313
commissaires:necessaires, 278v°
histoires:noires, 311
histoires:memoyres, 283
souspirs:desirs, 337
palais:laidz, 267
jamais:mais, 308v°
jadis:paradis, 266v°
paradis:dis, 292v°
remis:soubzmys, 348
commis:soubzmis, 304, 307
promis:amys, 338
permis:mis, 331
bannis:punys, 344
pris:depris, 289v°
pris:compris, 324
pris:espris, 321v°
pris:mys, 330
apris:gris, 299v°
apris:pris, 280, 281v°, 317v°, 333, 344
apris:espritz, 306v°
entrepris:pris, 269v°
espris:pris, 266v°, 287
espris:compris, 303
pluresis:assis, 332v°
assis:massifz, 272

130

133

134

135

PRINCIPAL WORKS CONSULTED

BIBLIOGRAPHIES

Cioranescu, Alexandre. *Bibliographie de la littérature française du seizième siècle.* Paris: Klincksieck, 1959.

Giraud, Jeanne. *Manuel de bibliographie littéraire pour les XVI°, XVII°, et XVIII° siècle.* Paris: Fayard, 1951.

Grente, Mgr. G. (sous la direction de), *Dictionnaire des Lettres françaises, Le XVI° siècle.* Paris: Fayard, 1951.

Klapp, Otto. *Bibliographie des französichen Literaturwissenschaft.* Frankfurt am Main: Klosterman, 1960.

Lanson, Gustave. *Manuel bibliographique de la littérature française moderne: XVI°, XVII°, XVIII°, et XIX°, siècles.* Nouvelle edition revue et augmentée. Paris: Hachette, 1921.

Schutz, A. H. *A Critical Bibliography of French Literature,* D. C. Cabeen General Editor. Vol. II, *The Sixteenth Century.* Syracuse: 1956.

Tchemerzine, Avenir. *Bibliographie d'éditions originales et rares d'auteurs français des XV°, XVI° ... siècles.* 10 vols. Paris: 1932.

LANGUAGE STUDIES

Brunot, Ferdinand. *Histoire de la langue française des origines à 1900. Le Seizième Siècle.* Paris: Colin, 1967.

Grammont, Maurice. *Le Vers français, ses moyens d'expression, son harmonie,* Paris: Delagrave, 1967.

Guiraud, Pierre. *Le Moyen français.* Que Sais-Je? Paris: Presses Universitaries de France, 1963.

Marty-Laveaux, Charles. *La Langue de la Pléiade.* 2 vols. Paris: Lemerre, 1896-98.

Wartburg, Walther von. *Évolution et structure de la langue française,* 5th ed. Berne: Francke, 1958.

PALEOGRAPHY

Franklin, B. *Dictionnaire des abbréviations latines et françaises usitées dans les inscriptions lapidaires et métalliques, les manuscrits, et les chartes du moyen âge.* 5th ed. Youngstown, Ohio: University Press, 1973.

Thompson, S. Harrison. *Latin Bookhands of the Later Middle Ages.* Cambridge: University Press, 1969.

DICTIONARIES AND ENCYCLOPEDIAS

Cary M. and others. *Oxford Classical Dictionary.* Oxford: Clarendon Press, 1949.

Cotgrave, Randall. *A Dictionarie of the French and English Tongues.* from 1611 edition. Columbia, S.C., 1950-68.

Darmsteter, Arsène, Adolphe Hatzfeld, and Antoine Thomas. *Dictionnaire général de la langue française du commencement du XVI° siècle jusqu'à nos jours.* 2 vols. Paris: Delagrave, 1924.

Godefroy, Frédéric. *Dictionnaire de l'ancienne langue française et de tous ses dialectes du IX° au XV° siècle.* 10 vols. Paris, 1880-1902.

Harvey, Paul and J. E. Hesseltine. *The Oxford Companion to French Literature.* Oxford, 1959.

Holman, A. J. "Bible Dictionary," in *The Holy Bible.* Philadelphia, 1901.

Huguet, Edmond. *Dictionnaire de la langue française du seizième siiècle.*

Joy, Charles R. compiler. *Harper's Topical Concordance,* 4th edition. New York: Harper, 1940.

Littré, Emile. *Dictionnaire de la langue française.* 4 vols. Paris, 1885.

Nicot, Jean. *Thresor de la langue françoise tant ancienne que moderne.* David Douceur, 1606. Fondation Singer-Polignac, Picard, 1960.

EDITIONS OF THE WORKS OF MARGUERITE DE NAVARRE

L'Heptaméron, ed. Felix Frank. 3 vols. Paris: Lisieux, 1897.

L'Heptaméron des Nouvelles, eds. Le Roux de Lincy and Anatole de Montaiglon. 4 vols. Paris, 1880. Geneva: Slatkine Reprints, 1970.

Les Marguerites de la Marguerite des Princesses, ed. Felix Frank. Texte de l'édition de 1547. 4 vols. Paris, 1873. Slatkine Reprints, 1970.

L'Heptaméron, ed. Michel François. Paris: Garnier, 1967.

Les Dernières Poésies de Marguerite de Navarre, ed. Abel Lefranc. Paris: Colin, 1896. Geneva: Slatkine Reprints, 1966.

La Navire ou Consolation du roi Francois à sa soeur Marguerite, ed. Robert Marichal. Paris: Champion, 1956.

Chansons Spirituelles, ed. Georges Dottin. Geneva: Droz, 1971.

Œuvres de Marguerite de Navarre, Comédies, ed. F. Ed. Schneegans. Strasbourg: Heitz, 1924.

Théâtre profane, ed. V.-L. Saulnier. Geneva: Droz, 1971.

La Coche, Ed Robert Marichal. Geneva: Droz, 1970.

Nouvelles, ed. Yves Le Hir. Paris: Presses Universitaires de France, 1967.

Œuvres Choisies, ed. H. P. Clive. New York: Appleton-Century-Crofts, 1968.

Lettres de Marguerite d'Angoulême, reine de Navarre, ed. F. Génin. 2 vols *Société de l'Histoire de France*. Paris: 1841.

Nouvelles Lettres, ed. F. Génin. Société de l'Histoire de France. Paris: Renouard, 1842.

Dialogue en forme de vision nocturne entre Marguerite de France et l'âme saincte de defuncte madame Charlotte de France, ed. Carlo Pellegrini. Catania, 1920.

Poésies du Roi Francois Ier, de Louise de Savoie, duchesse d'Angoulême, de Marguerite, reine de Navarre, ed. Aimé Champollion-Figeac. Paris, 1847. Geneva: Slatkine Reprints, 1969.

MICROFILM AND XEROX

L'Heptameron ou Histoire des Amants fortunés, les Nouvelles de la Royne de Navarre — Un poème en trois livres intitulé les Prisons, par la même Royne. in handwriting later than that of the MS. MS. 1522 (former 7576), Bibliothèque Nationale. Paris, France.

Derniers [sic] Œuvres de la Reyne de Navarre/ Lesquelles n'ont esté imprimées. MS. 24.298, Bouhier Collection. Bibliothèque Nationale. Paris, France.

BIOGRAPHY

Bourdeille, Pierre de, Seigneur de Brantême. M. Louis Moland, ed. Paris: Garnier, 1926.

Hackett, Francis. *Francis the First.* Garden City: Doubleday-Doran, 1935.

Jourda Pierre. *Une Princesse de la renaissance: Marguerite d'/Angoulême, reine de Navarre.* Paris: Desclée, de Brouwer et Cie., 1930.

_____ *Marguerite d'Angoulême, Duchesse d'Alençon, Reine de Navarre (1492-1549), Étude biographique et littéraire.* 2 vols. Paris: Champion, 1930. Bottega d'Erasmo Reprint, 1966.

Putnam, Samuel. *Marguerite of Navarre.* New York: Grosset and Dunlap, 1936.

Roelker, Nancy Lyman. *Queen of Navarre: Jeanne d'Albret.* Cambridge, Mass.: Harvard University Press, 1968.

Saintsbury, George. "Marguerite d'Angoulême" in *Encyclopedia Britannica.* 11th ed., xviii, 706. New York, 1911.

Sainte-Marthe, Charles de. "Oraison funèbre de la mort de l'incomparable Marguerite, Royne de Navarre et Duchesse d'Alençon," in Leroux de Lincy and Anatole de Montaiglon, *L'Heptameron des Nouvelles.* Paris, 1880, Geneva: Slatkine Reprints, 1969.

Schmidt, Charles. *Gérard Roussel, prédicateur de la reine de Navarre.* Strasbourg, 1845, Geneva: Slatkine Reprints, 1969.

LITERARY STUDIES

Comte, Charles. "Le Texte de Marguerite de Navarre" in *Revue de Métrique et de Versification*, III, N° 3, 1896, pp. 97-128.

Courteault, Paul. "Les Dernières poésies de Marguerite de Navarre" in *Revue Critique d'Histoire de littérature*, XXX, N° 26, 29 juin, 1896, 505-510.

Delègue, Y. "Autour de deux Prologues: l'*Heptaméron* est-il anti-Boccace?" in *Travaux de Linguistique et de Littérature*, IV, N° 2. Strasbourg, 1966, 23-37.

Febvre, Lucien. *Autour de l'Heptaméron: Amour sacré, amour profane*. Paris: Gallimard, 1944.

France, Anatole. "La Reine de Navarre," in *Le Génie latin*. Paris: Lemerre, 1916, pp. 11-36.

Frank, Felix. *Dernier Voyage de la reine de Navarre, Marguerite d'Angoulême . . . avec sa fille Jeanne d'Albret aux bains de Cauterets* (1549). Toulouse, 1897.

Frappier, Jean. "La Chastelaine de Vergi, Marguerite et Bandello" in *Publications de la Faculté des Lettres*. Strasbourg, N° 105, 1946 (*Mélanges 1945*, t. II), 89-150.

───────. "Sur Lucien Febvre et son interpretation psychologique du XVI° siècle," in *Mélanges d'histoire littéraire offerts à Raymond Lebègue*. Paris: Nizet, 1969, pp. 19-31.

Gelernt, Jules. *World of Many Loves: The Heptameron of Marguerite de Navarre*. Chapel Hill: University of North Carolina Press, 1966.

Hauser, Henri. "Les Dernières poésies de Marguerite de Navarre" in *Revue critique d'Histoire de littérature*, xxx, N° 26, Paris, 29 juin, 1896, 505-510.

Jourda, Pierre. *Tableau chronologique des publications de Marguerite de Navarre*. 2 vols. Paris, 1922.

───────. "Tableau chronologique des publications de Marguerite de Navarre," in *Revue du Seizième Siècle*, XII, 1925, 209-255.

───────. *Répertoire analytique et chronologique de la correspondance de Marguerite d'Angoulême* (1492-1549). Geneva: Slatkine Reprints, 1973.

───────. *Épîtres et comédies inédites*. Extr. de la *Revue du Seizième Siècle*. Paris, 1927.

───────. "Marguerite de Navarre, poétiques inédites," in *Revue du Seizième Siècle*, xvii, 1930, 42-63.

───────. "Récents écrits sur Marguerite de Navarre," in *Revue du Seizième Siècle*, XI, 1924, 273-88.

───────. "La dixième nouvelle de l'Heptaméron," in *Mélanges de philologie, d'histoire et de littérature offerts à Joseph Vianey*. Paris: Presses Françaises, 1934, 127-31.

───────. "L'Heptaméron: Livre préclassique," in *Studi in onore di Carlo Pelligrini*. Turin: Società Edtrice Italiana, 1963, pp. 133-36.

───────. "La première nouvelle de l'Heptaméron, in *Mélanges d'histoire littéraire (XVI° - XVIII° siècle) offerts à Raymond Lebègue*. Paris: Nizet, 1969, pp. 45-50.

Krailsheimer, Arthur J. "The Heptameron Reconsidered," in *The French Renaissance and its Heritage: Essays presented to Alan B. Boase*. London: Methuen, 1968, pp. 75-90.

───────, ed. *Three Sixteenth Century Conteurs*. Oxford: Clarendon, 1966.

Lanson, Gustave. "Compte-rendu de Abel Lefranc: *Les Dernières poésies de Marguerite de Navarre*" in *Revue d'Histoire littéraire de la France*, 1896, pp. 292-298.

Lebègue, Raymond. "Les Sources de l'Heptaméron et la pensée de Marguerite de Navarre." in *Comptes-rendus des séances de l'année 1956: Académie des Inscriptions et Belles-Lettres*. Paris, 1957, pp. 466-73.

───────. "De Marguerite de Navarre à Honore de Balzac," in *Comptes-rendus des séances de l'année 1957: Académie des Inscriptions et Belles-Lettres*. Paris, 1964, pp. 46-56.

───────. "Le second Miroir de Marguerite de Navarre," in *Comptes-rendus des séances de l'année 1963: Académie des Inscriptions et Belles-Lettres*. Paris, 1964, pp. 46-56.

───────. *La tragédie religieuse en France* (1514-1573). Part II: "Marguerite qui fit l'Heptaméron." Paris: Gallimard N.R.F., 1929, pp. 91-99.

Lefranc, Abel. "Marguerite de Navarre et le platonisme de la Renaissance," in *Grands Ecrivains de la Renaissance*. Paris: Champion, 1914.

_____ . *Dernières Poésies de Marguerite de Navarre.* Paris: Champion, 1896.

_____ . *Les Idées religieuses de Marguerite de Navarre d'après son œuvre poétique.* Extrait du *Bulletin de la Société de l'Histoire du protestantisme français,* 1897-1898. Paris: Fischbacher, 1898.

Le Hir, Yves. "L'Inspiration biblique le Triomphe de l'Agneau de Marguerite de Navarre," *Mélanges d'histoire littéraire de la Renaissance offerts à Henri Chamard.* Paris: Nizet, 1951, pp. 43-61.

Moore, Will Grayburn. *La Réforme allemande et la littérature française: Recherches sur la notoriété de Luther en France.* Publications de la Faculté des Lettres. Strasbourg, 1930.

Meylan, Edward F. "La Date de l'Oraison de l'ame fidèle et son importance pour la biographie de Marguerite de Navarre," in *Modern Language Notes,* lii, 1937, 562-58.

Mignon, Maurice. "L'Italianisme de Marguerite de Navarre," in *Les Affinités intellectuelles de l'Italie et de la France.* Paris: Hachette, 1923, pp. 116-77.

Paris, Gaston. compte rendu, "Les Dernières Poesies de Marguerite de Navarre," in *Journal des Savants,* June, 1896, pp. 273-368.

Pellegrini, C. *La Prima opera di Margherita di Navarre e la terza rima in Francia.* Biblioteca di storia crit. e lett. No. 9. Catania, 1920.

Rat, Maurice. "L'Amour courtois et l'*Heptaméron* de la Reine de Navarre. "in *Revue des Deux Mondes.*" Sept. 15, 1966, pp. 227-236.

Renaudet, Augustin. "Marguerite de Navarre à propos d'un ouvrage récent," in *Revue du Seizième Siècle,* xviii, 1931, 272-308.

_____ . *Humanisme et Renaissance: Dante, Pétrarque, Standonck, Erasme, Lefèvre d'Etaples, Marguerite de Navarre, Rabelais, Guichardin, Giordano Bruno.* Travaux H. et R., No. 30. Geneva: Droz, 1958.

Ritter, Raymond. *Les Solitudes de Marguerite de Navarre.* Paris: Champion, 1953.

Sainte-Beuve, Charles-A. "Marguerite de Navarre," in *Causeries du Lundi.* Paris: Garnier, 1850, vii, 434-54.

Saulnier, Verdun-L. "Marguerite de Navarre: Art médiéval et pensee nouvelle," *Revue Universitaire,* lxiii, 1954, 154-62.

_____ . "Martin Pontus et Marguerite de Navarre: La Réforme lyonnaise et les sources de l'Heptaméron," in *Revue Universitaire,* xxi, 1928, 557-94.

_____ . "Etudes cirtiques sur les comédies profanes de Marguerite de Navarre," in *Humanisme et Renaissance,* xi, 1947, 36-77.

Sckommodau, H. *Die religiösen Dichtungen Margaretes von Navarra.* Cologne: Westdeutscher Verlag, 1955.

_____ . *Petit (Œuvre dévot et contemplatif: Neuedition und versuch einer Erklärung.* Frankfort am Main: Klostermann, 1966.

Sturel, René, ed. *Poésies inédites de Marguerite de Navarre.* Extrait de la *Revue du Seizième Siècle.* Paris, 1914.

Telle, Emile Villemur. *L'Œuvre de Marguerite d'Angoulëme Reine de Navarre et la Querelle des Femmes.* Toulouse, 1937. Geneva: Slatkine Reprints, 1969.

Tetel, Marcel. *Marguerite de Navarre's Heptameron: Themes, Language, Structure.* Durham: Duke University Press, 1973.

_____ . "Marguerite de Navarre et Montaigne: Relativisme et Paradoxe," in *From Marot to Montaigne.* Lexington, Ky.: University of Kentucky Press, 1972, pp. 125-35.

Vernay, Henri. *Les divers sens du mot "raison" autour de l'œuvre de Marguerite, Reine de Navarre (1492-1549).* Heidelberg: Winter, 1962.

STUDIES OF RELATED SUBJECTS

Arnoux, Jules. *Un Précurseur de Ronsard: Antoine Héroët, néo-platonicien et poète (1492-1568).* Digne: Chaspoul, 1912.

Bainton, Roland H. *Erasmus of Christendom.* New York: Scribner, 1969.

Baridon, Silvio F., ed. *Le Roman de la Rose dans la version attribuée à* Clément Marot. 2 vols. Milan: Varese, 1954 and 1957.

Beguin, Albert. *Poésies de la presence de Chretien de Troyes à Pierre Emmanuel.* Paris: Editions du Seuil, 1957.

Busson, Henri. *Les Sources et le développement du rationalisme dans la Littérature française de la Renaissance* (1553-1601). Paris: Latouzey et Anet, 1922.

Camponigri, A. Robert, trans. *Pico della Mirandola: Oration on the Dignity of Man.* New York: Regnery, 1956.

Chamard, Henri. *Les Origines de la poésie française de la Renaissance.* Paris, 1920.

Clark, D. L. *Rhetoric and Poetry in the Renaissance.* New York, 1922.

Clark, John. *Epic Poetry: Post-Virgilian.* New York, Haskell, 1964.

Coleman, Elliott and Carley Dawson, trans. Georges Poulot: *The Metamorphoses of the Circle.* Baltimore, 1966.

Courcelle, Pierre Paul. *La Consolation de Philosophie dans la tradition littéraire, antécédents et postérité de Boèce.* Paris: 1967.

Domandi, Mario, trans. Ernst Cassirer: *The Individual and the Cosmos in Renaissance Philosophy.* New York; 1964.

Doutrepoint, Georges. *Jean Lemaire de Belges et la Renaissance.* Brussels: Lamartin, 1934.

Fergusson, Francis. *Dante's Drama of the Mind, a Modern Reading of the Purgatorio.* Princeton University Press, 1953.

Festugière, Jean. *La Philosophie de l'amour de Marsile Ficin et son influence sur la littérature française au seizième siècle.* Etudes de la philosophie médiévale. No. 31. Paris. 1941.

Gandillac, Maurice, trans. *Œuvres complètes du Pseudo-Denys.* Paris: 1934.

Gilson, Etienne. *La Philosophie de Saint Bonaventure.* Etudes de Philosophie médiévale No. 4. Paris: 1953.

Grandgent, C. H. *La Divina Commedia di Dante Alighieri.* Revised Edition. Boston: Heath, 1933.

Guégan, Bertrand, ed. *Œuvres complètes de Maurice Scève.* Paris, 1927. Geneva: Slatkine Reprints, 1967.

Guy, Henri. *Histoire de la poésie française au XVI° siècle.* Tome II: *Clément Marot et son école.* Paris, 1926.

Hutton, James. *The Greek Anthology in France and in the Latin Writers of the Netherlands to the Year 1800.* Ithaca: Cornell University Press, 1946.

Imbart de la Tour, P. *Les Origines de la Réforme.* VOL. III: *L'Evangelismo.* (1521-1538). Paris: Hachette, 1935.

Jodogne, P., ed. *Jean Lemaire de Belges.* Collection Anciens Auteurs Belges, No. 5. Brussels, 1964.

Jonas, Hans. *The Gnostic Religion.* 2nd edition. Boston: Beacon, 1963.

Marcel, Raymond, ed., *Marsile Ficin.* Paris: 1958.

Merrill, Robert Valentine. *Platonism in French Renaissance Poetry.* New York University Press, 1957.

Mourgues, Odette De. *Metaphysical, Baroque, and Précieux Poetry.* Oxford: Clarendon Press, 1953.

Plattard, Jean, *L'Œuvre de Rabelais, sources, inventions et composition.* Paris: Champion, 1920.

Reitzenstein, Richard and H. H. Schrader. *Studien zum antiken Syncretismus aus Iran und Griechenland.* Leipsig and Berlin: Teuber, 1926.

Ritter, Gerhard. *Luther, his Life and Work.* trans. C. S. Meyer. New York: Harper, 1964.

Rivaud, A. Platon: *Œuvres complètes.* Collection Budé. Paris: 1925.

Rotta, Paolo. *Nicolo Cusano.* Milan: Fratelli Bocca, 1942.

Rougemont, Denis de. *Love in the Western World.* trans. M. Belgion. New York: 1956.

Rouse, W. H. D. trans. *The Great Dialogues of Plato.* Eric W. Warmington and Philip G. Rouse, eds. New York: Mentor-New American Library, 1955-56.

Rutz-Reese, Caroline. *Charles de Sainte-Marthe.* New York: Columbia University Press, 1910.

Schmidt, Albert-M. *La Poésie scientifique en France au XVI° siècle.* Paris: Albin Michel, 1938.

—————— . *Poètes du XVI° siècle.* Pléiade. Paris: Gallimard, 1953.

Screech, Michael A. *Marot Evangélique.* Geneva: Droz, 1967.

_____ . *The Rabelaisian Marriage*. London: Adward Arnold, 1958.

_____ . "Some stoic Elements in Rabelais' Religious Thought" in *Etudes Rabelaisiennes*, I. Geneva: Droz, 1959.

_____ . "L'Evangelisme de Rabelais: Aspects de la satire religieuse au XVI° siècle," in *Etudes Rabelaisiennes*, II. Geneva: Droz, 1959.

Sturel, René. *Bandello en France au XVI° Siècle*. Extrait du *Bulletin Italien*, 1913-1918.

Sweetser, F.-P. ed. *Les Cent Nouvelles Nouvelles*. Geneva: Droz, 1967.

Tilley, Arthur J. *Studies in the French Renaissance*. New York: Barnes and Noble, 1968.

Weber, Henri. *La Création poétique au XVI° siècle en France de Maurice Scève à Agrippa d'Aubigné*. 2 vols. Paris: Nizet, 1956.

Willy, Basil. *The Seventeenth Century Background*. London: 1934.

Yates, Frances A. *Giordano Bruno and the Hermetic Tradition*. London: Routledge and Kegan Paul, 1964.

Doris Earnshaw

THE FEMALE VOICE IN MEDIEVAL ROMANCE LYRIC

American University Studies: Series II (Romance Languages and Literature). Vol. 68
ISBN 0-8204-0575-2   190 pages   hardcover US $ 34.95*

*Recommended price – alterations reserved

The spontaneous, audacious voice of the speaking woman in medieval *chansons de femme* has delighted and puzzled critics for many years. Some call the
voice 'folkloric' and others claim it is a courtly convention. This new sociolin-
guistic study examines the poetics of female speech within a dominantly male
voiced body of poetry. Using for material the extant lyrics in Mozarabic
Spanish, Galician-Portuguese, Provençal, Old French and Italian, the book first
discovers formal patterns of fragmentation and incorporation. Then the drama-
tic *persona* of the female speaker is identified by cultural characteristics of
speech style, economic class and political position. Finally, the conventions
that govern the use of female speech are shown to pre-date the medieval period
and persist to our own time.

PETER LANG PUBLSIHING, INC.
62 West 45th Street
USA – New York, NY 10036

Marlies Kronegger

THE LIFE SIGNIFICANCE OF FRENCH BAROQUE POETRY

American University Studies: Series II (Romance Languages and Literature). Vol. 81
ISBN 0-8204-0639-2   178 pages   hardcover US $ 30.50*

*Recommended price – alterations reserved

With baroque poets, the vocation of literature seems to be the exaltation of the elemental significance of life and of the human spirit. The tetrad pattern of the four elements – water, fire, air, and earth – provides their views of the cosmos as a whole, imprinting the elements' struggle with one another upon every level of creation. The four elements are the matrix of their relations to both themselves and a primordial Being. Their universe is in essence a universe of tension and uneasiness, for it is a universe of creation, revolt, and exaltation. Man does not simply submit to the forces of nature but is able by spiritual energy to regulate and control them.

"At the end of a passionate and not less fascinating multi-faceted study. M.E. Kronegger succeeds in convincing the reader that behind an ever-changing universe of forms and elements, there hides definitively the victory of the poetic Baroque mentality in reply to the dynamic life forces of both cosmos and human existence. New in methodology and stimulating in her conclusions, the new study of Kronegger lifts the veil on a primordial aspect of the French Baroque adventure. A precious book to explore the Age of Louis XIV ... and that of Saint-Amant."

(Jean-Claude Vuillemin, Pennsylvania State University)

PETER LANG PUBLSIHING, INC.
62 West 45th Street
USA – New York, NY 10036

Eglal Doss-Quinby

LES REFRAINS CHEZ LES TROUVERES DU XIIe SIECLE AU DEBUT DU XIVe

American University Studies: Series II (Romance Languages and Literature). Vol. 17

ISBN 0-8204-0153-6   318 pages   hardback US $ 32.00*

*Recommended price - alterations reserved

La conception courante du refrain comme répétition périodique à l'intérieur d'une forme chantée ne rend pas compte des divers principes de composition qui règlent la mise en oeuvre d'un genre qui a joué un rôle capital dans la constitution de la lyrique médiévale. Malgré l'intérêt et la complexité de la matière -- en raison de sa re-création à chaque reprise intra - ou intertextuelle -- une étude intégrale des refrains chez les trouvères, voire une définition (le pluriel s'avère plus exact), fait défaut. Tel est précisément l'objet de cet ouvrage: proposer des critères d'identification permettant d'opérer un classement rigoureux du corpus (vérifié à partir d'un échantillon statistique) et analyser la formulation, les manifestations, les modes d'integration du refrain ainsi que ses fonctions structurales et poétiques.

PETER LANG PUBLISHING, INC.
62 West 45th Street
USA — New York, NY 10036